A COMMENTARY ON THE COLLECTED PLAYS OF W. B. YEATS

A COMMENTARY ON
THE COLLECTED PLAYS
OF W. B. YEATS

A. Norman Jeffares
and
A. S. Knowland

STANFORD UNIVERSITY PRESS
Stanford, California
1975

Stanford University Press
Stanford, California

© 1975 by A. Norman Jeffares and A. S. Knowland

Originating publisher
The Macmillan Press, Ltd, London, 1975

Printed in Great Britain

ISBN 0–8047–0875–4
LC 74–82993

For Frank Wynne
and all our friends in Sligo

Contents

Preface

THIS commentary is intended to assist the reader of Yeats's *Co-lected Plays* (page references to this work are given in the margin in bold face type). Yeats's poetry and his prose have been quoted where they throw light on the meaning of particular plays: thus his notes to various editions are included as well as passages from his critical and autobiographical prose and from his letters.

Readers will be able to supplement the bibliographical information by referring to *The Variorum Edition of the Plays of W. B. Yeats* (ed. R. K. Alspach). *A Concordance to the Plays of W. B. Yeats* (ed. Eric Domville) affords a quick means of comparing the language, the images and symbols used by Yeats. A useful guide to published criticism of Yeats's work is *A Bibliography of Yeats Criticism 1887–1965* (ed. K. G. W. Cross and R. T. Dunlop).

Stirling   A. NORMAN JEFFARES
Oxford   A. S. KNOWLAND
1974

The quotations from the work of W. B. Yeats are reprinted by kind permission of Senator Michael Butler Yeats.

Abbreviations

OTHER BOOKS

PYP	George Brandon Saul, *Prolegomena to the Study of Yeats's Poems* (1957)
PYPl	George Brandon Saul, *Prolegomena to the Study of Yeats's Plays* (1958)
RI	Frank Kermode, *Romantic Image* (1957)
S&S	Thomas R. Whitaker, *Swan and Shadow: Yeats's Dialogue with History* (1964)
SQ	Maud Gonne MacBride, *A Servant of the Queen* (1938)
TD	Leonard E. Nathan, *The Tragic Drama of W. B. Yeats* (1965)
WBY	J. M. Hone, *W. B. Yeats 1865–1939* (1942; rev. ed. 1962). References are to the 1962 edition.
WMA	Giorgio Melchiori, *The Whole Mystery of Art* (1960)
Y	Harold Bloom, *Yeats* (1970)
Y&GI	Donald T. Torchiana, *Yeats and Georgian Ireland* (1966)
Y&T	F. A. C. Wilson, *W. B. Yeats and Tradition* (1958)
YCE	*W. B. Yeats 1865–1939 Centenary Essays*, ed. D. E. S. Maxwell and S. B. Bushrui (1965)
YCI	B. Rajan, *W. B. Yeats. A Critical Introduction* (1965)
YI	F. A. C. Wilson, *Yeats's Iconography* (1960)
Y:M&M	Richard Ellmann, *Yeats: the Man and the Masks* (1948; rev. ed. 1961). References are to the 1948 edition.
Y:M&P	A. Norman Jeffares, *Yeats: Man and Poet* (1949, rev. ed. 1962). References are to the 1962 edition.
YTDR	David R. Clark, *W. B. Yeats and the Theatre of Desolate Reality* (1965)
YTP	Peter Ure, *Yeats the Playwright* (1963)
YV	Helen Hennessy Vendler, *Yeats's Vision and the Later Plays* (1963)
YVP	S. B. Bushrui, *Yeats's Verse Plays: The Revisions 1900–1910* (1965)
YW	Curtis Bradford, *Yeats at Work* (1965)

JOURNALS

DUM	*Dublin University Magazine*
ELH	*Journal of English Literary History*
NO	*National Observer*

Chronology of Yeats's Life

1865   William Butler Yeats, the son of John Butler Yeats and his wife, Susan (*née* Pollexfen), born at Georgeville, Sandymount Avenue, Dublin, 13 June.

1867   John Butler Yeats moves with his family to 23 Fitzroy Road, Regent's Park, London. Robert (d. 1873), John Butler (Jack), Elizabeth Corbet (Lolly) were born here. Susan Mary (Lily), the elder daughter, was born at Sligo. Frequent visits were made to Sligo to Mrs Yeats's parents, the Pollexfens.

1874   The family moves to 14 Edith Villas, West Kensington.

1875   Yeats goes to the Godolphin School, Hammersmith. Holidays spent in Sligo.

1876   The family moves to 8 Woodstock Road, Bedford Park.

1880   John Butler Yeats's income from lands in Kildare ceases because of Land War. Family returns to Ireland, is lent Balscadden Cottage, Howth, Dublin. W. B. Yeats goes to the High School, Harcourt Street, Dublin (until 1883).

1881   Family moves to Island View, small house overlooking Howth Harbour. Yeats thinks himself in love with his cousin Laura Johnston.

1883   W. B. Yeats enters School of Art, Dublin.

1885   Family moves to 10 Ashfield Terrace, off Harold's Cross Road, Dublin. First published poems and an article on esoteric Buddhism appear in the *Dublin University Review*. Founder member of Dublin Hermetic Society. Becomes friend of Katharine Tynan and John O'Leary.

1886   First experience of séance. Attacks Anglo-Irish, begins to read Irish poets who wrote in English and translations of Gaelic sagas.

1887   Family moves to 58 Eardley Crescent, Earls Court, London. Mrs Yeats has two strokes. W. B. Yeats visits William Morris at Kelmscott House. Joins London Lodge of Theosophists.

1888   Family installed in 3 Blenheim Road, Bedford Park (J. B. Yeats's home till 1902). Last of Yeats family land sold in accordance with Ashbourne Act (1888). Contributions to American journals. Visits Oxford to work in Bodleian. Joins esoteric section of Theosophists.

1889   Mild collapse. Prepares selections for Walter Scott. *The Wanderings of Oisin and Other Poems*. Visits W. E. Henley, meets Oscar Wilde, John Todhunter, York Powell, John Nettleship, and Edwin Ellis (with whom he decides to edit Blake's poems). Edits *Fairy and Folk Tales of the Irish Peasantry*. Meets Florence Farr. Maud Gonne visits Bedford Park; he falls in love with her; offers to write *The Countess Cathleen* for her.

1890   'The Lake Isle of Innisfree'. Asked to resign from Theosophists. Initiated into the Order of the Golden Dawn.

1891   *Representative Irish Tales. John Sherman and Dhoya*. The Rhymers' Club founded in London. Friendship with Johnson and Dowson. Asks Maud Gonne to marry him. She goes to France. He meets her on her return on ship with Parnell's body. Writes poem on Parnell. Founds London-Irish Literary Society with T. W. Rolleston. Founds National Literary Society in Dublin with John O'Leary as President.

1892   *The Countess Kathleen and Various Legends and Lyrics. Irish Fairy Tales*.

1893   *The Celtic Twilight. The Works of William Blake* (ed. Ellis and Yeats, 3 vols).

1894   First visit to Paris; stays with MacGregor Mathers and proposes to Maud Gonne again. Sees *Axel*. Meets 'Diana Vernon'. Revises *The Countess Cathleen* in Sligo while staying with George Pollexfen and conducting experiments with symbols. *The Land of Heart's Desire* produced. Visits Gore-Booths at Lissadell.

1895   *Poems.* Not on good terms with Dowden and Mahaffy. Lionel Johnson drinking heavily. Shares rooms in the Temple with Arthur Symons for a few months (between 1895 and 1896, date uncertain).

1896   Takes rooms in Woburn Buildings; affair with 'Diana Vernon' lasts a year. Visits Edward Martyn with Arthur Symons, meets Lady Gregory, visits Aran Islands. Meets Synge in Paris, when there to found order of Celtic Mysteries. Member of I.R.B.; forms idea of uniting Irish political parties.

1897   *The Adoration of the Magi. The Secret Rose.* Disturbed by effects of Jubilee Riots in Dublin. Visits Coole; collects folklore there with Lady Gregory; writing *The Speckled Bird* (unpublished novel).

1898   Accompanies Maud Gonne on tour of Irish in England and Scotland. Forms idea of creating Irish Theatre with Lady Gregory and Edward Martyn.

1899   *The Wind Among the Reeds.* In Paris, again proposes marriage to Maud Gonne. *The Countess Cathleen* and Martyn's *Heather Field* produced in Ancient Concert Rooms, Dublin, as programme of Irish Literary Theatre.

1900   Proposes marriage to Maud Gonne in London. Leaves I.R.B. (probably in 1900). Forms new order of Golden Dawn after trouble with Mathers and Aleister Crowley. Helps George Moore to rewrite Martyn's *The Tale of a Town*, which became *The Bending of the Bough*.

1902   Lectures on the psalteries. *Diarmuid and Grania* written in collaboration with George Moore. Becomes President of Irish National Dramatic Society. *Cathleen ni Houlihan* performed in Dublin with Maud Gonne in title role.

1903   Maud Gonne marries John MacBride. *The Countess Cathleen, The Pot of Broth* and *The Hour Glass* produced in visit of Irish National Dramatic Company to London. First lecture tour in U.S., arranged by John Quinn.

1905   Abbey Theatre opens with Yeats as producer-manager. *The King's Threshold* and *On Baile's Strand.*

1905   Limited company replaces National Theatre. Co-director with Lady Gregory and Synge.

1906   *Stories of Red Hanrahan. Poems 1895–1905.*

1907   Crisis over Synge's *The Playboy of the Western World.* Visits Italy with Lady Gregory and her son. Works on *The Player Queen.*

1908   *Collected Works* (in 8 vols). Stays with Maud Gonne in Normandy. Father goes to New York.

1910   Resigns managership. Crisis in affair with unmarried woman. *The Green Helmet and other poems.*

1911   Accompanies Abbey players to U.S.

1912   Stays with Maud Gonne in Normandy. Meets Ezra Pound.

1913   Receives Civil List pension of £150 p.a. *Poems Written in Discouragement* (dealing with Lane Gallery controversy). Stays at Stone Cottage, Holmans Hatch, Sussex, in autumn with Ezra Pound.

1914   Visits U.S. (January). Returns for Ezra Pound's marriage to Mrs Shakespear's daughter. Investigates miracle at Mirabeau with Maud Gonne MacBride and the Hon. Everard Fielding (June). *Responsibilities: poems and a play.* Becomes interested in family history; finishes *Reveries* (first part of *Autobiographies*).

1915   Hugh Lane goes down with *Lusitania.* Refuses knighthood.

1916   With Ezra Pound (winter). First of the *Plays for Dancers* produced in Lady Cunard's house, London (March). Easter Rising. Writes 'Easter 1916'. In Normandy proposes marriage to Maud Gonne. Reads French poets with Iseult Gonne.

1917   Buys Castle at Ballylee. Proposes to Iseult Gonne. Marries Georgie Hyde-Lees on 21 October. *The Wild Swans at Coole.*

1918   They stay at Oxford, then Glendalough, then visit Sligo; stay at Coole (and supervise restoration of tower), later at 73 St Stephen's Green (Maud Gonne's house) until December. *Per Amica Silentia Luae.*

1919   Anne Butler Yeats born (26 February) in Dublin. Summer at Ballylee. Winter spent in Oxford in Broad Street.

1920   American lecture tour until May. Yeats in Ireland in autumn.

1921   Michael Butler Yeats born (22 August). *Michael Robartes and the Dancer. Four Plays for Dancers.*

1922   Buys Georgian house, 82 Merrion Square, Dublin. J. B. Yeats dies in New York. D.Litt. of Dublin University. Spends summer at Ballylee. *The Trembling of the Veil. Later Poems. The Player Queen.* Becomes Senator of Irish Free State.

1923   Nobel Prize for Poetry. Visits Stockholm in December for award of Nobel Prize.

1924   *Essays. The Cat and the Moon and certain poems.* Year mainly spent in final work on *A Vision.* Reading history and philosophy. High blood pressure. Visits Sicily (November).

1925   Visits Capri, Rome, Milan (February). May at Ballylee. Reading Burke and Berkeley. Speech on divorce in Senate. *A Vision* (dated 1925, published January 1926).

1926   *Estrangement.* Chairman of Coinage Committee in Senate.

Visits St Otteran's School in Waterford ('Among School Children').

1927   Ballylee in summer. *October Blast*. Congestion of lungs (October). Algeciras, Seville (lung bleeding). Cannes.

1928   Cannes (till February). *The Tower*. Rapallo (April). Dublin house sold. Ballylee (June). Furnished house at Howth (July). Last Senate Speech (July).

1929   Rapallo (winter). Summer in Ireland, in flat (Fitzwilliam Square, Dublin), at Coole and Ballylee, then at Howth. *A Packet for Ezra Pound* (August). *The Winding Stair* (October). Rapallo. Malta fever (December). Ezra Pound and George Antheil at Rapallo.

1930   Portofino (April). Writes 'Byzantium'. Renvyle, Connemara (June). Coole. *Words upon the Window-pane* produced at Abbey Theatre (November). Visits Masefield at Boar's Hill, Oxford, thirtieth anniversary of their first meeting. Spends winter in Dublin, in furnished house on Killiney Hill.

1931   Writes 'The Seven Sages'. D.Litt. at Oxford (May). Writes much verse at Coole in summer. Broadcast B.B.C. Belfast (September). Spends winter at Coole, reading Balzac; Lady Gregory dying.

1932   Works on 'Coole Park and Ballylee 1931'. Winter and spring at Coole. Lady Gregory dies. Foundation of Irish Academy of Letters (September). Last American tour (October). *Words for Music Perhaps and other poems* (November).

1933   Leases Riversdale, Rathfarnham, Co. Dublin. Interested in O'Duffy's blueshirt movement. *The Winding Stair and other poems* (September). *Collected Poems* (November).

1934   Steinach operation. Rapallo (June). Rome (autumn). *Wheels and Butterflies. Collected Plays. The King of the Great Clock Tower.*

1935   Majorca (winter). Shri Purohit Swami collaborates in translation of *Upanishads* there. *Dramatis Personae. A Full Moon in March* (November).

1936   Seriously ill; heart missing beat (January); nephritis. Returns to Riversdale. Broadcasts on modern poetry, B.B.C., London (summer).

1937   Elected member Athenaeum. Broadcasts B.B.C. London (April, July, September). *A Speech and Two Poems* (August). Visits Lady Gerald Wellesley. *Oxford Book of Modern Verse (1892–1935). A Vision* (October). Mentone (winter). *Essays 1931–1936* (December).

1938   *The Herne's Egg* (January). Visits Sussex, stays with Lady Gerald Wellesley, and with Edith Shackleton Heald. *New Poems* (May). Sussex (June). Last public appearance at Abbey Theatre for performance of *Purgatory* (August). Maud Gonne visits him at Riversdale (late summer). Sussex (September).

1939   Dies 28 January, buried at Roquebrune. *Last Poems and Two Plays* (June). *On the Boiler*.

1948   Body reinterred at Drumcliffe Churchyard, Sligo.

The Contents of the Collected Plays

Page numbers in bold are those of the *Collected Plays*; those of the Commentary are in ordinary figures.

Ballylee (*W. B. Yeats*)
Sandymount (*Yeats's birthplace*)
Rathfarnham (*Yeats's last Irish residence*)
Aran Islands (*J. M. Synge*)
Coole Park (*Lady Gregory*)
French Park (*Douglas Hyde*)

Tulira (*Edward Martyn*)
Lissoy (*? The Deserted Village*)
Moore Hall (*George Moore*)
Elphin (*Oliver Goldsmith*)
Cloyne (*Bishop Berkeley*)
Ballyshannon (*Wm. Allingham*)

YEATS'S IRELAND

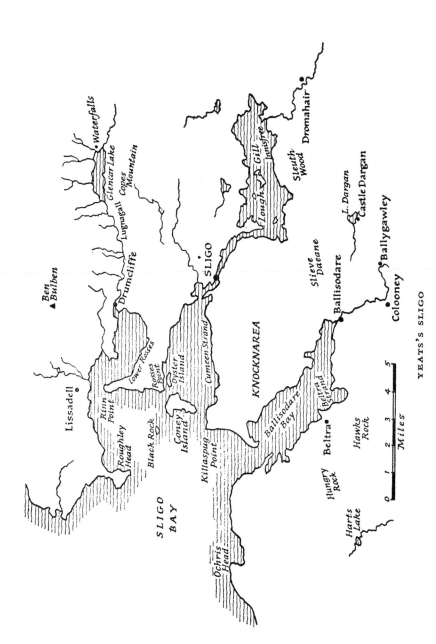

YEATS'S SLIGO

The Countess Cathleen

This was Yeats's first play and his constant reworkings of it – the
date, 1892, refers only to the first version – demonstrate not only
his painstaking apprenticeship to the craft of the playwright but
also the special affection of a parent for the first-born. Even in
1923, when he had come to a just appreciation of its deficiencies, he
said it gave him more pleasure in the memory than any of his
plays (*PC* vi).

For a full account of the genesis and evolution of the play before
its first publication in 1892 see M. J. Sidnell's article, *Yeats's First
Work for the Stage* (*YCE* 167f). Of this first printed version, in
which the title appears as *The Countess Kathleen*, Yeats made this
comment: 'If I had not made magic my constant study I could not
have written a single word of my Blake book, nor would *The Countess
Kathleen* have ever come to exist. The mystical life is the centre of
all that I do and all that I think and all that I write' (*L* 211), and in
the preface to this version he explained:

> The chief poem is an attempt to mingle personal thought and
> feeling with the beliefs and customs of Christian Ireland;
> whereas the longest poem in my earlier book [*The Wanderings of
> Oisin*] endeavoured to set forth the impress left on my imagi-
> nation by the Pre-Christian cycle of legends. The Christian
> cycle being mainly concerned with contending moods and
> moral motives needed, I thought, a dramatic vehicle (*CK*).

There is also the account in the unpublished Autobiography:

> She [Maud Gonne] spoke to me of her wish for a play that she
> could act in Dublin . . . I told her of a story I had found when
> compiling my *Fairy and Folk Tales of the Irish Peasantry*, and
> offered to write for her the play I have called *The Countess
> Cathleen*. When I told her I wished to become an Irish Victor
> Hugo, was I wholly sincere? – for though a volume of bad
> verse translations from Hugo had been my companion at
> school, I had begun to simplify myself with great toil. I had

seen upon her table *Tristram of Lyonesse* and *Les Contemplations* and besides it was natural to command myself by claiming a very public talent, for her beauty as I saw it in those days seemed incompatible with private, intimate life. (*MS* 41)

He revised and expanded the play in the light of theatrical experience gained as a result of the performance in London of *The Land of Heart's Desire* in March 1894 and printed the revision in *Poems* (1895), the title appearing as *The Countess Cathleen* (rev. and repr. 1899, 1901, 1904, 1908, 1912, 1913, 1919, 1920, 1922 twice, 1923, 1924, 1927, 1929). It also appeared in *The Poetical Works of William B. Yeats*, Vol. II, Dramatical Poems, New York and London, 1907 (1909, 1911); *The Collected Works in Verse and Prose of William Butler Yeats*, Vol. III, Stratford-upon-Avon, 1908; *The Countess Cathleen*, London, 1912; *The Poetical Works of William B. Yeats*, Vol. II, Dramatic Poems, rev. and repr. New York and London, August 1912 (1914, 1916, 1917, 1919, 1921); *A Selection from the Poetry of W. B. Yeats*, Leipzig (Tauchnitz), January 1913 (1922); *The Countess Cathleen*, London, 1916 (1916, 1920, 1922, 1924); *Selected Poems*, New York, 1921; *Plays and Controversies*, London, 1923, New York, 1924 (repr. London, 1927); *The Countess Cathleen and The Land of Heart's Desire*, London, 1924 (1925, 1929); *The Collected Plays of W. B. Yeats*, London, 1934, New York, 1935; *The Collected Plays of W. B. Yeats*, London, 1952, New York, 1953 (repr. London, 1953, 1960, 1963, 1966).

The first performance of the play was given at The Antient Concert Rooms, Dublin on 8 May 1899, and for this a third revision was made, printed in *Poems* (1901). For Yeats's account of the rehearsals and the performance, see 'Dramatis Personae', where he comments:

The play itself was ill-constructed, the dialogue turning aside at the lure of word or metaphor, very different, I hope, from the play as it is today after many alterations, every alteration tested by performance. It was not, nor is it now, more than a piece of tapestry. The Countess sells her soul, but she is not transformed (*A* 416–17).

The play had been called heretical, and Yeats's defence was as follows:

The play is symbolic: the two demons who go hither and thither buying souls are the world, and their gold is the pride of the eye. The Countess herself is a soul which is always, in all laborious and self-denying persons, selling itself into captivity and unrest that it may redeem 'God's children', and finding the peace it has not sought because all high motives are of the substance of peace. The symbols have other meanings, but they have this principal meaning (*L* 319).

See R. Ellmann, *James Joyce*, New York, 1953, pp. 68–9, for Joyce's reactions to the play, referred to in Chapter v of *A Portrait of the Artist as a Young Man*.

The third version appeared in *Poems* (1895) rev. and repr. London, 1904; in *The Poetical Works of William B. Yeats*, New York, 1907; *Poems* (1895) rev. and repr. London, 1908; *The Collected Works in Verse and Prose of William Butler Yeats*, Vol. III, Stratford-upon-Avon, 1908.

A fourth version was first printed in 1912, and a fifth and final version in *Poems* (1919), and in *PC*, the text of *CPl*.

The fullest studies of these revisions are to be found in David R. Clark's essay 'Vision and Revision: Yeats's *The Countess Cathleen*', in *The World of W. B. Yeats*, ed. Robin Skelton and Ann Saddlemyer, Dublin, 1965, and in Peter Ure's *Yeats the Playwright*, London, 1963. The most striking feature of them is the progressive enlargement of the role of Aleel [Kevin, in the 1892 version], until in the final one he is present in every scene. This enlargement complicates the simplicity of the original story by adding to what could have been a straightforward moral conflict between the Countess and the Demons the internal dilemma within her soul of the choice between responsibility on the one hand and on the other escape to the land of dreams, whose representative Aleel finally becomes.

VPl prints the 1892 version of the play (with collations of all other versions) and also Yeats's long note in the 1927 revision of *Poems* (1895):

I found the story of the Countess Cathleen in what professed to be a collection of Irish folklore in an Irish newspaper some years ago. I wrote to the compiler, asking about its source, but got no answer, but have since heard that it was translated from *Les Matinées de Timothé Trimm* a good many years ago, and has been drifting about the Irish press ever since. Léo Lespès gives it as an Irish story, and though the editor of *Folklore* has kindly advertised for information, the only Christian variant I know of is a Donegal tale, given by Mr. Larminie in his *West Irish Folk Tales and Romances*, of a woman who goes to hell for ten years to save her husband, and stays there another ten, having been granted permission to carry away as many souls as could cling to her skirt. Léo Lespès may have added a few details, but I have no doubt of the essential antiquity of what seems to me the most impressive form of one of the supreme parables of the world. The parable came to the Greeks in the sacrifice of Alcestis, but her sacrifice was less overwhelming, less apparently irremediable.

Then follows Léo Lespès' version in French. After giving the cast of the 1899 performance in Dublin, Yeats continued:

Some of the characters so represented have dropped out of the play during revision. The players had to face a very vehement opposition stirred up by a politician and a newspaper, the one accusing me in a pamphlet, the other in long articles day after day, of blasphemy because of the language of the demons or of Shemus Rua, and because I made a woman sell her soul and yet escape damnation, and of a lack of patriotism because I made Irish men and women, who, it seems, never did such a thing, sell theirs. The politician or the newspaper persuaded some forty Catholic students to sign a protest against the play, and a Cardinal, who avowed that he had not read it, to make another, and both politician and newspaper made such obvious appeals to the audience to break the peace, that a score or so of police were sent to the theatre to see that they did not. I had, however, no reason to regret the result, for the stalls, containing almost all that was distinguished in Dublin, and a gallery of artisans alike insisted on the freedom of literature.

After the performance in 1899 I added the love scene between Aleel and the Countess, and in this new form the play was revived in New York by Miss Wycherley, as well as being played a good deal in England and America by amateurs. Now at last I have made a complete revision to make it suitable for performance at the Abbey Theatre. The first two scenes are almost wholly new, and throughout the play I have added or left out such passages as a stage experience of some years showed me encumbered the action; the play in its first form having been written before I knew anything of the theatre. I have left the old end, however, in the version printed in the body of this book, because the change for dramatic purposes has been made for no better reason than that audiences – even at the Abbey Theatre – are almost ignorant of Irish mythology – or because a shallow stage made the elaborate vision of armed angels upon a mountainside impossible. The new end is particularly suited to the Abbey stage, where the stage platform can be brought out in front of the proscenium and have a flight of steps at one side up which the Angel comes, crossing towards the back of the stage at the opposite side. The principal lighting is from two arc lights in the balcony which throw their lights into the faces of the players, making footlights unnecessary. The room at Shemus Rua's house is suggested by a great grey curtain – a colour which becomes full of rich tints under the stream of light from the arcs. The short front scene before the last is just long enough when played with incidental music to allow the scene set behind it to be changed. The play when played without interval in this way lasts a little over an hour.

The note concludes with the simplified ending adopted for the 1911 performance at the Abbey Theatre, 4 December, with Maire O'Neill as the Countess, from the point where the Merchants rush out – p. 45.

The pamphlet referred to above, *Souls for Gold*, by Frank Hugh O'Donnell, together with related correspondence, can now be seen in *Our Irish Theatre*, by Lady Gregory, Gerrards Cross, 1972.

The French story itself tells a straightforward tale of the arrival in a poverty-stricken Ireland of two demon-merchants who make great display of their wealth, buying the souls of the poor and the needy. The countess Kitty O'Connor, 'un ange de beauté', sells all her treasure, retaining only her castle and its surrounding pastures, in order to save the peasants. The merchants, helped by a wicked valet, thereupon rob her of her money. The peasants are left destitute – with no choice but to die of hunger or sell their own souls. Relief from the 'lands of the East' is on its way but will take eight days to arrive. After a night of agony the Countess decides to sell her own soul for the highest price she can get – 150,000 *écus d'or*. Three days later she is found dead of grief. But the sale of her soul, entered into out of charity, is declared null and void by God.

In developing the role of Aleel in the course of his treatments of this story, Yeats was influenced by his own love for Maud Gonne (to whom the 1892 version was dedicated) by her rejection of his proposals of marriage, and by his progressive disillusionment with her absorption in politics. It would be dangerous, however, to identify Maud Gonne with the Countess on the basis of the lines in *The Circus Animals' Desertion* (*CP* 391):

> And then a counter-truth filled out its play,
> The Countess Cathleen was the name I gave it;
> She, pity-crazed, had given her soul away,
> But masterful heaven had intervened to save it.
> I thought my dear must her own soul destroy,
> So did fanaticism and hate enslave it.

It is impossible to think of the Countess as enslaved by these qualities. Cf. however, the following note on these lines: 'The Countess was like Yeats's early interpretation of Maud Gonne's character. He told her that after they had met in London in 1891 (the year he first proposed marriage to her) he had come to understand the tale of a woman selling her soul to buy bread for her starving people as a symbol of all souls who lose their peace or fineness of soul or beauty of spirit in political service, but chiefly as a symbol of her soul that seemed to him incapable of rest.' (*Comm*, 509) It is more appropriate to regard the play as the 'counter-truth' to *The Wanderings of Oisin*, in which Oisin chooses the Fenians and rejects St Patrick. Here, the choice is in effect reversed. Misleading, too, is the comment he made in 'Estrangement', which is interesting more as an expression of intention than of achievement:

In Christianity what was philosophy in Eastern Asia became life, biography and drama. A play passes through the same process in being written. At first, if it has psychological depth, there is a bundle of ideas, something that can be stated in philosophical terms; my *Countess Cathleen*, for instance, was once the moral question, may a soul sacrifice itself for a good end? but gradually philosophy is eliminated until at last the only philosophy audible, if there is even that, is the mere expression of one character or another. (*A* 468)

The cast at the first performance on 8 May 1899 was as follows: First Demon, Marcus St John; Second Demon, Trevor Lowe; Shemus Rua, Valentine Grace; Teig Rua, Charles Sefton; Maire Rua, Madame San Carolo; Aleel, Florence Farr; Oona, Anna Mather; Herdsman, Claude Holmes; Gardener, Jack Wilcox; Sheogue, Dorothy Paget; Peasant Woman, M. Kelly; Servant, T. E. Wilkinson; the Countess Cathleen, May Whitty.

quern: a small hand-mill.   **3**

turf: peat for the fire.

famine-struck: the view of Ireland starving is often taken at a nationalistic level, as the result of English exploitation, but it is worth noting that there is plenty of food in the presumably Irish countess's house and on the mountains. The starvation is symbolic of the spiritual poverty which is the consequence of men selling their souls to the devils of materialism. For a later development of this idea see 'At Galway Races', *CP* 108, 'Pardon, Old Fathers . . .', *CP* 113, 'September 1913', *CP* 120.

horned owls: associated, according to Yeats's note in *CK*, in popular   **4**
belief with evil fairies. See also note on **50**, lines 2–9.

though the whole land . . . weasel's tooth: cf. 'Nineteen Hundred and Nineteen', *CP* 233, line 32, '*Who are but weasels fighting in a hole*' and *CP* 236, line 92, '*The weasel's twist, the weasel's tooth*'. Yeats had seen weasels fighting at Coole. Lady Gregory recorded their bad name with gamekeepers, the need other country people expressed 'to behave well to them' and the advice of an old acquaintance not to insult one – 'For they are enchanted and understand all things' (*Coole*, 1971, p. 26). Lady Wilde (*AL*, I, 62), recorded that they are 'spiteful and malignant, and old withered witches sometimes take this form'. See also her *Ancient Cures, Charms and Usages of Ireland*, 1890, p. 69. Yeats may have been influenced by his reading of Landor, who placed in Sheridan's mouth an argument that there should be no church establishment for less than one hundred adults:

> But seriously, in turning this acid on such putridity there would be a violent fermentation; there would be animosities and conflicts. However, what harm if there should be? Turn out the weasel against the rat, and, at least while they are fighting neither of them can corrode the rafters or infect the larder. (W. S. Landor, 'Conversations with Windham and Sheridan', *Collected Works*, III, p. 127)

to wake them: to give them a wake, a funeral celebration.   **5**

the needle's eye: the eternity of death. Cf. 'Veronica's Napkin',   **6**
CP 270, lines 1–6:

> The Heavenly Circuit: Berenice's Hair:
> Tent-pole of Eden: the tent's drapery:
> Symbolical glory of the earth and air!
> The Father and His angelic hierarchy
> That made the magnitude and glory there
> Stood in the circuit of a needle's eye.

In an account of the origin of the poem 'On a Picture of a Black Centaur by Edmund Dulac', *CP* 242, given in Hone, *WBY* 326–8, Cecil Salkeld recalls a conversation with Yeats while on a walk:

> Suddenly, he pulled up short at a big stone and said: 'Do you realise that eternity is not a long time, but a *short* time . . . ?' I just said, I didn't quite understand. 'Eternity', Yeats said, 'Eternity is in the glitter on the beetle's wing . . . it is something infinitely short . . .'

Cf. also 'A Needle's Eye', Supernatural Songs, xi, *CP* 333:

> All the stream that's roaring by
> Came out of a needle's eye.

SD   Cathleen, Oona, and Aleel enter: Peter Ure points out (*YTP* 21), that this entry was written into the 1895 version of the play and that the whole episode was retained in all subsequent versions, even though it was entirely redrafted for the final 1912 version. He thinks that the necessity it imposes upon the Countess of calling at one of her own cottages in order to find her way to her own castle is a trifle grotesque, but justifies it on two counts. First, it establishes a visual contrast between the hungry peasants and the gorgeous world of the Countess and so strengthens the thematic conflict of the choice facing her between retreat into dreams and the acceptance of responsibility. Second, by bringing the Countess into the play at this point, an earlier stage than at the opening of the second act, he links the two together more efficiently.

7   *singing like a wave of the sea*: cf. 'The Fiddler of Dooney', *CP* 82:

> And when the folk there spy me,
> They will all come up to me,
> With 'Here is the fiddler of Dooney!'
> And dance like a wave of the sea.

Henn (*LT* 305) compares Florizel's remark to Perdita, *A Winter's Tale*, IV, iv:

> When you do dance, I wish you
> A wave o' the sea.

dreams of terrors to come: a preparation for his visionary scene, 45f.
For my fathers served your fathers: cf. 'The Curse of Cromwell', *CP* 350:

> You ask what I have found, and far and wide I go:
> Nothing but Cromwell's house and Cromwell's
>   murderous crew,
> The lovers and the dancers are beaten into the clay,
> And the tall men and the swordsmen and the horsemen,
>   where are they?
> And there is an old beggar wandering in his pride —
> His fathers served their fathers before Christ was
>   crucified.

and Yeats's *Commentary* in *KGCT* on 'Parnell's Funeral', *CP* 319, that after the Battle of the Boyne 'At the base of the social structure, but hardly within it, the peasantry dreamed on in their medieval sleep; the Gaelic poets sang of the banished Catholic aristocracy; "My fathers served their fathers before Christ was crucified" sang one of the most famous.'

Who mocks . . . love: in view of the echoes from *King Lear* and **8** *Richard II* later in the play, possibly a glance at the opening line of *Twelfth Night*.

Two grey horned owls: see note on **50**, lines 2–9. See note on **4** above.   **9**

Scene II: **17**
  Aleel's part in this was added in the 1912 revision. His dramatic function here is that he appeals to that side of the Countess which would like to escape to the subjective, timeless and pagan world of dreams, beauty and art. This world is shattered by the successive entries of the Steward, and Teigue and Shemus. By the end of the

scene the Countess has chosen the objective, Christian world of self-sacrifice and responsibility.

Maeve: usually the wild queen of Connacht, but here the queen of the faery.

Knocknarea: a mountain near Sligo, its top supposedly the site of Maeve's burial cairn.

19   *You have not been christened*? Aleel as dreamer and poet looks forward to 'Vacillation', *CP* 286, line 87: *Homer is my example and his unchristened heart*.

20   *Cro-Patrick*: Croagh Patrick, a mountain in south-west Co. Mayo, one of the traditional Irish centres of pilgrimage, from which St Patrick is said to have banished snakes from Ireland.

A learned theologian . . . sinless: like those ecclesiastical authorities quoted in the pamphlet that Maud Gonne, James Connolly and Arthur Griffith wrote in connection with the starving peasantry of Co. Kerry in 1897, in support of the view that starvation justifies robbery. Maud Gonne wrote, *SQ*:

> In 1847 our people died by thousands of starvation though every ship leaving an Irish port was laden with food in abundance. The Irish people might have seized that food, cattle, corn and all manner of provisions before it reached the sea-ports – have prevented famine and saved their country from ruin, but did not do so, believing such action to be sinful and dreading to peril their souls to save their bodies. In this belief, we know now that they were entirely mistaken . . . (quoted by M. J. Sidnell, 'Yeats's First Work for the Stage', *YCE* 176).

21   *There is no soul . . . world*: cf. 'Paudeen', *CP* 122:

> Indignant at the fumbling wits, the obscure spite
> Of our old Paudeen in his shop, I stumbled blind
> Among the stones and thorn-trees, under morning light:
> Until a curlew cried and in the luminous wind
> A curlew answered: and suddenly thereupon I thought
> That on the lonely height where all are in God's eye,

There cannot be, confusion of our sound forgot,
A single soul that lacks a sweet crystalline cry.

and a passage in 'The Stirring of the Bones': 'The love of God is infinite for every human soul because every human soul is unique; no other can satisfy the same need in God' (*A* 379).

sell all . . . meal: with this passionate, reckless generosity of sacri- **23** fice, the antithesis of the demons' materialism, cf. 'Pardon, Old Fathers . . .', *CP* 113; 'To a Wealthy Man . . .', *CP* 119; 'September 1913', *CP* 121; 'The Rose Tree', *CP* 206.

One walked: the reference is to Aengus, the Celtic god of youth, **25** beauty and poetry, who reigned in Tir-nan-ogue, the country of the young. The birds are his kisses transformed. Cf. 'The Song of Wandering Aengus', *CP* 66.

he bids me call . . . are done: cf. *The Land of Heart's Desire*, **61,** line 7. This appeal to the world of faery is echoed frequently in the early verse. See, especially, 'The Stolen Child', *CP* 20, 'Who Goes with Fergus?', *CP* 48, 'The Hosting of the Sidhe', *CP* 61, and Yeats's note:

The powerful and wealthy called the gods of ancient Ireland the Tuatha De Danaan, or the Tribes of the goddess Danu, but the poor called them, and still sometimes call them, the Sidhe, from Aes Sidhe or Sluagh Sidhe, the people of the Faery Hills, as these words are usually explained. Sidhe is also Gaelic for wind, and certainly the Sidhe have much to do with the wind. They journey in whirling winds, the winds that were called the dance of the daughters of Herodias in the Middle Ages, Herodias doubtless taking the place of some old goddess. When the country people see the leaves whirling on the road they bless themselves, because they believe the Sidhe to be passing by. They are almost always said to wear no covering upon their heads, and to let their hair stream out; and the great among them, for they have great and simple, go much on horseback. If any one becomes too much interested in them, and sees them over much, he loses all interest in ordinary things. I shall write a great deal elsewhere about such enchanted persons, and can give but an example or two now.

A woman near Gort, in Galway, says: 'There is a boy, now, of the Cloran's; but I wouldn't for the world let them think I spoke of him; it's two years since he came from America, and since that time he never went to Mass, or to Church, or to fairs, or to market, or to stand on the cross roads, or to hurling, or to nothing. And if anyone comes into the house, it's into the room he'll slip, not to see them; and as to work, he has the garden dug to bits, and the whole place smeared with cow dung; and such a crop as was never seen; and the alders all plaited till they look grand. One day he went as far as the chapel; but as soon as he got to the door he turned straight round again, as if he hadn't power to pass it. I wonder he wouldn't get the priest to read a Mass for him, or something; but the crop he has is grand, and you may know well he has some to help him.' One hears many stories of the kind; and a man whose son is believed to go out riding among them at night tells me that he is careless about everything, and lies in bed until it is late in the day. A doctor believes this boy to be mad. Those that are at times 'away', as it is called, know all things, but are afraid to speak. A countryman at Kiltartan says, 'There was one of the Lydons – John – was away for seven years, lying in his bed, but brought away at nights, and he knew everything; and one, Kearney, up in the mountains, a cousin of his own, lost two hoggets, and came and told him, and he knew the very spot where they were, and told him, and he got them back again. But *they* were vexed at that, and took away the power, so that he never knew anything again, no more than another.' This wisdom is the wisdom of the fools of the Celtic stories, that was above all the wisdom of the wise. Lomna, the fool of Fiann, had so great wisdom that his head, cut from his body, was still able to sing and prophesy; and a writer in the 'Encyclopaedia Britannica' writes that Tristram, in the oldest form of the tale of Tristram and Iseult, drank wisdom, and madness the shadow of wisdom, and not love, out of the magic cup (*W*R).

Cf. 'A Host of the Air', *CP* 63, and Yeats's note:

Some writers distinguish between the Sluagh Gaoith, the host of the air, and Sluagh Sidhe, the host of the Sidhe, and describe the host of the air of a peculiar malignancy. Dr. Joyce says, 'of all the different kinds of goblins . . . air demons were most dreaded by the people. They lived among clouds, and mists, and rocks, and hated the human race with the utmost malignity.'

A very old Arann charm, which contains the words 'Send God, by his strength, between us and the host of the Sidhe, between us and the host of the air', seems also to distinguish among them. I am inclined, however, to think that the distinction came in with Christianity and its belief about the prince of the air, for the host of the Sidhe, as I have already explained, are closely associated with the wind.

They are said to steal brides just after their marriage, and sometimes in a blast of wind. A man in Galway says, 'At Aughanish there were two couples came to the shore to be married, and one of the newly married women was in the boat with the priest, and they going back to the island; and a sudden blast of wind came, and the priest said some blessed words that were able to save himself, but the girl was swept.'

This woman was drowned; but more often the persons who are taken 'get the touch', as it is called, and fall into a half dream, and grow indifferent to all things, for their true life has gone out of the world, and is among the hills and the forts of the Sidhe. A faery doctor has told me that his wife 'got the touch' at her marriage because there was one of them wanted her; and the way he knew for certain was, that when he took a pitchfork out of the rafters, and told her it was a broom, she said, 'It is a broom'. She was, the truth is, in the magical sleep to which people have given a new name lately, that makes the imagination so passive that it can be moulded by any voice in any world into any shape. A mere likeness of some old woman, or even old animal, some one or some thing the Sidhe have no longer a use for, is believed to be left instead of the person who is 'away'; this some one or some thing can, it is thought, be driven away by threats, or by violence (though I have heard country women say that violence is wrong), which perhaps awakes the soul out of the magical sleep. The story in the poem is founded on an old Gaelic ballad that was sung and translated for me by a woman at Ballisodare in County Sligo; but in the ballad the husband found the keeners keening his wife when he got to his house. She was 'swept' at once; but the Sidhe are said to value those the most whom they but cast into a half dream, which may last for years, for they need the help of a living person in most of the things they do. There are many stories of people who seem to die and be buried – though the country people will tell you it is but some one or some thing put in their place that dies and is buried – and yet are brought back afterwards. These tales are perhaps memories of true awakenings out of the magical sleep, moulded by the imagination, under the influence of a mystical doctrine which it understands too literally, into the shape of some well-known traditional tale. One does not hear them as one hears the others, from the persons who are 'away', or from their wives or husbands; and one old man, who had often seen the Sidhe, began one of them with 'Maybe it is all vanity.'

Here is a tale that a friend of mine heard in the Burren hills, and it is a type of all:

'There was a girl to be married, and she didn't like the man, and she cried when the day was coming, and said she wouldn't go along with him. And the mother said, "Get into the bed, then, and I'll say that you're sick." And so she did. And when the man came the mother said to him, "You can't get her, she's sick in the bed." And he looked in and said, "That's not my wife that's in the bed, it's some old hag." And the mother began to cry and to roar. And he went out and got two hampers of turf and made a fire, that they thought he was going to burn the house down. And when the fire was kindled, "Come out now," says he, "and we'll see who you are, when I'll put you on the fire." And when she heard that, she gave one leap, and was out of the house, and they saw, then, it was an old hag she was. Well, the man asked the advice of an old woman, and she bid him go to a faery-bush that was near, and he might get some word of her. So he went there at night, and saw all sorts of grand people, and they in carriages or riding on horses, and among them he could see the girl he came to look for. So he went again to the old woman, and she said, "If you can get the three bits of blackthorn out of her hair, you'll get her again." So that night he went again, and that time he only got hold of a bit of her hair. But the old woman told him that was no use, and that he was put back now, and it might be twelve nights before he'd get her. But on the fourth night he got the third bit of blackthorn, and he took her, and she came away with him. He never told the mother he had got her; but one day she saw her at a fair, and, says, she "That's my daughter; I know her by the smile and by the laugh of her," and she with a shawl about her head. So the husband said, "You're right there, and hard I worked to get her." She spoke often of the grand things she saw underground, and how she used to have wine to drink, and to drive out in a carriage with four horses every night. And she used to be able to see her husband when he came to look for her, and she was greatly afraid he'd get a drop of the wine, for then he would have come underground and never left it again. And she was glad herself to come to earth again, and not to be left there.'

The old Gaelic literature is full of the appeals of the Tribes of the goddess Danu to mortals whom they would bring into their country; but the song of Midher to the beautiful Etain, the wife of the king who was called Echaid the ploughman, is the type of all.

'O beautiful woman, come with me to the marvellous land where one listens to a sweet music, where one has spring flowers in one's hair, where the body is like snow from head to foot, where no one is sad or silent, where teeth are white and eyebrows are black ... cheeks red like foxglove in flower ... Ireland is beautiful, but not so beautiful as the Great Plain I call you to. The beer of Ireland is heady, but the beer of the Great Plain is much more heady. How marvellous is the country I am speaking of! Youth does not grow old there. Streams with warm flood flow there; sometimes mead, sometimes wine. Men are charming and without a blot there, and love is not forbidden there. O woman, When you come into my powerful country you will wear a crown of gold upon your head. I will give you the flesh of swine, and you will have beer and milk to drink, O beautiful woman. O beautiful woman, come with me!' (*WR*)

He was angelical . . . to sleep: Aengus is 'not angelical' in the sense **27** that he does not share the orthodox Christian belief in sacrifice and the shared burden of sin, but Aleel, the representative of Aengus, by his capacity for love and poetic vision, asserts the ultimate supremacy of the spiritual world over the material.

her: the Virgin Mary. The line is echoed in **50**, line 4.

Country-under-Wave: Tir-fa-tonn (Tir-fo-thoinn), one of the old **28** Irish conceptions of the Other World. Cf. 'Under the Moon', *CP* 91, lines 6-7:

> Land-under-Wave, where out of the moon's light
>   and the sun's
> Seven old sisters wind the threads of the long-lived
>   ones

Here the seven old sisters may be the planets.

29   *the ninth and mightiest Hell*: in Dante's *Inferno* the ninth and lowest circle of Hell is reserved for traitors.

30   *the bog of Allen*: in Co. Kildare.
Fair Head: a point in the north-east of Co. Antrim, east of Ballycastle Bay.

37   *Thanks to that lie . . . sick*: refer back to **30**, lines 2–6.
hurried in like feathers: in similar feathers, i.e. as an owl.

40   *I may not touch it*: the demons may not touch Aleel's soul because he has given it in love to the Countess.

41   *His gaze . . . dreadful fear*: a premonition of their final defeat seen by Aleel at the end of the play in the artist's vision of an ultimate reality.

44   *Sign . . . in Hell*: see note on **50**, lines 6–8.

45   *The brazen door . . . bitterness*: this speech is rewritten in the alternative Abbey ending, losing its references to Irish mythological figures. See Yeats's note on page 4.
Balor: the Irish Chimaera, the leader of the hosts of darkness at the great battle of good and evil, life and death, light and darkness, which was fought out on the strands of Moytura, near Sligo (*P* (1895)).
eyes: although according to legend Balor had only one. Saul, *PYPl* 29.
Barach: acted as Concubar's pawn in the fate of the children of Usna by enticing Fergus away to a feast – Fergus having made an oath never to refuse a feast from him – so that the sons of Usna, Ardan and Ainle, could be killed in his absence.
the lascivious race: led by Orchil. See note on **46**, line 7.

Cailitin: a wizard in the Ulster Cycle of Irish legend who with his sons warred on Cuchulain with his magical arts.

Sualtim . . . Dectora: the father and mother of Cuchulain.

that great King: Conchubar, who pursued Deirdre and her lover Naoise, and finally killed him by treachery.

Naoise and Deirdre: the hero and 'the heroine of the most tender of old Gaelic stories. She was loved by Concobar, but fled from him with Naisi, only to be recaptured by treachery. She is the sad and beautiful woman of the Red Branch cycle . . .' (*P* (1895)).

their heads are twisted: like the twisted faces of the Diviners, Augurers, Sorcerers etc. of *Inferno* xx.

First, Orchil . . . take mine: these lines are cut in the Abbey **46** ending.

Orchil: a sorceress of the Fomoroh, 'the name of the gods of night and death and cold. The Fomoroh were mis-shapen and had now the heads of goats and bulls, and now but one leg, and one arm that came out of the middle of their breasts. They were the ancestors of the evil faeries and, according to one Gaelic writer, of all mis-shapen persons' (*P* (1895)). In the 1899 edition of *Poems* (1895), Yeats wrote that he had forgotten all he may once have known about her.

And while . . . sudden a storm: these lines are cut in the 1911 Abbey **47** ending.

SD Bring me the looking-glass: see note on **8**, line 23.   **48**

And I . . . bottomless space: these lines are cut in the 1911 Abbey ending.

Time and Fate and Change: cf. *The Land of Heart's Desire*, **59**, line 21, where they stand for the temporal world.

Angels and devils . . . helms: for this battle cf. 'The Valley of the **49** Black Pig', *CP* 73, and Yeats's own note after the title:

The Irish peasantry have for generations comforted themselves, in their misfortunes, with visions of a great battle, to be
fought in a mysterious valley called, 'The Valley of the Black
Pig', and to break at last the power of their enemies. A few
years ago, in the barony of Lisadell, in County Sligo, an old
man would fall entranced upon the ground from time to time,
and rave out a description of the battle; and I have myself
heard [it] said that the girths shall rot from the bellies of the
horses, because of the few men that shall come alive out of the
valley.

A longer note in *WR* read:

All over Ireland there are prophecies of the coming rout of the
enemies of Ireland, in a certain Valley of the Black Pig, and
these prophecies are, no doubt, now, as they were in the Fenian
days, a political force. I have heard of one man who would not
give any money to the Land League, because the Battle could
not be until the close of the century; but, as a rule, periods of
trouble bring prophecies of its near coming. A few years before
my time, an old man who lived at Lisadell, in Sligo, used to
fall down in a fit and rave out descriptions of the Battle; and a
man in Sligo has told me that it will be so great a battle that the
horses shall go up to their fetlocks in blood, and that their
girths, when it is over, will rot from their bellies for lack of a
hand to unbuckle them. The battle is a mythological battle, and
the black pig is one with the bristleless boar, that killed Dear-
mod, in November, upon the western end of Ben Bulben;
Misroide MacDatha's son, whose [an errata slip in the first
printing of *WR* read 'Misroide MacDatha's sow, whose']
carving brought on so great a battle; 'the croppy black sow,'
and 'the cutty black sow' of Welsh November rhymes (*Celtic
Heathendom*, 509–516); the boar that killed Adonis; the boar
that killed Attis; and the pig embodiment of Typhon (*Golden
Bough*, II, 26, 31). The pig seems to have been originally a genius
of the corn, and, seemingly because the too great power of their
divinity makes divine things dangerous to mortals, its flesh was
forbidden to many eastern nations; but as the meaning of the
prohibition was forgotten, abhorrence took the place of reverence, pigs and boars grew into types of evil, and were described
as the enemies of the very gods they once typified (*Golden Bough*,
II, 26–31, 56–7). The Pig would, therefore, become the Black
Pig, a type of cold and of winter that awake in November, the
old beginning of winter, to do battle with the summer, and

with the fruit and leaves, and finally, as I suggest; and as I believe, for the purposes of poetry; of the darkness that will at last destroy the gods and the world. The country people say there is no shape for a spirit to take so dangerous as the shape of a pig; and a Galway blacksmith – and blacksmiths are thought to be especially protected – says he would be afraid to meet a pig on the road at night; and another Galway man tells this story: 'There was a man coming the road from Gort to Garry-land one night, and he had a drop taken; and before him, on the road, he saw a pig walking; and having a drop in, he gave a shout, and made a kick at it, and bid it get out of that. And by the time he got home, his arm was swelled from the shoulder to be as big as a bag, and he couldn't use his hand with the pain of it. And his wife brought him, after a few days, to a woman that used to do cures at Rahasane. And on the road all she could do would hardly keep him from lying down to sleep on the grass. And when they got to the woman she knew all that happened; and, says she, it's well for you that your wife didn't let you fall asleep on the grass, for if you had done that but even for one instant, you'd be a lost man.'

It is possible that bristles were associated with fertility, as the tail certainly was, for a pig's tail is stuck into the ground in Courland, that the corn may grow abundantly, and the tails of pigs, and other animal embodiments of the corn genius, are dragged over the ground to make it fertile in different countries. Professor Rhys, who considers the bristleless boar a symbol of darkness and cold, rather than of winter and cold, thinks it was without bristles because the darkness is shorn away by the sun. It may have had different meanings, just as the scourging of the man-god has had different though not contradictory meanings in different epochs of the world. [The note in *CW* reads: If one reads Professor Rhys' *Celtic Heathendom* by the light of Professor Frazer's *Golden Bough*, and puts together what one finds there about the boar that killed Diarmuid, and other old Celtic boars and sows, one sees that the Battle is mythological, and that the Pig it is named from must be a type of cold and winter doing battle with the summer, or of death battling with life. For the purposes of poetry, at any rate, I think it a symbol of the darkness that will destroy the world . . .]

The Battle should, I believe, be compared with three other battles; a battle the Sidhe are said to fight when a person is being taken away by them; a battle they are said to fight in November for the harvest; the great battle the Tribes of the goddess Danu fought, according to the Gaelic chroniclers, with the Fomor at Moy Tura, or the Towery Plain.

I have heard of the battle over the dying both in County Galway and in the Isles of Arann, an old Arann fisherman having told me that it was fought over two of his children, and that he found blood in a box he had for keeping fish, when it was over; and I have written about it, and given examples elsewhere. A faery doctor, on the borders of Galway and Clare, explained it as a battle between the friends and enemies of the dying, the one party trying to take them, the other trying to save them from being taken. It may once, when the land of the Sidhe was the only other world, and when every man who died was carried thither, have always accompanied death. I suggest that the battle between the Tribes of the goddess Danu, the powers of light, and warmth, and fruitfulness, and goodness, and the Fomer, the powers of darkness, and cold and barrenness, and badness upon the Towery Plain, was the establishment of the habitable world, the rout of the ancestral darkness; that the battle among the Sidhe for the harvest is the annual battle of summer and winter; that the battle among the Sidhe at a man's death is the battle of life and death; and that the battle of the Black Pig is the battle between the manifest world and the ancestral darkness at the end of all things; and that all these battles are one, the battle of all things with shadowy decay. Once a symbolism has possessed the imagination of large numbers of men, it becomes, as I believe, an embodiment of disembodied powers, and repeats itself in dreams and visions, age after age.

Yeats also, in 1902, wrote that when he was discussing the Battle of the Black Pig with a Sligo countrywoman this seemed to her a battle between Ireland and England but to him an Armageddon which would quench all things in Ancestral Darkness again (*M* 111). Cf. *The Land of Heart's Desire*, **58**, lines 2–3.

Moytura: see note on **45**, line 9, though the reference is specifically to the 'Second Battle of Moytura' in which Balor lost his 'death-pouring eye'. Saul, *PYPl* 29.

SD Considerably altered in the 1911 Abbey ending. Balor and Moytura make way for Belial. The *Old Man* is cut, and the elaborate scenic vision is replaced by the entry at line 9 of a '*Winged Angel, carrying a torch and sword . . . from the R, with eyes fixed upon some distant thing. The Angel is about to pass out to the L, when Aleel speaks.*

The Angel stops a moment and turns.' Aleel then addresses lines 12–15
to the Angel, who '*turns again and is about to go, but is seized by Aleel.'*

For the description of the angels, cf. 'When I was in my twenties
I saw a drawing or etching by some French artist of an angel
standing against a midnight sky. The angel was old, wingless, and
armed like a knight, as impossibly tall as one of those figures at
Chartres Cathedral, and its face was worn by time and by innumerable battles . . . that image remained and I imitated it in the old
angels at the end of *The Countess Cathleen.'* ('Pages from a Diary in
1930', *E* 305–6)

The Light . . . deed alone: in *DP* Yeats wrote that 'the selling of the   50
souls', these lines and lines 4–7, **44,** which were 'considered an
attack on the Pope', caused disturbances at the first performances:

Every disturbance was drowned by cheers. Arthur Griffith,
afterwards slanderer of Lane and Synge, founder of the Sinn
Fein Movement, first President of the Irish Free State, and at
that time an enthusiastic anti-cleric, claimed to have brought
'a lot of men from the Quays and told them to applaud everything the Church would not like'. I did not want my play
turned into an anti-clerical demonstration, and decided from
the general feeling of discomfort when an evil peasant in my
first act trampled upon a Catholic shrine that the disturbances
were in part my own fault. In using what I considered traditional
symbols I forgot that in Ireland they are not symbols but
realities. But the attacks in the main, like those upon Synge
and O'Casey, came from the public ignorance of literary method.
The play itself was ill-constructed, the dialogue turning aside
at the lure of word or metaphor, very different I hope, from
the play as it is to-day after many alterations, every alteration
tested by performance. It was not, nor is it now, more than a
piece of tapestry. The Countess sells her soul, but she is not
transformed. If I were to think out that scene to-day, she would,
the moment her hand has signed, burst into loud laughter,
mock at all she has held holy, horrify the peasants in the midst
of their temptations. Nothing satisfied me but Florence Farr's
performance in the part of Aleel. Dublin talked of it for years,
and after five-and-thirty years I keep among my unforgettable
memories the sense of coming disaster she put into the words:
                              but now
Two grey horned owls hooted above our heads. (*A* 416–17)

The Land of Heart's Desire

This was first performed at the Avenue Theatre, Northumberland Avenue, London, in a double-bill with Shaw's *Arms and the Man*, on 29 March 1894, where it proved popular, running for a little over six weeks. Yeats tells us that he wrote it in response to Florence Farr's request for a one-act play in which her niece, Dorothy Paget, a girl of eight or nine, might make her first stage appearance. It was not founded on any particular Irish story. (For a brief comment on the theme, see p.29 below.) Writing to AE in 1904, Yeats had grown critical of its 'exaggeration of sentiment and sentimental beauty' (*L* 434), its popularity – it had been played under the auspices of the Irish Literary Society of New York and in San Francisco – coming, he thought, not from its merits but because of this weakness. Yeats revised it for a performance at the Abbey on 22 February 1912, having grown to dislike it without quite knowing what he disliked in it. During the course of this revision he cast it back in time 'because the metrical speech would have sounded unreal if spoken in a country cottage now that we have so many dialect comedies' (*P* (1895) repr. 1912). When he issued the play in 1923, it was introduced by the following preface:

> This play contains more of my first experiments in blank verse than any other in my books, for *The Countess Cathleen*, though published before it, was all re-written for later editions. Many passages that pleased me when I wrote them, and some that please me still, are mere ornament without dramatic value. A revival of the play but a few days ago at the Abbey Theatre enabled me to leave out these and other passages and to test the play without them. I think that it gained greatly, became indeed for the first time tolerable drama; certainly for the first time for many years gave its author pleasure. Amateurs perform it more often than any other play of mine, and I urge them to omit all lines that I have enclosed in brackets. It should sound simple and natural if played with the text I recommend,

and it may be that it would read better too, being a more perfect action, but I hesitate to leave out altogether what many people like, what, it may be, I can no longer judge. Somebody, Dr. Todhunter, the dramatic poet, I think, had said in my hearing that dramatic poetry must be oratorical, and I think that I wrote partly to prove that false; but every now and then I lose courage, as it seems, and remembering that I had some reputation as a lyric poet wrote for the reader of lyrics. When I saw it played with all needless and all mere lyrical passages cut away, I recalled the kind of pleasure that I had sought to create, and at last listened with the hope that this pleasure had reached those about me. Mr. Lennox Robinson, the producer, had kept all the players except the fairy child as still and statuesque as possible, so that the blank verse where there is so little animation seemed their natural utterance.' (*PC*)

The play was first printed in London 1894, Chicago 1895, then in *Poems*, London, 1895; London and Boston, 1895 (rev. and repr. London, 1899, 1901, 1904, 1908, 1912, 1913, 1919, 1920, 1922 twice, 1923, 1924, 1927, 1929); a revised version was printed in *The Bibelot*, Portland, Maine, Vol. x, no. 6, 1903, and in book form in 1903, Portland, Maine (repr. thirteen times to 1925); it also appeared in: *The Poetical Works of William B. Yeats*, Vol. ii, Dramatical Poems, New York and London, 1907 (1909, 1911); *The Collected Works in Verse and Prose of William Butler Yeats*, Vol. iii, Stratford-upon-Avon, 1908; *The Land of Heart's Desire*, New York, 1909; *The Land of Heart's Desire*, London, 1912 (1913, 1916, 1919, 1922 twice, 1923, 1924 five times, 1925); *The Poetical Works of William B. Yeats*, Vol. ii, Dramatic Poems, rev. and repr. New York and London, August 1912 (1914, 1916, 1917, 1919, 1921); *Selected Poems*, New York, 1921; *Plays and Controversies*, London, 1923; New York, 1924 (repr. London, 1927); *The Countess Cathleen and The Land of Heart's Desire*, London, 1925 (repr. 1929 twice); *The Land of Heart's Desire*, San Francisco, 1926; *The Collected Plays of W. B. Yeats*, London, 1934; New York, 1935; *Nine One-Act Plays*, London, 1937; *The Collected Plays of W. B. Yeats*, London, 1952; New York, 1953 (repr. London, 1953, 1960, 1963, 1966).

The cast of the first production was as follows: Maurteen Bruin, James Welch; Shawn Bruin, A. E. W. Mason; Father Hart, G. R. Foss; Bridget Bruin, Charlotte Morland; Maire Bruin, Winifred Fraser; A Faery Child, Dorothy Paget.

53   *Persons in the Play:*

In a letter to Martin E. Browne, Yeats wrote: 'I named the characters in my play Harts and Bruins to the best of my memory because those names were common in the village of Rosses at Rosses Point, Sligo. There were pilots and innkeepers of the name of Bruin and probably also of the name Hart, though in the case of the Harts my memory is more vague' (*L* 908).

55   *Ocris Head*: probably Aughris Head, a promontory on Sligo Bay. Saul, *PYPl* 32.

57   *Good People*: the faeries.

quicken wood: quicken is mountain ash, a tree thought to be sacred.

they may steal new-married brides: cf. 'The Host of the Air', *CP* 63 and Yeats's note:

> Any one who tastes fairy food or drink is glamoured and stolen by the fairies. This is why Bridget sets O'Driscoll to play cards. 'The folk of the air' is a Gaelic name for the fairies.

58   *When God . . . into pieces*: see note on **49**, lines 5–6.

59   *May Eve*: the time when the power of the faeries, for good or evil, is strongest.

Fate and Time and Change: see note on **48**, line 21.

61   *Come, faeries . . . a flame*: cf. Aleel's appeal to the Countess Cathleen, **25**, lines 12 ff, and notes on pp. 11–15.

too crafty and too wise: Maurteen.

too godly and too grave: Father Hart.

more bitter than the tide: Bridget.

Of drowsy love and my captivity: Shawn.

63   *Coolaney*: Coolooney, a village near Sligo.

From dawn . . . is old: cf. 'The Song of the Old Mother', *CP* 67: **64**

> I rise in the dawn, and I kneel and blow
> Till the seed of the fire flicker and glow;
> And then I must scrub and bake and sweep
> Till stars are beginning to blink and peep;
> And the young lie long and dream in their bed
> Of the matching of ribbons for bosom and head.
> And their day goes over in idleness,
> And they sigh if the wind but lift a tress:
> While I must work because I am old,
> And the seed of the fire gets feeble and cold.

The tortured thing: cf. *The Resurrection*, **584**, lines 18–19: *That makes* **66**
me shudder. The utmost possible suffering as an object of worship!
SD   Father Hart takes crucifix . . . room: note the irony by which it
is Father Hart's action that releases Mary from the protection of his
moral orthodoxy.

Ballygawley Hill: in Co. Sligo or Co. Tyrone.   **68**

Nuala and *Finvara* (lines 14, 17): the Arch-King and Queen of **69**
the faery host of Connacht.
Aengus of the Birds: see note on *The Countess Cathleen*, **25**, line 9.
Fiachra: one of the children of Lir.

White: the characteristic colour of faeryland. Cf. 'The White **71**
Birds', *CP* 46. This poem first appeared in *NO* (7 May 1892). The
title in this printing had a note after it which read '(*The birds of
fairyland are said to be white as snow. The Danaan Islands are the islands
of the fairies*)' 'The Danaan Shore is, of course, *Tier-nan-Oge*, or
fairyland.' (*CK*)
Madame MacBride (to whom, as Maud Gonne, the poem was
written) told A. N. Jeffares that she and Yeats had been walking
on the cliffs at Howth one afternoon (the day after Yeats had first
proposed to her and been rejected) and were resting when two

seagulls flew over their heads and on out to sea. She had said that if she was to have the choice of being any bird she would choose to be a seagull above all, a commonplace remark, but 'in three days he sent me the poem with its gentle theme, ''I would that we were my beloved, white birds on the foam of the sea''.'

72   'At the Abbey Theatre, where the platform of the stage comes out in front of the curtain, the curtain falls before the priest's last words. He remains outside the curtain and the words are spoken to the audience like an epilogue.' (*LHD* 1912)

Cathleen Ni Houlihan

An item in *The United Irishman*, 5 May 1902 included the texts of the lyrics and gave Yeats's interpretation of this play, which he sent in reply to questions submitted by the paper:

My subject is Ireland and its struggle for independence. The scene is laid in the West of Ireland at the time of the French landing. I have described a household preparing for the wedding of the son of the house. Everyone expects some good thing from the wedding. The bridegroom is thinking of his bride, the father of the fortune which will make them all more prosperous, and the mother of a plan of turning this prosperity to account by making her youngest son a priest, and the youngest son of a greyhound pup the bride promised to give him when she marries. Into this household comes Kathleen Ni Houlihan herself, and the bridegroom leaves his bride, and all the hopes come to nothing. It is the perpetual struggle of the cause of Ireland and every other ideal cause against private hopes and dreams, against all that we mean when we say the world. I have put into the mouth of Kathleen Ni Houlihan verses about those who have died or are about to die for her, and these verses are the key of the rest. She sings of one yellow-haired Donough in stanzas that were suggested to me by some old Gaelic folk-song:

> I will go cry with the woman,
>   For yellow-haired Donough is dead,
> With a hempen-rope for a neck-cloth,
>   And a white cloth on his head.
>
> I am come to cry with you woman,
>   My hair is unbound and unwound;
> I remember him ploughing his field,
>   Turning up the red side of the ground.
>
> And building his barn on the hill,
>   With the good-mortared stone;
> Oh, we'd have pulled down the gallows,
>   Had it happened at Enniscrone.

And just before she goes out she sings:

> Do not make a great keening
>   When the graves have been dug to-morrow
> Do not call the white-scarfed riders
>   To the buryings that shall be to-morrow;
> Do not spread the food to call strangers,
>   To the wakes that shall be to-morrow,

And after a few words of dialogue she goes out crying:

> They shall be remembered for ever;
> They shall be alive for ever;
> They shall be speaking for ever,
> The people shall hear them for ever.

I have written the whole play in the English of the West of Ireland, the English of people who think in Irish. My play, 'The Land of Heart's Desire', was, in a sense, the call of the heart, the heart seeking its own dream [see commentary, pp. 22–3]; this play is the call of country, and I have a plan of following it up with a little play about the call of religion, and printing the three plays together some day. (Article in *The United Irishman*, 5 May 1902; *VPl* 234–5.)

When dedicating two volumes of his plays to Lady Gregory, Yeats wrote in February 1903:

When I was a boy I used to wander about at Rosses Point and Ballisodare listening to old songs and stories. I wrote down what I heard and made poems out of the stories or put them into the little chapters of the first edition of 'The Celtic Twilight', and that is how I began to write in the Irish way.

Then I went to London to make my living, and though I spent a part of every year in Ireland and tried to keep the old life in my memory by reading every country tale I could find in books or old newspapers, I began to forget the true countenance of country life. The old tales were still alive for me indeed, but with a new, strange, half unreal life, as if in a wizard's glass, until at last, when I had finished 'The Secret

Rose', and was half-way through 'The Wind Among the Reeds', a wise woman in her trance told me that my inspiration was from the moon, and that I should always live close to water, for my work was getting too full of those little jewelled thoughts that come from the sun and have no nation. I had no need to turn to my books of astrology to know that the common people are under the moon, or to Porphyry to remember the image-making power of the waters. Nor did I doubt the entire truth of what she said to me, for my head was full of fables that I had no longer the knowledge and emotion to write. Then you brought me with you to see your friends in the cottages, and to talk to old wise men on Slieve Echtge, and we gathered together, or you gathered for me, a great number of stories and traditional beliefs. You taught me to understand again, and much more perfectly than before, the true countenance of country life.

One night I had a dream almost as distinct as a vision, of a cottage where there was well-being and firelight and talk of a marriage, and into the midst of that cottage there came an old woman in a long cloak. She was Ireland herself, that Cathleen ni Houlihan for whom so many songs have been sung and about whom so many stories have been told and for whose sake so many have gone to their death. I thought if I could write this out as a little play I could make others see my dream as I had seen it, but I could not get down out of that high window of dramatic verse, and in spite of all you had done for me I had not the country speech. One has to live among the people, like you, of whom an old man said in my hearing, 'She has been a serving-maid among us', before one can think the thoughts of the people and speak with their tongue. We turned my dream into the little play, 'Cathleen ni Houlihan', and when we gave it to the little theatre in Dublin and found that the working people liked it, you helped me to put my other dramatic fables into speech. Some of these have already been acted, but some may not be acted for a long time, but all seem to me, though they were but a part of a summer's work, to have more of that countenance of country life than anything I have done since I was a boy. (*Where There is Nothing*, London, 1903; *VPl* 232)

He remembered the play in 1908:

Miss Maud Gonne played very finely, and her great height made Cathleen seem a divine being fallen into our mortal infirmity. Since then the part has been twice played in America by women who insisted on keeping their young faces, and one of these when she came to the door dropped her cloak, as I have been told, and showed a white satin dress embroidered with shamrocks. Upon another, – or was it the same occasion? – the player of Bridget wore a very becoming dress of the time of Louis the Fourteenth. The most beautiful woman of her time, when she played my Cathleen, 'made up' centuries old, and never should the part be played but with a like sincerity. This was the first play of our Irish School of folk-drama, and in it that way of quiet movement and careful speech which has given our players some little fame first showed itself, arising partly out of deliberate opinion and partly out of the ignorance of the players. Does art owe most to ignorance or to knowledge? Certainly it comes to its deathbed full of knowledge. I cannot imagine this play, or any folk-play of our school, acted by players with no knowledge of the peasant, and of the awkwardness and stillness of bodies that have followed the plough, or too lacking in humility to copy these things without convention or caricature.

The lines beginning 'Do not make a great keening' and 'They shall be remembered for ever' are said or sung to an air heard by one of the players in a dream. This music is with the other music at the end of the third volume. (Appendix II, *Cathleen ni Houlihan, CW* IV; *VPl* 233)

A 'Note on the Music' in *The Hour Glass, Cathleen Ni Houlihan, The Pot of Broth* (1904) reads:

The little song in 'Cathleen ni Houlihan' beginning, 'I will come and cry with you, woman,' is sung by our players to an old Irish air, and the lines beginning, 'Do not make a great keening' and 'They shall be remembered for ever' to an air heard in a dream by one of the players. (*VPl* 234)

Stephen Gwynn's account of the performance in *Irish Drama*, 1936, p. 158, is noteworthy:

The effect of *Cathleen ni Houlihan* on me was that I went home asking myself if such plays should be produced unless one was prepared for people to go out to shoot and be shot. Yeats was not alone responsible; no doubt but Lady Gregory had helped him to get the peasant speech so perfect; but above all Miss Gonne's impersonation had stirred the audience as I have never seen another audience stirred.

Yeats himself alluded to the play in his old age in 'The Man and the Echo' (*CP* 393):

> Did that play of mine
> Send out certain men the English shot?

And this play was discussed by Yeats with an awareness of the dangers of using drama to arouse opinion as early as 1903:

> I am a Nationalist, and certain of my intimate friends have made Irish politics the business of their lives, and this made certain thoughts habitual with me, and an accident made these thoughts take fire in such a way that I could give them dramatic expression. I had a very vivid dream one night, and I made *Cathleen ni Houlihan* out of this dream. But if some external necessity had forced me to write nothing but drama with an obviously patriotic intention, instead of letting my work shape itself under the casual impulses of dreams and daily thoughts, I would have lost, in a short time, the power to write movingly upon any theme. I could have aroused opinion, but I could not have touched the heart ... (*E* 116)

This play was first performed by W. G. Fay's Irish National Dramatic Co. at St Teresa's Abstinence Association Hall, Clarendon Street, Dublin on 2 April, 1902. The cast was: Cathleen, Miss Maud Gonne; Delia Cahel, Miss Maire nic Sheublagh; Bridget Gillan, Miss M. T. Quinn; Patrick Gillan, Mr C. Caufield; Michael Gillan, Mr T. Dudley Digges; Peter Gillan, Mr W. G. Fay. It was first printed in *Samhain*, October 1902, and subsequently appeared as follows: *Cathleen Ni Houlihan*, London, 1902; *The Hour-Glass and Other Plays*, New York and London, 1904 (1906, 1909, 1911, 1912, 1914, 1915, 1919; the title in these editions is *Cathleen ni Hoolihan*); *The Hour-Glass, Cathleen-Ni-Houlihan, The Pot of Broth*, London, 1904 (repr. Dublin, 1905); *Cathleen Ni Houlihan*, London, 1906; *The Unicorn from the Stars and Other Plays*, New York, 1908 (1915); *The Collected Works*, Vol. IV, Stratford-upon-Avon, 1908; *Cathleen ni Houlihan*, London, 1909; *Cathleen ni Houlihan*, Stratford-upon-Avon, 1911; *Plays for an Irish Theatre*, London and Stratford-upon-Avon, 1911 (1913); *Plays in Prose and Verse*, London, 1922; New York, 1924 (repr. London, 1922, 1926, 1931); *The Collected Plays of W. B. Yeats*, London, 1934; New York, 1935; *Nine One-Act Plays*, London, 1937; *The Collected Plays of W. B. Yeats*, London, 1952;

New York, 1953 (repr. London, 1953, 1960, 1963, 1966). It is included in the *Variorum Edition*, ed. Russell D. Alspach, 1966; *Selected Plays*, Papermac edition, ed. A. Norman Jeffares, London, 1964; and *Eleven Plays of William Butler Yeats*, ed. A. Norman Jeffares, New York, 1964. The play was translated into Irish by Tomás Luibhéid, and produced in the Abbey Theatre, Dublin, 20 April 1946.

75 *Title:*

Cathleen (or Kathleen) ni Houlihan: a symbol of Ireland. Yeats spelt the name Cathleen ny Houlihan in the *Samhain* text, *Cathleen Ni Hoolihan* in *Cathleen Ni Hoolihan* (1902) and *Cathleen ni Hoolihan* in *The Hour-Glass and Other Plays* (1904). Subsequently the name is spelt Cathleen ni Houlihan. He used the spelling Kathleen in his reply to queries in *The United Irishman*, 5 May 1902.

In *Cathleen Ni Hoolihan* (1908) an epigraph was included:

> Young she is, and fair she is, and would be
>   crowned a queen
> Were the King's son at home with
>   Kathaleen-Ny-Houlahan.

This edition, only, was dedicated 'To the Memory of William Rooney'. Senator Michael Yeats, 'W. B. Yeats and Irish Folk Song', *Southern Folk Lore Quarterly*, xxxi, June 1966, thinks the title was inspired by a song written by the Gaelic poet Blind William Heffernan.

SD Killala, in 1798: Killala is in Co. Mayo, in the West of Ireland, where a French force of a thousand republican soldiers commanded by General Humbert landed on 22 August 1798. They were joined by many unarmed peasants, marched inland to Castlebar, where they defeated a large body of yeomanry. They were surrounded by Lord Cornwallis at Ballinamuck and forced to surrender. The *Hoche*, a French ship, later arrived in Lough Swilly and had to surrender to an English squadron. Wolfe Tone was on board. As a leader of the United Irishmen, he had earlier despaired of altering the position of the Irish Parliament and joined in the creation of a revolutionary movement which began in the mid-1790s. Tone went to America and then arrived in Paris in 1796, where he rapidly became friendly with Carnot, who gave him the rank of adjutant-general in the French army. As J. C. Beckett has remarked of the state of affairs in Ireland at the time, 'the grip which the Irish government had on the situation was a precarious one and it was certain that if any considerable French force should land, a dangerous and possibly disastrous rebellion would break out'. (*A Short History of Ireland*, 1952, p. 136) In December 1796 he sailed in a fleet of forty-three ships some of which reached Bantry Bay. The weather – an easterly gale – and mismanagement caused the return of this expedition to France. Tone's *Diary* gives a despairing account of this failure. A second French fleet – intended to convey 14,000 men to Ireland – was defeated at Camperdown in October 1791. The Directory of the United Irishmen gave up hope of large-scale French aid, and the 1798 Rebellion began.

The play draws upon memories of the period when great numbers of the population, according to Edmund Curtis, 'now preferred a "union with France" to a "union with Britain" if such had to be. According to the current patriotic song "the Shan Van Vocht", the French were already "on the sea" and during two years several expeditions menaced English rule in Ireland.' (*A History of Ireland*, 1936, p. 338). For the latest detailed account of the period, see Thomas Pakenham, *The Year of Liberty. The Story of the great Irish Rebellion of 1798*, 1969.

hurling: 'hurling-match' is read in the *Samhain* text and up to *The Unicorn from the Stars and Other Plays* (1908). Hurley or hurling is an Irish game, resembling hockey. It is mentioned in the Red Branch stories, and was encouraged by the Gaelic Athletic Association which preceded the Gaelic League (established in 1893). Its mention here has patriotic, nationalist resonances.

Maurteen: spelt thus in *Samhain* text, in *The Hour-Glass and Other* **76** *Plays* (1904) and the text of the *Collected Plays* (1934 and 1952). Other editions use the spelling Murteen.

and I after making it: a Gaelic syntactical construction.

77   *and you feeding them*: a Gaelic syntactical construction.
Ballina: a country town in north-east Mayo.
stook: a bundle.

78   *Enniscrone*: G. B. Saul (*PYPl* 35), suggests Inchicronan, Co. Clare, but Enniscrone (now a small seaside resort) in the extreme west of Sligo, not far from Ballina, is probably intended.

79   *tramping the country like a poor scholar*: the existence of the 'hedge scholars' was caused by one of the Penal Laws which followed the victories of William of Orange. This made it illegal for Catholics to go abroad for education or keep a public school in Ireland. The Gaelic tradition survived through 'Courts of Poetry', informal gatherings of poets in barns or kitchens, and through the illegal schools maintained by travelling 'hedge schoolmasters'. Aodh de Blacam sums up the effect of the poets in terms which also apply to the hedge schoolmasters: 'With a prodigious zeal for learning, they sometimes mastered the Classic languages, but their individual achievements could not prevail against the standards of the times, which demanded in literature only what was comprehensible to the illiterate, although spiritually refined and sensitive, people . . . Gaelic poetry had become democratic' (*A First Book of Irish Literature*, Dublin, n.d., p. 134).

81   *Too many strangers in the house*: presumably the English in Ireland (and the Scots in Ulster).
My land . . . taken from me: a reference to the 'Plantations' of Ireland by England.
four beautiful green fields: the four provinces of Ireland – Ulster, Munster, Leinster and Connaught.
Kilglass: spelt Kilglas in *Samhain* version and in *The Hour-Glass and Other Plays* (1904). A village near Killala.

yellow-haired Donough . . . Galway: the folk song 'Donnchadh Bán'   **82**
or 'Flaxen-haired Donough' was the source for this song. See
Myles Dillon, *Early Irish Literature*, 1948, p. 185. The lament or
keen for Fair-haired Donough was sometimes thought to have been
composed by Anthony Raftery (*c*. 1784–1835) of Mayo, a blind
poet and fiddler. See Michael Yeats, 'W. B. Yeats and Irish Folk
Song'.

a red man of the O'Donnells: probably 'Red' Hugh Roe O'Donnell   **83**
(*c*. 1571–1602) who escaped from prison in Dublin, was inaugurated
as 'The O'Donnell' (1592), overran Connacht, shared in the Irish
victory at the Battle of the Yellow Ford on the Blackwater, failed to
reduce Mountjoy's forces at Kinsale, went to Spain for aid, and was
reputedly poisoned there at Salamanca. O'Donnell was the last of
the old Gaelic Kings.

a man of the O'Sullivans: probably Donal O'Sullivan Beare (1560–
1618), who, when Philip III's fleet occupied Kinsale, Co. Cork in
September 1607, received a Spanish garrison in his fort at Dunbay.
Dunbay was the only castle which resisted the English forces after
the battle of Kinsale. O'Sullivan fought his way north, and thence
to London. Failing to obtain restitution from James, he went to
Spain where a refugee killed him.

Brian . . . Clontarf: Brian Boru, the High King of Ireland, was
killed in the Battle of Clontarf, 1014, in which the Danes were
decisively defeated.

Poor Old Woman: the Shan van vocht, another image of Ireland.   **85**
Cathleen the daughter of Houlihan: cf. Yeats's lyric poem 'Red Hanrahan's Song about Ireland' (*CP* 90).

keening: an Irish form of mourning over the dead, raising the
caoine.

white-scarfed riders: white robed priests at funerals.   **86**
wakes: gatherings in honour of the dead; a watching over the
body.

the touch: to be infected.

87   *Killala*: see note on **75,** *SD*.

88   *a young girl, and she had the walk of a queen*: the part suited Yeats's memories of first meeting Maud Gonne:

> Her movements were worthy of her form, and I understood at last why the poet of antiquity, where we would but speak of face and form, sings, loving some lady, that she paces like a goddess. (*MS* 40)

And there is the more finished portrait in *Autobiographies*:

> ... that day she seemed a classical impersonation of the Spring, the Virgilian commendation 'She walks like a goddess' made for her alone (*A* 123).

Cf. references to Helen who 'walked with her boy' at Troy ('When Helen lived', *CP* 124) and the line in 'Fallen Majesty' which records the change in Maud Gonne after her marriage and subsequent separation from John MacBride: 'Whereon a thing once walked that seemed a burning cloud' (*CP* 138). Maud Gonne was directly compared to a queen in 'Presences' (*CP* 174): 'And one, it may be a queen.' Her long flowing line as she walked was commended in 'A Thought from Propertius' (*CP* 172). Her stature, praised in 'Peace' (*CP* 103) and elsewhere, was very effective in the initial production of the play as Yeats has recorded:

> Miss Maud Gonne played very finely, and her great height made Cathleen seem a divine being fallen into our mortal infirmity. (Appendix II, *Cathleen ni Houlihan*, *CW* v; *VPl* 233)

One of Yeats's own comments on *Cathleen ni Houlihan* is worth recording; in his unpublished notes written for Horace Plunkett's use in the 1904 inquiry into the Abbey Theatre's patent he wrote:

> It may be said that it is a political play of a propagandist kind. This I deny. I took a piece of human life, thoughts that men had felt, hopes that they had died for, and I put this into what I believe to be a sincere dramatic form. I have never written a play to advocate any kind of opinion and I think that such a play would be necessarily bad art, or at any rate a very humble kind of art. At the same time I feel that I have no right to exclude for myself or for others, any of the passionate material of drama. (Quoted by R. Ellmann, *IY* 295–6)

The first performance of this 'trivial, unambitious retelling of an
old folk-tale [which] showed William Fay for the first time as a
most loveable comedian' (*A* 452), was given in Dublin, 30 October
1902, in the Antient Concert Rooms. It was written with Lady
Gregory's help, but 'neither Lady Gregory nor I could yet distinguish between the swift-moving town dialect – the dialect of the
Irish novelists no matter what part of Ireland they wrote of – and
the slow-moving country dialect' (*A* 451). It proved hardly less
popular than *Cathleen ni Houlihan.*

The play was first printed in *The Gael*, New York, September
1903, and subsequently in: *The Hour Glass and Other Plays*, New
York and London, 1904 (1904, 1906, 1909, 1911, 1912, 1914, 1915,
1919); *The Hour Glass, Cathleen Ni Houlihan, The Pot of Broth*,
London, 1904 (repr. Dublin, 1905); *The Pot of Broth*, London, 1905;
The Pot of Broth, London, 1911; *Plays in Prose and Verse*, London,
1922; New York, 1924 (repr. London, 1922, 1926, 1931); *The
Collected Plays of W. B. Yeats*, London, 1934; New York, 1935;
Nine One-Act Plays, London, 1937; *The Collected Plays of W. B.
Yeats*, London, 1952; New York, 1953 (repr. London, 1953, 1960,
1963, 1966).

The cast of the first performance was as follows: A Beggarman,
W. G. Fay; Sibby, Maire T. Quinn; John, her husband, P. J. Kelly.
In a note to *PPV*, Yeats wrote:

I did not include this play in Mr. Bullen's collected edition of
my work, as it seemed too slight a thing to perpetuate, but I
found a little time ago that my own theatre had put it into
rehearsal without asking my leave; and that some American
had written for rights in it, and another American produced it
without rights. I have therefore retouched it a little, and changed
a song that I had always hated, and once more admit it to my
canon. If it has a lasting interest, it is that it was the first comedy
in dialect, of our movement, and gave Mr. William Fay his

first opportunity as a comedian. I have no record of the cast on its first production, in, I think, 1902, for that was before the Abbey Theatre and its records; except that Mr. William Fay was Tramp, and played it not only with great humour but with great delicacy and charm. In some country village an audience of farmers once received it in stony silence, and at the fall of the curtain a farmer stood up and said nobody there had ever seen a play. Then Mr. William Fay explained what a play was, and the farmer asked that it might be performed again, and at the second performance there was much laughter and cheers. I hardly know how much of the play is my work, for Lady Gregory helped me as she has helped in every play of mine where there is dialect, and sometimes where there is not. In those first years of the Theatre we all helped one another with plots, ideas, and dialogue, but certainly I was the most indebted as I had no mastery of speech that purported to be of real life. This play may be more Lady Gregory's than mine, for I remember once urging her to include it in her own work, and her refusing to do so. The dialect, unlike that of *Cathleen ni Houlihan*, which was written about the same date, has not, I think, the right temper, being gay, mercurial, and suggestive of rapid speech. Probably we were still under the influence of the Irish novelists, who never escaped, even when they had grown up amid country speech, from the dialect of Dublin. The dialect of *Cathleen ni Houlihan* is, I think, true in temper but it has no richness, no abundance. The first use of Irish dialect, rich, abundant, and correct, for the purposes of creative art was in J. M. Synge's *Riders to the Sea*, and Lady Gregory's *Spreading the News*.

91   *Fiannta-h-Eireann*: a species of legendary professional infantry who supposedly spent half the year hunting and camping. Saul, *PYPl* 37.

92   *kippeens*: small sticks or chicken bones.

93   *Jack the journeyman*: this figure turns up in *Words for Music Perhaps*, 'Crazy Jane and Jack the Journeyman', *CP* 292.

Slanlus: lichen. Saul, *PYPl* 37.   **96**

Fearavan: creeping buttercup or crowfoot. Saul, *PYPl* 37.   **97**
Athair-talav: ground ivy. Saul, *PYPl* 37.

stirabout: a sort of porridge of meal.   **98**

Lochlann: Norway. Saul, *PYPl* 37.   **99**

My Paistin Finn: white, or fair Finn. Printed as one of 'Two Songs   **100**
Rewritten for the Tune's Sake', *CP* 325. *Paistin Finn* is a Munster
folk tune, sung to a lively air. It may be a popularised version of a
song from the Ossianic cycle as the title means 'Little child of
Fionn'. Fionn was Oisin's father. Since the Ossianic cycle was more
popular than the Ulster cycle it is not unlikely, Dr Brendan Kennelly
suggests, that Paistin Finn, which is purely folk, was originally
heroic in the Fenian manner.

speckled shin: a sign of old age.   **101**

Biddy Early: a wise woman, who lived between Feakle and Tulla   **104**
in Co. Clare, in the nineteenth century. Lady Gregory collected
many stories about her in *Visions and Beliefs in the West of Ireland*,
to which Yeats contributed two essays and some notes.
boreen: a grassy lane.

The King's Threshold

This play was first performed by the Irish National Theatre Society at the Molesworth Hall, Dublin on 7 October 1903. The cast was: Seanchan, Frank Fay; King Guaire, Mr P. Kelly; Lord High Chamberlain, Mr Shamus O'Sullivan; Soldier, Mr William Conroy; Monk, Mr S. Sheridan-Neill; Mayor, Mr William Fay; A Cripple, Mr Patrick Columb; A Court Lady, Miss Honor Saville; Another Court Lady, Miss Dora Melville; A Princess, Miss Sara Allgood; Another Princess, Miss Dora Gunning; Fedelm, Miss Maire MacShinbhlaigh; A Servant, Mr P. MacShinbhlaigh; Another Servant, Mr P. Josephs; A Pupil, Mr G. Roberts; Another Pupil, Mr Cartia McChormac.

The play was financed by Miss E. F. Horniman, who designed and made the costumes. Yeats told Frank Fay that he was 'very glad' that William Fay had cast his brother as Seanchan 'an exhausting part . . . but you will find plenty to act and the best dramatic verse I have written to speak' (*L* 409). He told Stephen Gwynn that he thought *The King's Threshold* ('the most ambitious thing we have attempted') the best thing he had ever done in dramatic verse (*L* 410).

This play was first printed in *The United Irishman*, 9 September 1903. The text of the play subsequently appeared as follows: *The King's Threshold*, New York, 1904; *The King's Threshold and On Baile's Strand*, London, 1904; *The King's Threshold*, Dublin, 1905; in *Poems, 1899–1905*, London and Dublin, 1906; in *The Poetical Works of William B. Yeats*, Vol. II, Dramatical Poems, New York and London, 1907 (1909, 1911); in *The Collected Works in Verse and Prose of William Butler Yeats*, Vol. II, Stratford-upon-Avon, 1908 (Vol. VIII of this edition contains the Prologue to *The King's Threshold*, Stratford-upon-Avon, 1911); in *Plays for an Irish Theatre*,

London and Stratford-upon-Avon, 1911 (1913); in *The Poetical Works of William B. Yeats*, Vol. II, Dramatic Poems, rev. New York and London, 1912 (1914, 1916, 1917, 1919, 1921); *The King's Threshold*, Stratford-upon-Avon, 1915; in *Seven Poems and a Fragment*, Dundrum, 1922 (this contains 63 lines, 'A New End for The Kings' Threshold'); *Plays in Prose and Verse*, London 1922; New York, 1924 (repr. London, 1922, 1926, 1931); *The Collected Plays of W. B. Yeats*, 1934; New York, 1935; *The King's Threshold*, London, 1937; *The Collected Plays of W. B. Yeats*, London, 1952; New York, 1953 (repr. London, 1953, 1960, 1963, 1966).

The Prologue was written for the first production of the play in Dublin but, as Yeats stated in the *Collected Works*, was 'not used, as owing to the smallness of the company, nobody could be spared to speak it.' The Prologue as it appeared in *The United Irishman*, 9 September 1903 ran as follows:

An old man with a red dressing-gown, red slippers and red nightcap, holding a brass candlestick with a guttering candle in it, comes on, in front of curtain.

Old Man – 'I've got to speak the prologue. [*He shuffles on a few steps.*] My nephew, that's one of the players, came to me and I in my bed, and my prayers said, and the candle put out, and he told me there were so many characters in this new play, that all the company were in it, whether they had been long or short at the business, and that there wasn't one left to speak the prologue. Wait a bit, there's a draught here. [*He pulls the curtain closer together*] That's better. And that's why I'm here, and maybe I'm a fool for my pains.

'And my nephew said, there are a good many plays to be played for you, some tonight and some on other nights through the winter, and the most of them are simple enough, and tell out their story to the end. But as to the big play you are to see to-night, my nephew taught me to say what the poet had taught him to say about it. [*Puts down candlestick and puts right finger on left thumb.*] First, he who told the story of Seanchan on King Guaire's threshold long ago in the old books told it wrongly, for he was a friend of the king, or maybe afraid of the king, and so put the king in the right. But he that tells the story now, being a poet, has put the poet in the right.

'And then [*touches other finger*] I am to say: Some think it would be a finer tale if Seanchan had died at the end of it, and the king had the guilt at his door, for that might have served the poet's cause better in the end. But that is not true, for if he that is in the story but a shadow and an image of poetry had not risen up from the death that threatened him, the ending would not have been true and joyful enough to be put into the voices of players and proclaimed in the mouths of trumpets, and poetry would have been badly served. [*He takes up the candlestick again*]

'And as to what happened Seanchan after, my nephew told me he didn't know, and the poet didn't know, and it's likely there's nobody that knows. But my nephew thinks he never sat down at the king's table again, after the way he had been treated, but that he went to some quiet green place in the hills with Fedelm, his sweetheart, where the poor people made much of him because he was wise, and where he made songs and poems, and it's likely enough he made some of the old songs and the old poems the poor people on the hillsides are saying and singing to-day. [*A trumpet-blast.*]

'Well, it's time for me to be going. That trumpet means that the curtain is going to rise, and after a while the stage there will be filled up with great ladies and great gentlemen, and poets, and a king with a crown on him, and all of them as high up in themselves with the pride of their youth and their strength and their fine clothes as if there was no such thing in the world as cold in the shoulders, and speckled shins, and the pains in the bones and the stiffness in the joints that make an old man that has the whole load of the world on him ready for his bed.

'And it would be better for me, that nephew of mine to be thinking less of his play-acting, and to have remembered to boil down the knapweed with a bit of threepenny sugar, for me to be wetting my throat with now and again through the night, and drinking a sup to ease the pains in my bones.'

I have made this prologue for a book of plays which I have written for the Irish National Theatre Society. The first play in the volume will be 'On the King's Threshold', which is to be performed for the first time in the Molesworth Hall, on the 24th, 25th and 26th of this month. This and a volume of prose plays to be published at the same time will contain practically all my one-act plays. I have as far as possible taken the usual steps to retain the acting rights, but in some cases will be ready to give leave to societies of amateurs to perform them in country places, after consultation with Mr. Fay (*VPl* 313–14)

In the London edition of 1904, Yeats explained that both *The King's Threshold* and *On Baile's Strand* had been written for Mr Fay's

'Irish National Theatre'; both of them, he commented, were founded on Old Irish prose romances, but he had borrowed some ideas for the arrangement of his subject in *The King's Threshold* from *Sancan the Bard*, a play published ten years earlier by Edwin Ellis. It also owed something to a Middle Irish Tale *Immtheacht na Tromdaimhe* which Yeats probably read in *Trans. Ossianic Society*, v.1 and in Lady Wilde's *Ancient Legends of Ireland*, p. 159 ff. Miss D. M. Hoare, *The Works of Morris and Yeats in Relation to Early Saga Literature*, 1937, p. 121, has shown how Yeats departed from these sources. In Lady Wilde's *Seanchan the Bard and the King of the Cats*, Scanchan and Guaire are eventually reconciled. Here is her version of the legend:

There is an amusing legend preserved in Ossianic tradition of the encounter between Seanchan, the celebrated chief poet of Ireland, and the King of all the Cats, who dwelt in a cave near Clonmacnoise.

In ancient Ireland the men of learning were esteemed beyond all other classes; all the great ollaves and professors and poets held the very highest social position, and took precedence of the nobles, and ranked next to royalty. The leading men amongst them lived luxuriously in the great Bardic House; and when they went abroad through the country they travelled with a train of minor bards, fifty or more, and were entertained free of cost by the kings and chiefs, who considered themselves highly honoured by the presence of so distinguished a company at their court. If the reception was splendid and costly, the praise of the entertainer was chanted by all the poets at the feast; but if any slight were offered, then the Ard-Filé poured forth his stinging satire in such bitter odes, that many declared they would sooner die than incur the anger of the poets or be made subject of their scathing satire.

All the learned men and professors, the ollaves of music, poetry, oratory, and of the arts and sciences generally, formed a great Bardic Association, who elected their own president, with the title of Chief Poet of all Ireland, and they also elected chief poets for each of the provinces. Learned women, likewise, and poetesses, were included in the Bardic Association, with distinct and recognized privileges, both as to revenue and costly apparel. Legal enactments even were made respecting the number of colours allowed to be worn in their mantles – the poets being allowed six colours, and the poetess five in her robe and mantle; the number of colours being a distinct recognition and visible sign of rank, and therefore very highly esteemed. But in time, as a consequence of their many and great privileges, the pride and insolence of the learned class, the ollamhs, poets, and poetesses, became so insufferable, that even the kings trembled before them. This is shown in the Ossianic tale, from which we may gather that Seanchan the Bard, when entertained at the court of King Guaire, grew jealous of the attention paid to the nobles while he was present. So he sulked at the festival, and made himself eminently disagreeable, as will be seen by the following legend:—

When Seanchan, the renowned Bard, was made *Ard-Filé*, or Chief Poet of Ireland, Guaire, the king of Connaught, to do him honour, made a great feast for him and the whole Bardic Association. And all the professors went to the king's house, the great ollaves of poetry and history and music, and of the arts and sciences; and the learned, aged females, Grug and Crag and Grangait; and all the chief poets and poetesses of Ireland, an amazing number. But Guaire the king entertained them all splendidly, so that the ancient pathway to his palace is still called 'The Road of the Dishes'.

And each day he asked, 'How fares it with my noble guests?' But they were all discontented, and wanted things he could not get for them. So he was very sorrowful, and prayed to God to be delivered from 'the learned men and women, a vexatious class.'

Still the feast went on for three days and three nights. And they drank and made merry. And the whole Bardic Association entertained the nobles with the choicest music and professional accomplishments.

But Seanchan sulked and would neither eat nor drink, for he was jealous of the nobles of Connaught. And when he saw how much they consumed of the best meats and wine, he declared he would taste no food till they and their servants were all sent away out of the house.

And when Guaire asked him again, 'How fares my noble guest, and this great and excellent people?' Seanchan answered, 'I have never had worse days, nor worse nights, nor worse dinners in my life.' And he ate nothing for three whole days.

Then the king was sorely grieved that the whole Bardic Association should be feasting and drinking while Seanchan, the chief poet of Erin, was fasting and weak. So he sent his favourite serving-man, a person of mild manners and cleanliness, to offer special dishes to the bard.

'Take them away', said Seanchan; 'I'll have none of them.'

'And why, oh, Royal Bard?' asked the servitor.

'Because thou art an uncomely youth,' answered Seanchan. 'Thy grandfather was chip-nailed – I have seen him; I shall eat no food from they hands.'

Then the king called a beautiful maiden to him, his foster daughter, and said, 'Lady, bring thou this wheaten cake and this dish of salmon to the illustrious poet, and serve him thyself.' So the maiden went.

But when Seanchan saw her he asked: 'Who sent thee hither, and why hast thou brought me food?'

'My lord the king sent me, oh, Royal Bard,' she answered, 'because I am comely to look upon, and he bade me serve thee with food myself.'

'Take it away,' said Seanchan, 'thou art an unseemly girl, I know of none more ugly. I have seen thy grandmother; she sat on a wall one day and pointed out the way with her hand to some travelling lepers. How could I touch thy food?' So the maiden went away in sorrow.

And then Guaire the king was indeed angry; and he exclaimed, 'My malediction on the mouth that uttered that! May the kiss of a leper be on Seanchan's lips before he dies!'

Now there was a young serving-girl there, and she said to Seanchan, 'There is a hen's egg in the place, my lord, may I bring it to thee, oh, Chief Bard?'

'It will suffice,' said Seanchan; 'bring it that I may eat.'

But when she went to look for it, behold the egg was gone.

'Thou hast eaten it,' said the bard, in wrath.

'Not so, my lord,' she answered; 'but the mice, the nimble race, have carried it away.'

'Then I will satirize them in a poem,' said Seanchan; and forthwith he chanted so bitter a satire against them that ten mice fell dead at once in his presence.

''Tis well,' said Seanchan; 'but the cat is the one most to blame, for it was her duty to suppress the mice. Therefore I shall satirize the tribe of the cats, and their chief lord, Irusan, son of Arusan. For I know where he lives with his wife Spit-fire, and his daughter Sharp-tooth, with her brothers, the Purrer and the Growler. But I shall begin with Irusan himself, for he is king, and answerable for all the cats.'

And he said—'Irusan, monster of claws, who strikes at the

mouse, but less it go; weakest of cats. The otter did well who bit off the tips of they progenitor's ears, so that every cat since is jagged-eared. Let thy tail hang down; it is right, for the mouse jeers at thee.'

Now Irusan heard the words in his cave, and he said to his daughter, Sharp-tooth: 'Seanchan has satirized me, but I will be avenged.'

'Nay, father,' she said, 'bring him here alive, that we may all take our revenge.'

'I shall go then and bring him,' said Irusan; 'so send thy brothers after me.'

Now when it was told to Seanchan that the King of the Cats was on his way to come and kill him, he was timorous, and besought Guaire and all the nobles to stand by and protect him. And before long a vibrating, impressive, impetuous sound was heard, like a raging tempest of fire in full blaze. And when the cat appeared he seemed to them of the size of a bullock; and this was his appearance – rapacious, panting, jagged-eared, snub-nosed, sharp-toothed, nimble, angry, vindictive, glare-eyed, terrible, sharp-clawed. Such was his similitude. But he passed on amongst them, not minding till he came to Seanchan; and him he seized by the arm and jerked him up on his back, and made off the way he came before any one could touch him; for he had no other object in view but to get hold of the poet.

Now Seanchan, being in evil plight, had recourse to flattery. 'Oh, Irusan,' he exclaimed, 'how truly splendid thou art, such running, such leaps, such strength, and such agility! But what evil have I done, oh, Irusan, son of Arusan? spare me, I entreat. I invoke the saints between thee and me, oh, great King of the Cats.'

But not a bit did the cat let go his hold for all this fine talk, but went straight on to Clonmacnoise where there was a forge; and St. Kieran happened to be there standing at the door.

'What!' exclaimed the saint; 'is that the Chief Bard of Erin on the back of a cat? Has Guaire's hospitality ended in this?' And he ran for a red-hot bar of iron that was in the furnace, and struck the cat on the side with it, so that the iron passed through him, and he fell down lifeless.

'Now my curse on the hand that gave that blow!' said the bard, when he got upon his feet.

'And wherefore?' asked St. Kieran.

'Because,' answered Seanchan, 'I would rather Irusan had

killed me, and eaten me every bit, that so I might bring dis-
grace on Guaire for the bad food he gave me; for it was all
owing to his wretched dinners that I got into this plight.'

And when all the other kings heard of Seanchan's misfortunes, they sent to beg he would visit their courts. But he would
have neither kiss nor welcome from them, and went on his way
to the bardic mansion, where the best of good living was always
to be had. And ever after the kings were afraid to offend
Seanchan.

So as long as he lived he had the chief place at the feasts,
and all the nobles there were made to sit below him, and
Seanchan was content. And in time he and Guaire were reconciled; and Seanchan and all the ollamhs, and the whole
Bardic Association, were feasted by the king for thirty days
in noble style, and had the choicest of viands and the best of
French wines to drink, served in goblets of silver. And in return
for his splendid hospitality the Bardic Association decreed,
unanimously, a vote of thanks to the king. And they praised
him in poems as 'Guaire the Generous', by which name he was
ever after known in history, for the words of the poet are
immortal. (*AL* II, 24–30)

Yeats's play has also a hint of *Samson Agonistes* about it. In his notes
to *Poems* 1899–1905 Yeats added that the play had been revised:

a good many times since then [the first production on 7
October 1903], and although the play has not been changed in
the radical structure, the parts of the Mayor, Servant, and
Cripples are altogether new, and the rest is altered here and
there. It was written when our Society was having a hard
fight for the recognition of pure art in a community of which
one half was buried in the practical affairs of life, and the
other half in politics and a propagandist patriotism. I took
the plot of it from a Middle Irish story about the demands
of the poets at the court of King Guaire, but twisted it about
and revised its moral that the poet might have the best of it.
One of my fellow-playwrights is going, I have hope, to take
the other side and make a play that can be played after it, as in
Greece the farce followed the tragedy. (*VPl* 315)

The revisions of the play are discussed in detail by both Ure, *YTP*
31–42, and Bushrui, *YVP* 73–119. In the Cuala Press edition,
Seven Poems and a Fragment (1922), Yeats wrote a note on the new
end of the play:

Upon the revival of this play at the Abbey Theatre a few weeks ago it was played with this new end. There were a few other changes. I had originally intended to end the play tragically and would have done so but for a friend who used to say 'O do write comedy & have a few happy moments in the Theatre.' My unhappy moments were because a tragic effect is very fragile and a wrong intonation, or even a wrong light or costume will spoil it all. However the play remained always of the nature of tragedy and so subject to vicissitude. (*VPl* 316).

In the notes to *Plays in Prose and Verse* (1922; New York, 1924) he stated:

When I wrote this play neither suffragette nor patriot had adopted the hunger strike, nor had the hunger strike been used anywhere, so far as I know, as a political weapon.

I have given the play the tragic end I would have given it at first, had not a friend advised me to 'write comedy and have a few happy moments in the theatre'. My friend meant that tragic emotion, depending as it does upon gradually deepening reverie, is so fragile, that it is shattered by a wrong movement or cadence, or even by a light in the wrong place. (*VPl* 315–16)

It has been suggested by T. H. McGreevy, 'Mr. W. B. Yeats as a Dramatist', *Revue Anglo-Americaine*, VII (1929–30) 19–36, that Yeats's revision of the play was made after the Lord Mayor of Cork, Terence MacSwiney, had died on hunger strike in 1920.

107 *Persons in the Play:*

Guaire: an Irish King of Gort, Co. Galway. Pronounced Goó-ir-d.

Seanchan: pronounced Shanahan.

Kinvara: a village north-west of Gort.

Fedelm: pronounced Feelem.

SD *Gort*: a village in Co. Galway, west of the Slieve Aughty mountains, near Lady Gregory's house, Coole Park.

Time's chariot: possibly an echo of Marvell's lines in 'To his Coy Mistress':

> But at my back I always hear
> Time's winged chariot hurrying near.

high angels: the golden angel is probably a reference to the Greek myth of Helios, the Sun God, son of the Titans Hyperion and his sister Theia (or Euryphaessa). He emerged from the east every morning and drove his golden chariot, drawn by winged horses, high into the heavens, reaching the land of the Hesperides in the evening. The Silver Angel is his sister Selene, the moon Goddess who began her journey through the sky when her brother finished his. The third child of the Titans was Eos (Aurora) who brought dawn to mankind.

a custom: hunger striking was recorded in Irish tradition.   **108**
Makers of the Law: the Brehons.
the poets' right: this may go beyond the right of sitting at the Council (see **129**) and refer to the privileged position of the *filid* at court.

that old custom: of sitting on the council.   **109**

Almhuin: Finn's hall, the modern Allen. The New York edition   **110**
of 1904 spells this *Almhuim*, probably a misprint.
Finn and Osgar: Finn was the leader of the Fenians and Oisin was his son by Saeve (of the Sidhe, or Fairy People). Oisin's son was Oscar, who was killed at the Battle of Gabhra A.D. 284, in which the Fianna or Fenians were almost all killed. Yeats described it as the 'battle in which the power of the Fenians was broken' (*P* (1895)).
Grania: Yeats commented on her in *P* (1895) as follows:

'A beautiful woman who fled with Dermot to escape from the love of aged Finn. She fled from place to place over Ireland, but at last Dermot was killed at Sligo upon the seaward point of Ben Bulben, and Finn won her love and brought her, leaning upon her neck, into the assembly of the Fenians, who burst into inextinguishable laughter.'

crane: grus cinerea, a bird with long legs, neck, and bill, now extinct   **111**
in British Isles, used as name of heron in Ireland.

the moon changed everything: cf. *AV* (B) 105-84, the power of the moon to change is mentioned in Yeats's poems. Cf. 'On woman' (*CP* 165) 'The pestle of the moon/That pounds up all anew'; 'Nineteen Hundred and Nineteen' (*CP* 233) 'the circle of the moon/ That pitches common things about'; 'The Phases of the Moon' (*CP* 185) 'The thirteenth moon but sets the soul at war'.

moonstruck: lunatic, distracted.

Candlemas: the feast of the purification of the Virgin Mary, celebrated on 2 February.

school: a bardic school. Apprentice poets studied in the Irish bardic schools, in the ancient and medieval period, under master poets, the *filid* (or later baird) who remained in being as an organised literary caste until the seventeenth century. The filid preserved national memory, the legendary prowess of rulers and the bonds of kinship. They were trained to recite the historic tales to kings and chiefs 'from the Chief *Ollamh* with three hundred and fifty tales, to the lowest in degree with seven' (A. S. Green, *History of the Irish State to 1014*, Chapter 1). The bardic courts of the post-seventeenth century were their humble offspring, a faint echo of the earlier disciplined achievement of the poets within the Gaelic society that virtually collapsed after the Flight of the Earls in 1607.

112   *looking upon these images, might bear/Triumphant children*: in contrast with the woman 'That, looking on the cloven lips of a hare,/Brings forth a hare-lipped child.'

men of Dea: the De Danaans, the people of the Goddess Dana.

four treasures: these were the Lia Fail or Stone of Destiny, the cauldron of plenty of the Dagda Mor, and the sword and spear of Lugh.

Grail King: the Holy Grail in medieval legend was the vessel (the 'holy cup') used by Jesus at the Last Supper, in which the blood from the Saviour's spear-wound was received by Joseph of Arimathea at the Cross. Joseph brought the Grail to Glastonbury. It was guarded by King Pelles, who is presumably the 'Grail King'. The Grail was lost, and the search for it became an image used by medieval writers to represent man's search for spiritual truth. The land lay under a curse, until a knight should put certain questions about the Grail and the spear that pierced Christ's side. (T. S. Eliot linked this myth with that of the Fisher King, and referred his readers to Jessie Weston's *From Ritual to Romance*, 1920).

the Courtly life/Is the world's model: a foreshadowing of Yeats's own **113**
praise of aristocracy in the poems of *The Green Helmet* (1910); cf.
'Upon a House Shaken by the Land Agitation' (*CP* 106) and 'These
are the Clouds' (*CP* 107).

the clattering houses: presumably as opposed to the spaciousness of
the King's palace.

all falls/In ruin, poetry calls out in joy: cf. the 'tragic joy' of 'The **114**
Gyres' (*CP* 337) and the 'gaiety transfiguring all that dread' of
'Lapis Lazuli' (*CP* 338). Cf. Yeats's views on the joy of accepting
what life brings in his essay on 'J. M. Synge and the Ireland of his
Time' (*E&I* 322) and his remark that tragedy was not legitimate if
it did not bring some great character 'to his final joy' (*E* 448–9).
He also wrote on this theme in 'A General Introduction for my
work' (*E&I* 522–3). It has been suggested by J. Kleinstück, 'Yeats
and Shakespeare' (*YCE* 12–14), that the idea of tragic joy was
Nietzschean. See also the speech of the Oldest Pupil:

> King, he is dead; some strange triumphant thought
> So filled his heart with joy that it has burst,
> Being grown too mighty for our frailty,
> And we who gaze grow like him and abhor
> The moments that come between us and that death
> You promised us. (**141–2**)

Ogham stick: Ogham was an alphabet of twenty characters, created **115**
by a mythical inventor Ogma. The characters were formed by
combinations of points and short lines on and at both sides of a
middle stem line called a flesc. Ogham writing survived from the
pagan period into the Christian. The legends speak of Oghams cut
on rods of yew or oak and the mayor is using an Ogham stick as
we might use a note on paper as an aid to memory.

Inchy: one of the seven woods in Coole Demense.

Kiltartan: a village north of Gort, Co. Galway. The village gave its name to Lady Gregory's style in her translations.

blessed well: Ireland has a large number of holy wells; cf. Synge's *The Well of the Saints* and see note on **119**.

116 *wake*: Irish custom of keeping watch in the presence of a corpse.

between the stones: a comment on the stony nature of this area of Galway.

117 *dulse*: *duileass* – Irish, edible seaweed.

Duras: situated beyond Kinvara and on the sea coast. It was at Count Floremond de Basterot's house there that Yeats and Lady Gregory began serious planning for an Irish theatre.

119 *Saint Colman*: St Colman Maclenin was patron saint of a cathedral church (now in ruins) at Kilmacduagh, near Coole. St Colman's well was 'within a couple of miles of my Galway house, Thoor Ballylee and is sacred to St Colman, and began a few years ago to work miracles again, rejuvenated by a Gaelic League procession in its honour' (notes to *TCM*). This note of 1924 was made more precise in the Introduction to *W&B*: 'A couple of miles as the crow flies from my house is a blessed well. Some thirty years ago the Gaelic League organized some kind of procession or "pattern" there, somebody else put a roof over it, somebody else was cured of a lame leg or a blind eye or the falling sickness. There are many offerings at the well-side left by sufferers; I seem to remember bits of cloth torn perhaps from a dress, hairpins and little pious pictures.' This introduction was written in 1934, and the 'thirty years ago' brings us back to the year of *The King's Threshold*, suggesting that the Gaelic League's procession put the idea of the well in Yeats's mind.

Roast the lucky fish: this may reflect Yeats's reading Lady Wilde's account of Tober-na-alt, the well of the Alt, in Sligo (cf. 'In a cleft that's christened Alt', 'The Man and the Echo' (*CP* 393):

In Sligo there is a well called *Tober-na-alt*, beautifully shadowed by trees, the branches of which are thickly hung with all sorts of votive offerings from those who have been cured by the water; and miracle-men attended, who professed to heal diseases by charms, prayers, and incantations.

A man who had been born blind once recited his experiences there. 'Oh, Christians, look on me! I was blind from my birth and saw no light till I came to the blessed well; now I see the water and the speckled trout down at the bottom, with the white cross on his back. Glory be to God for the cure.' And when the people heard that he could really see the speckled trout, of course they all believed in the miracle. For a tradition exists that a sacred trout has lived there from time immemorial, placed in the well by the saint who first sanctified the water. Now there was an adventurous man who desired much to get possession of this trout, and he watched till at last he caught it asleep. Then he carried it off and put it on the gridiron. The trout bore the grilling of one side very patiently; but when the man tried to turn it on the fire, the trout suddenly jumped up and made off as hard as it could back to the well, where it still lives, and can be seen at times by those who have done proper penance and paid their dues to the priest, with one side all streaked and marked brown by the bars of the gridiron, which can never be effaced. (*AL* II, 166–7).

Is it cry out for him? . . . curse him and abuse him: these speeches **120** probably reflect the Irish belief in the power of satire and the curse. Poets were feared for the power of their invective or satire.

tributary kings: Under Brehon law there were five main classes in **121** Ireland: kings of different grades from the King of the tuath or cantred up to the Ard-ri, or King of Ireland; nobles; freemen with property; freemen without property; non-free. There were 184 tuaths in Ireland; probably not all of them had kings.

get the clapper from the bell: be quiet. **122**

125 *meat . . . carried from too good a table*: there is perhaps an ironic contrast with the scene in the *Odyssey* where Odysseus cuts off a rich portion from the chine of a boar and sends it to the blind minstrel Demodocus.

126 *mouthfuls of sweet air*: cf. 'I made it out of a mouthful of air', 'He thinks of Those who Have spoken Evil of his Beloved' (*CP* 75); 'Being but a mouthful of air', *At the Hawk's Well* (*CPl* 219); 'For what have we in this life but a mouthful of air', *John Sherman*, 1891. See also note on **640**, p. 263.

127 *four rivers in the mountain garden*: see **136**, lines 14–21 where this image is explained by Seanchan as 'out of a poem I made long ago'.
    high circle: the gold crown of the king.
    whey-faced: silver.
    wasteful virtues: cf. 'Only the wasteful virtues earn the sun' in 'Pardon, Old Fathers' (*CP* 113).

128 *a great wind*: in 1903 a 'big wind' did a great deal of damage in Ireland, especially in the west.
    Lent: period of forty days, from Ash Wednesday to Easter eve, kept as a time of fasting, abstinence and penitence, to commemorate our Lord's fasting in the wilderness.
    hurley: Irish game, somewhat resembled by hockey, of great antiquity. See note on **75**.

131 *Finula*: Finnhua in 1904 edition.
    First Princess: 'Princess Buan' in 1904 edition.
    at his table: presumably at the Council table.

135 *high days of the year*: possibly the four great festivals in February, May, midsummer and November.

all the fowls of the air: possibly an echo of Cock Robin's   **136**

> All the birds of the air
> Fell a-sighing and a-sobbing

or, more likely, in view of the reference in Fedelm's next speech to 'Adam's Paradise', a memory or echo of Genesis 1, 26, 'the fowl of the air'.

spirits in the images of birds: in the essay 'Magic' Yeats recorded how a young Irishwoman who had been in a profound trance thought in her waking state that 'the apple of Eve was the kind of apple you can buy at the greengrocer's, but in her trance she saw the Tree of Life with ever-sighing souls moving in its branches instead of sap, and among its leaves all the fowls of the air, and on its highest bough one white fowl wearing a crown. When I went home I took from the shelf a translation of *The Book of Concealed Mystery* (translated by Mathers in *The Kabbalah Unveiled*), an old Jewish book, and cutting the pages came upon this passage, which I cannot think I had ever read: 'The Tree . . . is the Tree of the Knowledge of Good and Evil . . . in its branches the birds lodge and build their nests, the souls and the angels have their place' (*E&I* 44–5).

miraculous beast out of Ezekiel: cf. 'old Ezekiel's cherubim' of 'To   **141** a Young Beauty' (*CP* 157) and the possible echo of Ezekiel x in the 'shape with lion body' in 'The Second Coming' (*CP* 280). There does not seem to be any specific echo from Ezekiel here.

O silver trumpets: J. M. Hone (*WBY* 187) suggests that Nietzsche's   **143** influence lay behind this speech. Yeats's attitude had emerged strongly from pre-Raphaelism. A letter written to AE in April 1904 indicates how he viewed his own earlier work:

> In my *Land of Heart's Desire*, and in some of my lyric verse of that time, there is an exaggeration of sentiment and sentimental beauty which I have come to think unmanly. The popularity of *The Land of Heart's Desire* seems to me to come not from its merits but because of this weakness. I have been fighting the prevailing decadence for years, and have just got it under foot in my own heart – it is sentiment and sentimental sadness,

womanish introspection. My own early subjectiveness rises at rare moments and yours nearly always rises above sentiment to a union with a pure energy of the spirit, but between this energy of the spirit and the energy of the will out of which epic and dramatic poetry comes there is a region of brooding emotions full of fleshly waters and vapours which kill the spirit and the will, ecstasy and joy equally. Yet this region of shadows is full of false images of the spirit and of the body. I have come to feel towards it as O'Grady feels towards it sometimes, and even a little as some of my own stupidest critics feel. As so often happens with a thing one has been tempted by and is still a little tempted by, I am roused by it to a kind of frenzied hatred which is quite out of my control. Beardsley exasperated some people in this way but he has never the form of decadence that tempted me and so I am not unjust to him, but I cannot probably be quite just to any poetry that speaks to me with the sweet insinuating feminine voice of the dwellers in that country of shadows and hollow images. I have dwelt there too long not to dread all that comes out of it. We possess nothing but the will and we must never let the children of vague desires breathe upon it nor the waters of sentiment rust the terrible mirror of its blade. I fled from some of this new verse you have gathered as from much verse of our day, knowing that I fled that water and that breath. Yours ever   W B YEATS

P.S. When the spirit sinks back weary from its flight towards the final whiteness it sinks into the dim shadowy region more often than less aspiring spirits. I am angry when I see it, whether it is my spirit or your spirit, as in *Deirdre*, or the spirit of some of these young poets of yours. Some day you will become aware as I have become of an uncontrollable shrinking from the shadows, for as I believe a mysterious command has gone out against them in the invisible world of [?] inner energies. Let us have no emotions, however abstract, in which there is not an athletic joy. (*L* 434-5)

Yeats had been introduced to Nietzsche by John Quinn, the Irish-American lawyer and patron of Irish writers and artists: he had found Nietzsche's division of the soul's main moments into Apollonian and Dionysiac attractive and decided that his own Dionysiac period was over. The image of an heroic great man recurs, notably in *On Baile's Strand*, and his father wrote reprovingly to him in 1906 apropos his new theories which derived from Nietzsche:

As you have dropped affection from the circle of your needs, have you also dropped love between man and woman? Is this the theory of the overman, if so, your demi-godship is after all but a doctrinaire demi-godship. Your words are idle – and you are far more human than you think. You would be a philosopher and are really a poet. (*LTHS* 97)

Peter Ure has suggested a useful passage (*YTP* 40) from Nietzsche's *Birth of Tragedy* in connection with *The King's Threshold*, that illustrates some of the ideas Yeats found stimulating in the German writer:

We are to perceive how all that comes into being must be ready for a sorrowful end . . . We are really for brief moments Primordial Being itself, and feel its indomitable desire for being and joy in existence; the struggle, the pain, the destruction of phenomena, now appear to us as something necessary. We are pierced by the maddening sting of these pains at the very moment when we have become, as it were, one with the immeasurable primordial joy in existence, and when we anticipate, in Dionysan ecstasy, the indestructibility and eternity of this joy. (*Works*, trans. Levy, I, pp. 128–9)

The Shadowy Waters

This is a very different play from *The Shadowy Waters* as printed in *CP* 469 ff, which was first published in 1906, and was itself the result of much reshaping of a work that Yeats began as a boy, possibly as early as 1885. In 1894 he wrote to his father that he was doing nothing but the play *The Shadowy Waters*, and by November of that year it appears to have been completed and about to be despatched to the publisher Elkin Matthews. By 1896 a version seems to have been ready for actual publication, and although in 1897 he told Fiona MacLeod that he was recasting it, nothing appeared in print until 1900. Still basically a poem in dramatic form, it was performed by the Irish National Theatre Society at the Molesworth Hall, Dublin, on 4 January 1904, with Florence Farr as Dectora. The play was then completely rewritten and a new version – the text of *CP* – published in 1906. Still dissatisfied, Yeats reshaped the play for a performance at the Abbey Theatre on 8 December 1906, and this, the Acting Version, was published separately in 1907. The date given in *CPl*, 1911, is misleading, in that it refers to its publication in *PAIT*.

The reader can easily perceive the differences between the 1906 and the 1907 versions by comparing the two in *CP* and *CPl* respectively. The general direction of the revisions is, as is to be expected, towards a reduction in symbolism, a closer approximation to the rhythms of colloquial speech, including the use of prose for minor characters, a sharper delineation of the characters both in isolation and in contrast. The fullest discussions of these revisions are to be found in Bushrui, *YVP* and T. Parkinson, *W. B. Yeats, Self-Critic: A Study of his Early Verse*, Berkeley, 1951.

Yeats tells us that the earliest version began in boyhood sailing expeditions 'to find what sea-birds began to stir before dawn', and that it would have been 'full of observation' had he been able to write it when it was first planned (*A* 73–4). But by 1897 it had become 'magical and mystical beyond anything' he had done (*L* 280).

Two years later, having absorbed much Irish mythology and acquired 'a rich background for whatever I want to do and endless symbols to my hand', he was trying to get into the play 'a kind of grave ecstasy' (*L* 322).

In a letter to Frank Fay in 1904, although regarding it as 'legitimate art', in that 'the whole picture as it were moves together – sky and sea and cloud are as it were actors . . . almost religious . . . more a ritual than a human story', he thought it was unsuitable for stage performance: 'I would not now do anything so remote, so impersonal' (*L* 425).

Nevertheless the play was given again, at the Abbey Theatre on 9 July 1905, and to assist his audience because he felt that it was still obscure, Yeats provided the following programme note for the occasion:

> The main story expresses the desire for a perfect and eternal union that comes to all lovers, the desire of Love to 'drown in its own shadow'. But it has also other meanings. Forgael seeks death; Dectora has always sought life; and in some way the uniting of her vivid force with his abyss-seeking desire for the waters of Death makes a perfect humanity. Of course, in another sense, these two are simply man and woman, the reason and the will, as Swedenborg puts it.
>
> The second flaming up of the harp may mean the coming of a more supernatural passion, when Dectora accepts the death-desiring destiny. Yet in one sense, and precisely because she accepts it, this destiny is not death; for she, the living will, accompanies Forgael, the mind, through the gates of the unknown world. Perhaps it is a mystical interpretation of the resurrection of the body. (*IY* 81)

To assist his readers, he printed the following note when he published the play in *The Arrow* in November 1906.

> I began 'The Shadowy Waters' when I was a boy, and when I published a version of it six or seven years ago, the plot had been so often re-arranged and was so overgrown with symbolical ideas that the poem was obscure and vague. It found its way on to the stage more or less by accident, for our people had taken it as an exercise on the speaking of verse, and it pleased a few friends, though it must have bewildered and bored the greater portion of the audience. The present version

is practically a new poem, and is, I believe, sufficiently simple, appealing to no knowledge more esoteric than is necessary for the understanding of any of the more characteristic love poems of Shelley or of Petrarch. If the audience will understand it as a fairy-tale, and not look too anxiously for a meaning, all will be well.

Once upon a time, when herons built their nests in old men's beards, Forgael, a Sea-King of ancient Ireland, was promised by certain human-headed birds love of a supernatural intensity and happiness. These birds were the souls of the dead, and he followed them overseas towards the sunset, where their final rest is. By means of a magic harp, he could call them about him when he would and listen to their speech. His friend Aibric, and the sailors of his ship, thought him mad, or that this mysterious happiness could come after death only, and that he and they were being lured to destruction. Presently they captured a ship, and found a beautiful woman upon it, and Forgael subdued her and his own rebellious sailors by the sound of his harp. The sailors fled upon the other ship, and Forgael and the woman drifted on alone following the birds, awaiting death and what comes after, or some mysterious transformation of the flesh, an embodiment of every lover's dream.

In the light of his experience of its performances in 1904 and 1905, he began to 'set it to rights as a stage play' (*Poems*, 1899–1905). He told Florence Farr that he was 'changing it greatly, getting rid of needless symbols, making the people answer each other, and making the groundwork simple and intelligible. I find I am enriching the poetry and the character of Forgael in the process' (*L* 453). His aim was to strengthen poetic language with 'common idiom', to get what he called 'creaking shoes' and 'liquorice-root' into abstract speech, and combine poetic construction with 'common passion' (*L* 462). The process also involved him in technical difficulties such as are mentioned in his note to the play as published in 1906:

... I hope I have set it to rights now, and that if it finds an audience familiar with the longing of a lover for impossible things, and longings that are like his, it will hold the attention and have some pleasure in it for the players. I have not yet seen this new version played, but have rehearsed it, and Mr. Robert Gregory has designed the boat and sail. The colours of all will be as at the first performance, dark blue and dark green, but for Dectora a lighter green against the darker tints in sky and boat, with some glimmer of copper here and there, and the lighting a not very bright moonlight. The effect of this monotony of colour was to my eyes beautiful, and made the players seem like people in a dream. I have described these colours a little in the stage directions, not because I think of them as a necessary part of the play, but because it is necessary for some remote and decorative picture of the action, to float up into the mind's eye of the reader, who must imagine some sort of a stage scenery. When we began to get together the properties in this new version, the stage carpenter found it very difficult to make the crescent-shaped harp that was to burn with fire; and besides, no matter how well he made the frame, there was no way of making the strings take fire. I had, therefore, to give up the harp for a sort of psaltery, a little like the psaltery Miss Farr speaks to [see 'The Players Ask for a Blessing on the Psalteries and on Themselves', *CP* 93, and *Comm* 97] where the strings could be slits covered with glass or gelatine on the surface of a shallow and perhaps semi-transparent box ... This necessitated changing the lines where the word 'harp' occurred ...' (*Poems*, 1899–1905)

But he was still not satisfied with the new version, and rewrote it once more in order to make it more suitable for the stage. This final rewriting, the Acting Version, was completed in time for a performance at the Abbey on 8 December 1906, and was published separately in 1907. This version, the text of *CPl*, is notable for its general condensation, its greater skill in stage-craft, and the introduction of prose.

The Acting Version subsequently appeared in: *The Poetical Works of William B. Yeats*, Vol. ii, Dramatical Poems, New York and London, 1907 (1909, 1911); *The Collected Works of William Butler Yeats*, Vol. ii, Stratford-upon-Avon, 1908; *Plays for an Irish Theatre*, London and Stratford-upon-Avon, 1911 (1913); *The Poetical Works of William B. Yeats*, Vol. ii, Dramatic Poems, rev. and repr. New York and London, 1912 (1914, 1916, 1917, 1919, 1921); *Plays in Prose and Verse*, London, 1922; New York, 1924; *The Collected Plays of W. B. Yeats*, London, 1934; New York, 1935; *Nine One-Act Plays*, London, 1937; *The Collected Plays of W. B. Yeats*, London, 1952; New York, 1953 (repr. London, 1953, 1960, 1963, 1966).

The cast for the performance on 8 December 1906 was as follows: Aibric, Arthur Sinclair; Forgael, Frank Fay; Dectora, Miss Darragh.

147 *the sea*: see 'He Bids his Beloved be at Peace' (*CP* 69) and Yeats's note:

> Some neo-platonist, I forget who, describes the sea as a symbol of the drifting indefinite bitterness of life, and I believe there is like symbolism intended in the many Irish voyages to the islands of enchantment, or that there was, at any rate, in the mythology out of which these stories have been shaped. I follow much Irish and other mythology, and the magical tradition, in associating the North with night and sleep, and the East, the place of sunrise, with hope, and the South, the place of the sun when at its height, with passion and desire, and the West, the place of sunset, with fading and dreaming things. (*WR*)

148 *man-headed bird*: see Yeats's note on p. 60 above.
the west: see note on **147,** line 3.

151 *But he that gets . . . finished*: cf. in general 'Solomon to Sheba' (*CP* 155) and 'Solomon and the Witch' (*CP* 199).

152 *I have but . . . cries*: cf. in general 'To the Rose Upon the Rood of Time' (*CP* 35). Yeats used roses decoratively in very early poems, but by 1891 he had begun to use the rose as an increasingly complex symbol. In doing so he was influenced by current English poetic practice and by the work of Irish poets in whose work it had stood for Ireland: 'It has given a name to more than one poem, both Gaelic and English, and is used, not merely in love poems but in addresses to Ireland, as in De Vere's line, ''The little black rose shall be red at last'', and in Mangan's ''Dark Rosaleen''. I do not of course, use it in this latter sense' (*CK*). Rose was the name of a girl with black hair in Irish patriotic poetry; she was Róisín Dubh, Dark Rosaleen, and personified Ireland. Yeats also alluded to the use of the Rose symbol in religious poems 'like the old Gaelic which speaks of ''the Rose of Friday'' meaning the Rose of Austerity' (*P*(1895)). He added that he had written a good deal on it in the notes to *WR* and these notes are included in the comments in

Comm on 'The Poet pleads with the Elemental Powers' (*CP* 80);
'He thinks of his Past Greatness . . .' (*CP* 81); 'He hears the Cry
of the Sedge' (*CP* 75). The Rose symbolises spiritual and eternal
beauty. Its meaning as a symbol was intensified by Yeats's member-
ship of the Golden Dawn, an occult society or Rosicrucian order
(see note (*Comm* 141) on 'The Mountain Tomb' (*CP* 136)) into
which he was initiated by MacGregor Mathers, the author of
The Kabbalah Unveiled, on 7 March 1890. From him and from the
rituals of the Golden Dawn (which included Egyptian, Kabbalist
and Christian imagery) Yeats learned of a series of geometric symbols that he could classify according to the four elements, and what
the ancients called the fifth element and sub-divisions of these. In
his unpublished Autobiography he wrote: 'I allowed my mind to
drift from image to image and these images began to affect my
writing, making it more sensuous and vivid.' In the Rosicrucian
symbolism a conjunction of rose (with four leaves) and cross forms
a fifth element – a mystic marriage – the rose possessing feminine
sexual elements, the cross masculine; the rose being the flower that
blooms upon the sacrifice of the cross. The Rose was a central
symbol in the Order of the Golden Dawn, and Ellmann (*Y: M&M*
97) quotes Stanislas de Guaita (founder in Paris in 1888 of a Kabbalistic Order of the Rosy Cross) who wrote in *Rosa Mystica*:

> The Rose that I invite you to pluck – sympathetic friend who
> turn these pages – does not flower on the shores of far-away
> countries; and we shall take, if you please, neither the express
> train nor the transatlantic steamer.
>   Are you susceptible to a deep emotion of the intellect? and
> do your favourite thoughts so haunt you as to give you at
> times the illusion of being real? . . . You are then a magician,
> and the mystic Rose will go of her own accord, however little
> you desire it, to bloom in your garden.

Yeats wrote to Ernest Boyd in February 1915 that his interest in
mystic symbolism did not come from Arthur Symons or any other
contemporary writers but from his own study of the mystic tradition
which dated from 1887; he had found in writers such as Valentin
Andrea authority for his use of the Rose (*L* 592). Wade commented
that Yeats probably read Johannes Valentine Andreae or Andreas
(1586–1654), the German theologican and mystic, in Foxcroft's
translation of *The Hermetic Romance or the Chymical Wedding* (1690)

originally written in High Dutch by C[hristian] R[osenkreuz]; this was reprinted in A. E. Waite, *The Real History of the Rosicrucians* (1887). In July 1892 Yeats wrote to John O'Leary that he could not have written his Blake book nor *The Countess Cathleen* had he not made magic his constant study – 'The mystical life is the centre of all that I do and all that I think and all that I write.' The study of magic was 'next to my poetry, the most important pursuit of my life' (*L* 210).

The Rose symbolism had other elements: physical and spiritual, pagan and Christian, and Yeats described them in an autobiographical passage:

> I planned a mystical Order ... and for ten years to come my most impassioned thought was a vain attempt to find philosophy and to create ritual for that Order. I had an unshakable conviction, arising how or whence I cannot tell, that invisible gates would open as they opened for Blake, as they opened for Swedenborg, as they opened for Boehme, and that this philosophy would find its manuals of devotion in all imaginative literature, and set before Irishmen for special manual an Irish literature which, though made by many minds, would seem the work of a single mind, and turn our places of beauty or legendary association into holy symbols. I did not think this philosophy would be altogether pagan, for it was plain that its symbols must be selected from all those things that had moved men most during many, mainly Christian, centuries.
>
> I thought that for a time I could rhyme of love, calling it *The Rose* because of the Rose's double meaning; of a fisherman who had 'never a crack' in his heart; of an old woman complaining of the idleness of the young, or of some cheerful fiddler, all those things that 'popular poets' write of, but that I must some day – on that day when the gates began to open – become difficult or obscure. With a rhythm that still echoed Morris I prayed to the Red Rose, to Intellectual Beauty. [He then quoted from the second stanza of 'To the Rose upon the Rood of Time'.] (*A* 253)

The 'mystical Order' was to include Maud Gonne; Yeats's uncle George Pollexfen and MacGregor Mathers were helpful but the idea was his own, and in the 1890s he envisaged the order centring on an empty castle on the Castle Rock in Lough Key which he had seen when visiting Douglas Hyde:

There is this small island entirely covered by what was a still habitable but empty castle. The last man who had lived there had been Dr Hyde's father who, when a young man, lived there for a few weeks. All round were the wooded and hilly shores, a place of great beauty. I believed that the castle could be hired for little money, and had long been dreaming of making it an Irish Eleusis or Samothrace. An obsession more constant than anything but my love itself was the need of mystical rites – a ritual system of evocation and meditation – to reunite the perception of the spirit, of the divine, with natural beauty. I believed that instead of thinking of Judea as holy we should [think] our own land holy, and most holy where most beautiful. Commerce and manufacture had made the world ugly; the death of pagan nature-worship had robbed visible beauty of its inviolable sanctity. I was convinced that all lonely and lovely places were crowded with invisible beings and that it would be possible to communicate with them. I meant to initiate young men and women in this worship, which would unite the radical truths of Christianity to those of a more ancient world, and to use the Castle Rock for their occasional retirement from the world.

For years to come it was in my thought, as in much of my writing, to seek also to bring again in[to] imaginative life the old sacred places – Slievenamon, Knocknarea – all that old reverence that hung – above all – about conspicuous hills. But I wished by my writings and those of the school I hoped to found to have a secret symbolical relation to these mysteries, for in that way, I thought, there will be a greater richness, a greater claim upon the love of the soul, doctrine without exhortation and rhetoric. Should not religion hide within the work of art as God is within His world, and how can the interpreter do more than whisper? I did not wish to compose rites as if for the theatre. They must in their main outline be the work of invisible hands.

My own seership was, I thought, inadequate; it was to be Maud Gonne's work and mine. Perhaps that was why we had been thrown together. Were there not strange harmonies amid discord? My outer nature was passive – but for her I should never perhaps have left my desk – but I knew my spiritual nature was passionate, even violent. In her all this was reversed, for it was her spirit only that was gentle and passive and full of charming fantasy, as though it touched the world only with the point of its finger. When I had first met her I had used as a test the death symbol, imagining it in my own mind, but not wishing to alarm her had asked that it should take the form not of a human but of a dog's skull. She said, 'I see a figure holding out its hand with a skull on it. No, there is a bruise* on the hand, but I was compelled to say it was a skull.' I, who could not influence her actions, could dominate her inner being. I could therefore use her clairvoyance to produce forms that would arise from both minds, though mainly seen by one, and escape therefore from what is mere[ly] personal. There would be, as it were, a spiritual birth from the soul of a man and a woman. I knew that the incomprehensible life could select from our memories and, I believed, from the memory of the race itself; could realize of ourselves, beyond personal predilection, all it required, of symbol and of myth. I believed we were about to attain a revelation.

Maud Gonne entirely shared these ideas, and I did not doubt that in carrying them out I should win her for myself. Politics were merely a means of meeting, but this was a link so perfect that [it] would restore at once, even [after] a quarrel, the sense of intimacy. At every moment of leisure we obtained in vision long lists of symbols. Various trees corresponded to cardinal points, and the old gods and heroes too, their places gradually in a symbolic fabric that had for its centre the four talismans of the Tuatha de Danaan, the sword, the stone, the spear and the cauldron, which related themselves in my mind with the suits of the Tarot. (*MS* 123–5)

This Order of Celtic mysteries was regarded by Yeats as a means of escaping from active life and politics as well as a means of gaining Maud Gonne's love. He wrote to George Russell (AE) on 23 January 1898:

I am deep in 'Celtic Mysticism', the whole thing is forming an elaborate vision. Maud Gonne and myself are going for a week or two perhaps to some country place in Ireland to get as you do the forms of gods and spirits and to get some sacred earth for our evocation. Perhaps we can arrange to go somewhere where you are so that we can all work together. Maud Gonne has seen [a] vision of a little temple of the heroes which she proposes to build somewhere in Ireland when '98 is over [celebrations to commemorate Wolfe Tone and the Rebellion of 1798] and to make the centre of our mystical and literary movements. (*L* 295)

* Doubtful reading.

The Rose also symbolises Maud Gonne, who told A. N. Jeffares that Yeats intended to allude to her by the symbol, and through her to Ireland. In 'The Rose upon the Rood of Time' the Rose is eternal beauty and something of its meaning is indicated in his remark that Timon of Athens and Cleopatra sorrow for all men's fate. 'Tragic joy' was a quality Yeats appreciated and he wrote of it:

> That shaping joy has kept the sorrow pure, as it had kept it were the emotion love or hate, for the nobleness of the arts is in the mingling of contraries, the extremity of sorrow, the extremity of joy, perfection of personality, the perfection of its surrender, overflowing turbulent energy, and marmorean stillness; and its red rose opens at the meeting of the two beams of the cross, and at the trysting-place of mortal and immortal, time and eternity. (*E&I*, 255)

There! there! They come . . . meadows of the dawn. These birds are **153** basically the souls of the dead – see Yeats's note on p. 60 – and their thronging appearance, carrying with it the overwhelming conviction of a supernatural reality, anticipates the 'nine-and-fifty swans' of 'The Wild Swans at Coole', *CP* 147. Lady Gregory quotes George Moore's description of them:

> It was then I forgot Yeats and Edward [Martyn] and everything else in the delight caused by a great clamour of wings, and the snowy plumage of thirty-six great birds rushing down the lake, striving to rise from its surface. At last their wings caught the air, and after floating about the lake they settled in a distant corner where they thought they could rest undisturbed. Thirty-six swans rising out of a lake and floating round it, and settling down in it, is an unusual sight; it conveys a suggestion of fairyland, perhaps because thirty-six wild swans are so different from the silly China swan which sometimes floats and hisses in melancholy whiteness up and down a stone basin. That is all we know of swans – all I knew until the thirty-six rose out of the hushed lake at our feet, and prompted me to turn to Yeats, saying, You're writing your poem in its natural atmosphere. (George Moore, *Hail and Farewell, Ave*, 1947 ed., p. 190)

Cf. also 'Coole Park and Ballylee, 1931' (*CP* 275):

> At sudden thunder of the mounting swan
> I turned about and looked where branches break
> The glittering reaches of the flooded lake.
>
> Another emblem there! That stormy white
> But seems a concentration of the sky;
> And, like the soul, it sails into the sight
> And in the morning's gone, no man knows why:
> And is so lovely that it sets to right
> What knowledge or its lack had set awry,
> So arrogantly pure, a child might think
> It can be murdered with a post of ink.

They've gone up thither . . . their beloved ones in the air. Cf. 'The Wild Swans at Coole' (*CP* 147, lines 19–21):

> Unwearied still, lover by lover,
> They paddle in the cold
> Companionable streams or climb the air

and Shelley's Alastor (lines 277 ff):

> A swan was there,
> Beside a sluggish stream among the reeds.
> It rose as he approached, and with strong wings
> Scaling the upward sky, bent its bright course
> High over the immeasurable main.
> His eyes pursued its flight: – 'Thou hast a home,
> Beautiful bird! thou voyagest to thine home,
> Where thy sweet mate will twine her downy neck
> With thine, and welcome thy return with eyes
> Bright in the lustre of their own fond joy.
> And what am I that I should linger here,
> With voice far sweeter than thy dying notes,
> Spirit more vast than thine, frame more attuned
> To beauty, wasting these surpassing powers
> In the deaf air, to the blind earth, and heaven
> That echoes not my thoughts?' A gloomy smile
> Of desperate hope wrinkled his quivering lips.
> For Sleep, he knew, kept most relentlessly
> Its precious charge: and silent Death exposed,
> Faithless perhaps as Sleep, a shadowy lure,
> With doubtful smile mocking its own strange charms.

Cf. also Shelley's preface to *Alastor*, describing the poet imagining the Being whom he loves, attaching all of the wonderful, wise or beautiful which could be envisaged by poet, philosopher or lover, to a single image, and then searching in vain for a prototype of his conception.

Iollan: either Iollan, son of Fergus MacRoy or Finn's uncle by **160** marriage. Saul, *PYP* 187.

For love . . . hatred in it: cf. 'Crazy Jane Grown Old Looks at the **162** Dancers' (*CP* 295):

> I found that ivory image there
> Dancing with her chosen youth,
> But when he wound her coal-black hair
> As though to strangle her, no scream
> Or bodily movement did I dare,
> Eyes under eyelids did so gleam;
> *Love is like the lion's tooth.*
>
> When she, and though some said she played
> I said that she had danced heart's truth,
> Drew a knife to strike him dead,
> I could but leave him to his fate;
> For no matter what is said
> They had all that had their hate!
> *Love is like the lion's tooth.*

The source of the poem is revealed in a letter Yeats wrote to Mrs Shakespear from Rapallo on 2 March 1929:

> Last night I saw in a dream strange ragged excited people singing in a crowd. The most visible were a man and woman who were I think dancing. The man was swinging round his head a weight at the end of a rope or leather thong, and I knew that he did not know whether he would strike her dead or not, and both had their eyes fixed on each other, and both sang their love for one another. I suppose it was Blake's old thought 'sexual love is founded upon spiritual hate' – I will probably find I have written it in a poem in a few days – though my remembering my dream may prevent that – by making my criticism work upon it. (At least there is evidence to that effect.) (*L* 758)

The passage on sexual love and spiritual hate in 'Anima Hominis' is concerned with similar matters, where Yeats sees the warfare of man and Daimon as imaged in love. (See *M* 336–7; cf. also **409, lines** 18 ff)

167 *Dragon*: the serpent of nature. See 'The Poet Pleads with the Elemental Powers' (*CP* 80):

> The Powers whose name and shape no living creature knows
> Have pulled the Immortal Rose:
> And though the Seven lights bowed in their dance and wept,
> The Polar Dragon slept,
> His heavy rings uncoiled from glimmering deep to deep:
> When will he wake from sleep?

Ellmann (*IY* 78) remarks that if we look at the cover of *TSR* we find the serpent's folds encircling the trunk of the tree of life as if it were indeed the 'Guardian of the Rose'. He continues:

> In Kabbalism this serpent is the serpent of nature in its benign aspect, and the occultist is said to follow the serpent's winding path upwards through many initiations, corresponding to each of the *Sephiroth*, until he reaches the top of the tree. Since in the poem the polar dragon sleeps, like earth in the 'Introduction' to Blake's *Songs of Experience*, the meaning seems to be that the natural world has become uncoiled or detached from beauty.

bird among the leaves: the purified soul in the topmost branches of the Tree of Life. Cf. in general 'The Two Trees', *CP* 54. Cf. also the passage from Yeats's essay on Magic (*E&I* 28–52), quoted on p. 55, which describes the trance of a young woman, and Yeats's later reading 'an old Jewish book' which described the Tree of the knowledge of Good and Evil (*E&I* 44).

O silver fish: cf. the 'silver trout' of 'The Song of Wandering Aengus' (*CP* 66), the object of Aengus's quest. Dectora addresses Forgael as the object of her quest, now achieved.

O Morning star: 'that wars against the principle of evil' and is 'a symbol of love, or liberty, or wisdom, or beauty, or of some other expression of "Intellectual Beauty".' 'Ideas of Good and Evil', *E&I* 88–9.

white fawn: cf. 'Ideas of Good and Evil' (*E&I* 90), where it will 'lead' the visionary 'among the Gods' and is also associated with the 'morning and Evening Star'. It is that which leads man 'out of the darkness and passion of the world into some day of partial regeneration.' These are the only fossils of secondary symbolism left after Yeats's revisions, apart from the major ones of the sea as the material world, the boat as soul, the west as the place of mystical experience. For fuller discussions of the earlier, heavily symbol-laden versions, see *YVP*, *YI* and *IY*.

Deirdre

This play was first performed on 24 November 1906 at the Abbey Theatre by the National Theatre Society Ltd (the Abbey Company). (See notes to *Plays for an Irish Theatre*, London and Stratford-upon-Avon, 1911 (1913); also *A Selection from the Poetry of W. B. Yeats*, Leipzig, 1913, and *Selected Poems*, New York, 1921.) The cast was as follows: Musicians, Sara Allgood, Maire O'Neill, Brigid O'Dempsey; Fergus, *an old man*, Arthur Sinclair; Naisi, *a young King*, F. J. Fay; Deirdre, *his Queen*, Miss Darragh; A Dark-faced Messenger, U. Wright; Conchubar, *the old King of Uladh*, J. M. Kerrigan; and Dark-faced Executioner, A. Power. Miss Darragh, whose real name was Letitia Marion Dallas (d. 1917), was chosen 'to prevent depths and intimacy being disturbed more than could be helped by the glitter of artifice' (*YTP* 48). But her appointment upset the other players in the Abbey: it was, according to W. G. Fay and Catherine Carswell, *The Fays and the Abbey Theatre*, 1935, p. 208, 'like putting a Rolls Royce to run a race with a lot of hill ponies.' The scenery was designed and painted by Robert Gregory, the music for the musicians' songs written by Arthur Donlay. (Different dates for the first performance are given by Yeats: 27 November 1906 in Appendix to *The Poetical Works of William B. Yeats*, Vol. II, New York and London, 1907 (1909, 1911) and in the revised editions of 1912, 1914, 1916, 1917, 1919 and 1921; and 26 November 1906 in the Notes to *Plays in Prose and Verse*, London 1922; New York 1924.) The part of Deirdre was played subsequently by Miss Maria Limerick, Miss Sara Allgood, and Miss Maire O'Neill. Mrs Patrick Campbell played it, according to Yeats, in Dublin and London in 1907 and in 1908, and also with her own company in London in the autumn of 1909. But she actually only played it in 1908 in Dublin and London. (See Notes to *Plays for an Irish Theatre*, London and Stratford-upon-Avon, 1911; *The Poetical Works of William B. Yeats*, 1912; and *Plays in Prose and Verse*, London, 1922; New York, 1924.) She liked the prose version, but Yeats hesitated at first about giving it to her, as he wrote to his father (*L* 475) and Katharine Tynan (*L* 476).

In *CW* II, he described the problems the play created for him:

After the first performance of this play in the autumn of 1906, I rewrote the play up to the opening of the scene where Naisi and Deidre play chess. The new version was played in the spring of 1907, and after that I rewrote from the entrance of Deirdre to her questioning the musicians, but felt, though despairing of setting it right, that it was still mere bones, mere dramatic logic. The principal difficulty with the form of dramatic structure I have adopted is that, unlike the loose Elizabethan form, it continually forces one by its rigour of logic away from one's capacities, experiences, and desires, until, if one have not patience to wait for the mood, or to rewrite again and again till it comes, there is rhetoric and logic and dry circumstance where there should be life. After the version printed in the text of this book had gone to press, Mrs. Patrick Campbell came to our Abbey Theatre and, liking what she saw there, offered to come and play Deirdre among us next November, and this so stirred my imagination that the scene came right in a moment. It needs some changes in the stage directions at the beginning of the play. There is no longer need for loaf and flagon, but the women at the braziers should when the curtain rises by arraying themselves – the one holding a mirror for the other perhaps. The play then goes on unchanged till the entrance of Deirdre, when the following scene is substituted for that on pages 139–140. (Bodb is pronounced Bove.) (*VPl* 391)

The passage following is quoted in *VPl* 391–3. Further alterations are contained in *VPl* 393–6. The play was first printed as *Deirdre*, London and Dublin, 1907 (variant readings in this edition are recorded in *VPl*, xx), then it was included in *The Poetical Works of William B. Yeats*, Vol. II, New York and London, 1907 (1909 and 1911), and in the revised editions of 1912, 1914, 1916, 1917, 1919 and 1921. It was included in *The Collected Works in Verse and Prose of William Butler Yeats*, Vol. II, Stratford-upon-Avon, 1908. (The appendix gives a different version of Deirdre's entrance; see *VPl*, xx.) *Alterations in Deirdre* was published in London, 1908; and *Deirdre* in Stratford-upon-Avon, 1911. *Plays for an Irish Theatre*, London and Stratford-upon-Avon, 1911 (1913) included it, as did *A Selection from the Poetry of W. B. Yeats*, Leipzig, 1913 (1922).

Other printings included *Deirdre*, Stratford-upon-Avon, 1914; *Selected Poems*, New York, 1921; *Plays in Prose and Verse*, London, 1922; New York, 1924 (repr. London 1922, 1926, 1931); *The Collected Plays of W. B. Yeats*, London, 1934; New York, 1935; *Nine One-Act Plays*, London, 1937; *The Collected Plays of W. B. Yeats*, London, 1952; New York, 1953 (repr. London, 1953, 1960, 1963, 1966). It is included in *Selected Plays*, Papermac edition, ed. A. Norman Jeffares, London, 1964; and in *Eleven Plays of William Butler Yeats*, ed. A. Norman Jeffares, New York, 1964. A further passage in *Plays for an Irish Theatre*, London and Stratford-upon-Avon, 1911, relates to Gordon Craig's scene for the play:

> Deirdre, like the other plays in this book, has been altered many times after performance, till at last I had come to think I had put all my knowledge into it and could not, apart from the always incalculable pleasure good playing brings, look for greater pleasure than it had already given me. But now because of Mr. Craig's scene which is fitted to so many moods and actions, and makes possible natural and expressive light and shade, I have begun to alter it again and to find in this a new excitement. Sooner or later it will be tried at the Abbey Theatre with what is, I believe, a new stage effect. The barbarous dark-faced men, who have not hitherto been all I imagined (perhaps because our stage is shallow), will not show themselves directly to the eyes when they pass the door, nor will the dark-faced messenger when he comes and says that supper's ready, nor it may be Conchubar when he comes to spy and not to fight. I will see passing shadows and standing shadows only. Perhaps the light that casts them may grow blood-red as the sun sets, but of that I am not sure. I have tried these shadows upon the stage and thought them impressive, but as I have not tried them before an audience I leave the old directions for the present. Should these shadows become a permanent part of the representation I will have to abandon the windows and doors through which one sees at present, a wood and evening sky But, perhaps, shadows of leaves seen on the wall beside the door under a shifting light will accompany the Musician's long opening speech. (*VPl* 396)

Further textual changes consequent upon these remarks are listed in *VPl* 396–7, and influenced Yeats's rewriting of the play. He gave an account of his sources in *The Arrow*, 24 November 1906:

The legend on which 'Deirdre' is founded is, perhaps, the most famous of all Irish legends. The best version is that in Lady Gregory's 'Cuchulain of Muirthemne', and is made up out of more than a dozen old texts. All these texts differ more or less, sometimes in essential things, and in arranging the story for the bounds of a one-act play, I have had to leave out many details, even some important persons, that are in all the old versions. I have selected certain things which seem to be characteristic of the tale as well as in themselves dramatic, and I have separated these from much that needed an epic form or a more elaborate treatment. Deirdre was the Irish Helen, and Naisi her Paris, and Concobar her Menelaus, and the events took place, according to the conventional chronology of the Bards, about the time of the birth of Christ. Concobar was High King of Ulster and Naisi King of one of the sub-kingdoms, and the scene of the play is laid in a guest-house among woods in the neighbourhood of Armagh, where Concobar had his palace.

Fergus, who in the old poems is a mixture of chivalry and folly, had been High King before Concobar, but had been tricked into abdicating in his favour. I have made no use of this abdication in my play, except that it helps to justify the popular influence I have attributed to him. I have introduced three wandering musicians, who are not in the legend (*VPl* 389).

Yeats described his rewriting of the play. In a note in *Deirdre*, London and Dublin, 1907, he commented that he had cut a passage because it overweighted what should have been a swift movement in the play and subsequently on correcting the proofs realized it was necessary to prepare for the words of the messenger. This passage was to be restored after the entrance of Deirdre and Naisi and reads as follows:

[*NAISI lays down shield and spear and helmet, as if weary. He goes to the door opposite to the door he entered by. He looks out on to the road that leads to Conchubar's house. If he is anxious, he would not have Fergus or Deirdre notice it. Presently he comes from the door, and goes to the table where the chessboard is.*]
Fergus.   You are welcome, lady.
Deirdre.   Conchubar has not come.
   Were the peace honest, he'd have come himself
   To prove it so.

Fergus.   Being no more in love
      He stays in his own house, arranging where
      The curlew and the plover go, and where
      The speckled heath-cock in a golden dish.
Deirdre.   But there's no messenger.
Fergus.   He'll come himself
      When all's in readiness and night closed in,
      But till that hour, etc. (*VPl* 390–1)

For discussion of Yeats's revisions see Peter Ure, *YTP* 43–58, and S. B. Bushrui, *YVP* 120–67.

The effect of Yeats's rewriting of the play was to give Deirdre's role more importance and centrality. (A four page leaflet, *Alterations in Deirdre*, 1908, contains these alterations; see also *VPl*.) A prose version was written first. Yeats mentioned it in a letter to Lady Gregory in May 1905, and in the autumn of 1906 he wrote to Florence Farr to say he thought he had made a great play out of *Deirdre*; it was 'most powerful and even sensational' (*L* 482).

The source for the play was probably Lady Gregory's version in *Cuchulain of Muirthemne*, pp. 92–117. The sources she listed for her version were the text and translations published by the Society for the Preservation of the Irish Language; Hyde, *Literary History of Ireland*; Hyde, *Zeitschrift Celt. Philologie*; O'Curry; Whitley Stokes, *Irische Texte*; Windisch, *Irische Texte*; Cameron, *Reliquae Celticae*; O'Flanagan, *Translations of Gaelic Society*; O'Flanagan, *Reliquae Celticae*; Carmichael, *Transactions of Gaelic Society*; *Ultonian Ballads*; De Jubainville, *Epopée Celtique*; and Dottin, *Revue Celtique*.

170   *Dedication:*

Mrs. Patrick Campbell: Mrs Patrick Campbell (1865–1940), the leading actress of her time, who played in Pinero's *The Second Mrs. Tanquery*, Ibsen's *Ghosts* and Shaw's *Pygmalion* (as Eliza Doolittle). Shaw was one of her chief admirers and critics: their 'strangely innocent' relationship is probably echoed in his play *The Apple Cart*. Some of Shaw's letters to her were included in her autobiography *My Life and Some Letters* (1922) and A. Dent edited *Bernard Shaw and Mrs. Campbell: Their Correspondence* in 1952 (this formed the subject of a play *Dear Liar: a Comedy of Letters* which played from 1957–60).

Robert Gregory: Robert Gregory (1881–1918), Lady Gregory's son, was educated at Harrow, New College, Oxford, and the Slade. He worked in Paris at Jacques Blanche's atelier and exhibited his paintings in Chelsea in 1914. His work as a painter is discussed by D. J. Gordon and Ian Fletcher, see *IP* 30–4. Yeats described him in 'In Memory of Major Robert Gregory' (*CP* 148) as 'Our Sidney' because of his Elizabethan variety of interests and achievements: a good shot, a good bowler, a boxer, a fearless horseman. He joined the Connaught Rangers in 1915, the Royal Flying Corps in 1916. In 1917 he became Chevalier of the Légion d'Honneur and was awarded a Military Cross. He showed 'the highest courage and skill' as a pilot. He was killed (in error, by an Italian pilot) on 23 January 1918 on the north Italian front. Yeats wrote three poems on him in addition to 'In Memory'; these are 'An Irish Airman Foresees his Death' (*CP* 152), 'Shepherd and Goatherd' (*CP* 159), and 'Reprisals' (*Rann*, autumn 1948; *Icarus*, May 1956; and *VE* 791).

Persons in the Play: **171**
   Uladh: Ulster.
   chessboard: see Lady Wilde, *AL* II, 32:

> The game of chess is frequently referred to in the old bardic tales: and chess seems to have been a favourite pastime with the Irish from the most remote antiquity. The pieces must have been of great size, for it is narrated that the great Cuchullen killed a messenger who had told him a lie, by merely flinging a chessman at him, which pierced his brain. The royal chessboard was very costly and richly decorated. One is described in a manuscript of the twelfth century: 'It was a board of silver and pure gold, and every angle was illuminated with precious stones. And there was a man-bag of woven brass wire.' But the ancestors of the same king had in their hall a chess-board with the pieces formed of the *bones of their hereditary enemies.*

   guest-house: the Irish Kings were noted for hospitality.   **172**
   royal house: Conchubar's palace was at Armagh. It was burned after the Deirdre-Naoise tragedy.
   old witch: Lavarcam, daughter of Aedh, the muse.
   Usna: father of Naoise, Ainle, Emain Macha, and Ardan.

173   *Fergus*: Fergus Mac Roigh, a former king of Ulster; he married Ness (or Nessa) and later was tricked by Ness into giving up his throne to Conchubar, Ness's son by another man. He lived out his days feasting, fighting and hunting. The story of his abdication is told in the *Book of Leinster* (*Ériu*, IV, trans. Whitley Stokes, p. 22). Yeats alluded (in *WR*) to his promise 'never to refuse a feast from a certain comrade, and the mischief that came by his promise, and the vengeance he took afterwards'. This concerned *geasa*, an obligation laid upon a person. Fergus was invited to a feast by Barach, in one version of the Deirdre story, and thus exposed Naisi and Deirdre, who were under his safe conduct, to Conchubar's vengeance.

   Fergus, son of Rogh: Fergus Mac Roigh or Roy.

   in my charge: see preceding note.

174   *who casts no second line*: a fishing image?

176   *the High King*: the Ard Ri, the high King of Ireland.

   Lugaidh Redstripe: a mythological figure, a hero of the Red Branch cycle.

177   *Edain*: a beautiful woman wooed and won by Midhir, King of the Sidhe. He took her to the Otherworld. Here Fuamorach, his wife, changed her into a fly. She then was blown into this world and reborn three times before Midhir in a game of chess finally won her back to the Otherworld. The story of all this forms one of the major tales in the mythological cycle *The Wooing of Edain*. See notes on 'The Wanderings of Oisin' and 'Baile and Ailinn', *Comm* 522 and 530.

178   *raddle*: rouge.

   Surracha: possibly Sorcha, the Gaelic Otherworld. O'Rahilly explains the name as originally *Syriaca*, Syria, influenced by the native word *Sorcha*, bright. In later romantic literature it denotes an exotic country with no precise geographical location.

The hole of the badger and den of the fox: this is probably an echo of   **179**
Yeats's reading in Spenser. He selected *Poems of Spenser* (1906) and
in his essay 'Edmund Spenser' (1902) he alluded to Spenser's 'The
Death of the Earl of Leicester', and commented that Spenser
'laments that unworthy men should be in the dead Earl's place,
and compares them to the fox – an unclean feeder – hiding in the
lair "the badger" swept.' Cf. in his poem 'The Municipal Gallery
Revisited' (*CP* 368) the line 'No fox can foul the lair the badger
swept'.
   seamew: gull.

these wanderers: the musicians.   **181**

The hot Istain stone, and the cold stone of Fanes: Professor David   **183**
Greene suggests that these may come from some medieval lapidary
and have nothing to do with Irish tradition. See note on **196**.
   delicate house of ivory: skull.

golden tongue: Fergus was occasionally called 'Fergus Honey-   **185**
mouth'.

Libyan heel: the mercenary messenger, dark-skinned. One of the   **188**
'dark men' who may have brought Conchubar 'Libyan dragon-
skin', **175**.

the reaping-hooks: the local farmers.   **189**
the crib: a wicker snare for birds.

in a net: there are parallels to Agamemnon's being caught in a   **194**
net by Aegisthus in Aeschylus, *Agamemnon*.

196   *the stones/That make all sure*: presumably the hot Istain stone and the cold stone of Fanes. The hot Istain stone may have come from the 'hot brain' of a Libyan dragon, the cold stone from its heart (see **183,** and the allusion to the miser's dragon-stone, **182**).

197   *The daughter of the King of Leodas*: an invented Scottish King.

Saul (*PYPl* 46) suggests Leodas may be 'an imaginary Pictish king? – the "Lord of Duntreon"?' Dun Treóin is in Argyll. Leodas is from Leòdhas, Gaelic name of the Isle of Lewis. Since rhyme in modern Irish is that of vowels only Treóin and Leòdhais (gen. of Leòdhas) would be interchangeable in the verse quoted, if it translated an original. In versions of the Deirdre story the woman who causes jealousy is the daughter of the Earl of Dún Treóin. Information supplied by Professor David Greene.

Scottish kings: Naoise and Deirdre went to live in Scotland, with his brothers Ainle and Ardan, when they left Ulster.

This is the first of the plays Yeats wrote which were the product of the impact on his own theories of drama, as they had developed over a long period of time, of the Japanese Noh drama. As early as 1899 he was envisaging a theatre 'for ourselves and our friends' ('The Theatre', *E&I* 166), free from the demands of commercialism, where words could be restored to their sovereignty over gesture and scenery, and the element of ritual in drama rediscovered. These ideas were developed in the 1903 essay 'The Reform of the Theatre' (*E* 107), in which he desiderates a theatre reformed in its plays, its speaking, its acting and its scenery. Its plays, serving the cause of beauty and truth, which will be the only justification they need, must be such as will make the theatre a place of intellectual excitement. They will require a stronger feeling for beautiful and appropriate language than is found in the ordinary theatre. Gesture must become merely an accompaniment to speech, not its rival. Acting must be simplified, shedding everything that draws attention away from the sound of the voice. Scenery and costume, like the background to a portrait, must contribute to the total effect.

In the 1904 essay 'First Principles', he develops further the idea already formulated in 'The Reform of the Theatre', that everything must be eliminated that draws attention away from 'the few moments of intense expression, whether that expression is through the voice or through the hands' (*E* 109). Now he writes:

What attracts me to drama is that it is, in the most obvious way, what all the arts are upon a last analysis. A farce and a tragedy are alike in this, that they are a moment of intense life. An action is taken out of all other actions; it is reduced to its simplest form, or at any rate to as simple a form as it can be brought to without our losing the sense of its place in the world. The characters that are involved in it are freed from everything that is not a part of that action; and whether it is, as in the less important kinds of drama, a mere bodily activity, a hair-breadth escape or the like, or as it is in the more important kinds, an activity of the souls of the characters, it is an energy, an eddy of life purified from everything but itself. The dramatist must picture life in action, with an unpreoccupied mind, as the musician pictures it in sound and the sculptor in form (*E* 153–4)

This concept of drama as a moment of intense life received dramatic expression in *Deirdre* (performed 1906), where, as Peter Ure says, 'everything concentrates on the way the single heroic individual confronts her destiny' (*YTP* 47). Indeed in *Deirdre*, and the even earlier *On Baile's Strand* (1903), he was already moving in the direction of that unity of tone, setting, character and image which is the distinguishing feature of the later dance plays. The 1910 essay, 'The Tragic Theatre' (*E&I* 238), affirms his opposition to naturalistic drama based on the 'contest of character and character', and shows him groping towards a drama where character 'grows less and sometimes disappears', being replaced by a lyric intensity of 'rhythm, balance, pattern, images'. For Yeats, character is defined primarily in comedy, which deals in that which is merely typical – 'personifications of averages, statistics, or even personified opinions, or men and women so faintly imagined that there is nothing about them to separate them from the crowd', whereas what he was seeking was a 'tragic art, passionate art', in which 'the persons on the stage . . . greaten until they are humanity itself.' This sort of character, which is the concern of tragedy, 'must be typical of something which exists in all men because the writer has found it in his own mind', for 'a poet creates tragedy from his own soul, that soul which is alike in all men.' (*PC* 91–3) In general terms, 'tragedy must always be a drowning and breaking of the dykes that separate man, and . . . it is upon these dykes comedy keeps house.' In 'Poetry and Tradition' (1907, *E&I* 246), the concept of tragic ecstasy expressed in heroic action is associated both with the 'recklessness', the *sprezzatura* of the great aristocracies of the Italian Renaissance and also with the 'courtesy and self-possession, and in the arts style' of the Japanese. But it was not until 1913 (see 'Swedenborg, Mediums, Desolate Places', *E* 64), when Ezra Pound introduced him to the Japanese Noh drama, that Yeats was able to find a form in which he could express these ideas effectively. The Fenollosa-Pound versions of the Japanese Noh plays acted as a catalyst which precipitated the *Four Plays for Dancers* and the explanatory essay 'Certain Noble Plays of Japan', whose confident, almost exultant tone ('I have invented a form of drama, distinguished, indirect, and symbolic, and having no need of mob or Press to pay its way – an aristocratic form', *E&I* 221) reflects the creative excitement that often comes when discovery merges with corroboration.

Yeats does not, of course, slavishly reproduce the features of the Noh drama. He rejects its stage, modifies the function of the chorus, presses scenery into the single clarified impression he was seeking to create ('a playing upon a single metaphor', *E&I* 234), and draws his action to a climatic dance, which is not always the case with the Noh. Indeed, in the spirit of Renaissance *imitatio* he assimilates the conventions of the Noh to his own purpose. Its fusion of language, music and gesture, its stylisation of character – largely achieved by masks – its unity of imagery, all gave him just that 'distance from life which can make credible strange events' (*E&I* 221) even the supernatural. 'All imaginative art', he wrote, 'remains at a distance and this distance, once chosen, must be firmly held against a pushing world. Verse, ritual, music and dance in association with action require that gesture, costume, facial expression, stage arrangement must help in keeping the door.' (*E&I* 224) Only such a form could be appropriate to a conception of tragic drama which was to be acted out in 'the deeps of the mind'.

To the influence of Pound must be added that of Gordon Craig, whom Yeats met in 1902, and with whose attacks on realism in the theatre Yeats sympathised, and whose advocacy of mask and marionette was known to him through Craig's magazine, *The Mask*, in which a version of *The Hour Glass* was published. Yeats used Craig's screens and designs for costumes and masks in *On Baile's Strand, Deirdre, The Hour Glass* and *The Player Queen* – see the notes on these plays.

The dance plays ended his search for an 'unpopular theatre and an audience like a secret society where admission is by favour and never to many' (*E* 254), and in Lady Cunard, in whose drawing-room at Cavendish Square, London, *At the Hawk's Well* was first performed on 2 April 1916, he found the hostess he needed to replace advertisement in the press. In a letter to Lady Gregory Yeats wrote that it 'was a real success . . . The form is a discovery and the dancing and masks wonderful' (*L* 611). When it was first published in *Harper's Bazaar* in March 1917, it was preceded by the following preface:

A couple of years ago I was sitting in my stall at the Court Theatre in London watching one of my own plays, 'The King's Threshold'. In front of me were three people, seemingly a husband, a wife and a woman friend. The husband was bored; he yawned and stretched himself and shifted in his seat, and I watched him with distress. I was inclined to be angry, but reminded myself that music where there are no satisfying audible words bores me as much, for I have no ear or only a primitive one. Presently, when the little princesses came upon the stage in their red clothes, the woman friend, who had seemed also a little bored, said: 'They do things very well', and became attentive. The distinguished painter who had designed the clothes at any rate could interest her. The wife who had sat motionless from the first said when the curtain had fallen and the applause – was it politeness or enthusiasm? – had come to an end, 'I would not have missed it for the world'. She was perhaps a reader of my poetry who had persuaded the others to come, and she had found a pleasure the book could not give her in the combination of words and speech. Yet when I think of my play, I do not call her to the mind's eye, or even her friend who found the long red gloves of the little princesses amusing, but always that bored man; the worst of it is that I could not pay my players or the seamstress or the owner of the stage, unless I could draw to my plays those who prefer light amusement or have no ear for verse, and fortunately they are all very polite.

Being sensitive, or not knowing how to escape the chance of sitting behind the wrong people, I have begun to shrink from sending my muses where they are but half-welcomed; and even in Dublin, where the pit has an ear for verse, I have no longer the appetite to carry me through the daily rehearsals. Yet I need a theatre; I believe myself to be a dramatist; I desire to show events and not merely tell of them; and two of my best friends were won for me by my plays, and I seem to myself most alive at the moment when a room full of people share the one lofty emotion. My blunder has been that I did not discover in my youth that my theatre must be the ancient theatre that can be made by unrolling a carpet or marking out a place with a stick, or setting a screen against the wall. Certainly those who care for my kind of poetry must be numerous enough, if

I can bring them together to pay half a dozen players who can bring all their properties in a cab and perform in their leisure moments.

I have found my first model – and in literature if we would not be parvenus we must have a model – in the 'Noh' stage of aristocratic Japan. I have described in the introduction to Mr. Pound's 'Certain Noble Plays of Japan' (Cuala Press, Dundrum, Ireland) what has seemed to me important on that most subtle stage. I do not think of my discovery as mere economy, for it has been a great gain to get rid of scenery, to substitute for a crude landscape painted upon canvas three performers who, sitting before the wall or a patterned screen, describe landscape or event, and accompany movement with drum and gong, or deepen the emotion of the words with zither or flute. Painted scenery, after all, is unnecessary to my friends and to myself, for our imagination kept living by the arts can imagine a mountain covered with thorn-trees in a drawing-room without any great trouble, and we have many quarrels with even good scene-painting.

Then too the masks forced upon us by the absence of any special lighting, or by the nearness of the audience who surround the players upon three sides, do not seem to us eccentric. We are accustomed to faces of bronze and of marble, and what could be more suitable than that Cuchulain, let us say, a half-supernatural legendary person, should show to us a face, not made before the looking-glass by some leading player – there too we have many quarrels – but moulded by some distinguished artist? We are a learned people, and we remember how the Roman theatre, when it became more intellectual, abandoned 'make-up' and used the mask instead, and that the most famous artists of Japan modelled masks that are still in use after hundreds of years. It would be a stirring adventure for a poet and an artist working together to create once more heroic or grotesque types that, keeping always an appropriate distance from life, would seem images of those profound emotions that exist only in solitude and in silence. Nor has anyone told me after a performance that they have missed a changing facial expression, for the mask seems to change with the light that falls upon it, and besides in poetical and tragic art, as every 'producer' knows, expression is mainly in those movements that are of the entire body.

'At the Hawk's Well' was performed for the first time in April 1916, in a friend's drawing-room, and only those who cared for poetry were invited. It was played upon the floor, and the players came in by the same door as the audience, and the audience and the players and I myself were pleased. A few days later it was revived in Lady Islington's big drawing-room at Chesterfield Gardens for the benefit of a war charity. The cast was as follows: The Young Man, Mr. Henry Ainley; the Old Man, Mr. Adam Wade; the Guardian of the Well, Mr. Itow; and the three musicians, Mr. Dulac, Mrs. Mann and Mr. Foulds. The music was by Mrs. Mann and Mr. Foulds. And round the platform upon three sides were three hundred fashionable people including Queen Alexandra, and once more my muses were but half welcome. I remember, however, with a little pleasure that we found a newspaper photographer planting his camera in a dressing-room and explained to him that as fifty people could pay our expenses, we did not invite the press and that flashlight photographs were not desirable for their own sake. He was incredulous and persistent – a whole page somewhere or other was at our disposal – and it was nearly ten minutes before we could persuade him to go away. What a relief after directing a theatre for so many years – for I am one of the two directors of the Abbey Theatre in Dublin – to think no more of pictures unless Mr. Dulac or some other distinguished man has made them, nor of all those paragraphs written by young men, perhaps themselves intelligent, who must applaud the common taste or starve!

Perhaps I shall turn to something else now that our Japanese dancer, Mr. Itow, whose minute intensity of movement in the dance of the hawk so well suited our small room and private art, has been hired by a New York theatre, or perhaps I shall find another dancer. I am certain, however, that whether I grow tired or not – and one does grow tired of always quarrying the stone for one's statue – I have found out the only way the subtler forms of literature can find dramatic expression. Shakespeare's art was public, now resounding and declamatory, now lyrical and subtle, but always public, because poetry was a part of the general life of a people who had been trained by the Church to listen to difficult words and who sang, instead of the songs of the music-halls, many songs that are still beautiful. A man who had sung 'Barbara Allan' in his own house would not, as I have heard the gallery of the Lyceum Theatre, receive the love speeches of Juliet with an ironical chirruping. We must recognize the change as the painters did when, finding no longer palaces and churches to decorate, they made framed pictures to hang upon a wall. Whatever we lose in mass and in power we should recover in elegance and subtlety. Our lyrical and our narrative poetry alike have used their freedom and have approached nearer, as Pater said all the arts would if they were able, to 'the condition of music'; and if our modern poetical drama has failed, it is mainly because, always dominated by the example of Shakespeare, it would restore an irrevocable past.

There is no authority in the legends about Cuchulain for the actual story. Yeats has devised a situation for his hero, similar to the kind which he found in the Noh plays, where 'the adventure itself is often the meeting with ghost, god, or goddess at some holy place or much-legended tomb' (*E&I* 232). Bjersby suggests that something of three visions which Yeats and other members of the Society of the Golden Dawn had seen in 1897 and 1898 (see *ICL* 43 and *Y:M&M* 127) may have lingered in his memory, and a note by Mrs Dorothea Hunter to a letter to her written by Yeats in connection with these visions and with his plan to organize a Celtic mystical order mentions

> The magic well of Connla [which] lies at the foot of a mountain ash. Those who gaze therein may, if they can find a guide, be led to the Fount of Perpetual Youth. The ash berries fall into the waters and turn them to fire. Connla, the Druid, is Guardian of the Well. (*L* 293n)

Bjersby points out, however, that there are striking differences between the visions and the play. There is no hawk, for example, in them, nor any sense of evil or dangerous power associated with the Guardian of the well. Wilson, in his long account of the play (*YI*, ch. 2), which he sees as functioning both at the personal, autobiographical level – Yeats's sexual and spiritual unhappiness at the time he wrote it – and also at the level of philosophy – Yeats's theory of the Self – and finally as an archetypal statement – adduces parallels and analogues from alchemical tradition and Celtic myth, especially the myth of Connla's Well, at the edge of which there grew 'a hazel tree bearing nuts of bright crimson, which could endow with all knowledge those that might eat of them' (see Standish O'Grady, *History of Ireland*, 1881 p. 127), and the myth of Slieve Gullian, the Castalian well of Irish mythology, whose waters, guarded by goddesses, could impart 'the gift of prescience' – though in the play it is immortality, not knowledge, that the waters confer.

Cuchulain's encounter with the hawk may owe something to the legend of Cuchulain and the two yoked birds, Fand and Liba, which Yeats appended to Lady Gregory's *Visions and Beliefs*, I, 290, and his erotic desire for the Guardian of the well may owe something to the legend of Niall and his brothers, in which Niall makes love to the haggish guardian of the well (see Standish O'Grady, *Silva Gadelica*, London, 1892, pp. 370–2). Wilson also elaborates on the influence, first noticed by Bjersby, of William Morris's prose romance *The Well of the World's End*, and corroborated by Yeats's essay on Morris, 'The Happiest of the Poets':

> In *The Well at the World's End* green trees and enchanted waters are shown to us as they were understood by old writers, who thought that the generation of all things was through water; for when the water that gives a long and a fortunate life, and that can be found by none but such a one as all women love, is found at last, the Dry Tree, the image of the ruined land, becomes green. To him indeed, as to older writers Well and Tree are all but images of the one thing, of an 'energy' that is not less 'eternal delight' because it is half of the body. (*E&I* 54)

Bloom (*Y* 296) points out that the Guardian performs the role she has in Morris, entangling the seekers in her love and keeping them from drinking the waters.

The play was first published in *Harper's Bazaar*, March 1917, and subsequently in *To-Day* (London) June 1917; *The Wild Swans at Coole*, Dundrum, 1917; *Four Plays for Dancers*, London, 1921; New York, 1921; *Plays and Controversies*, London, 1923; New York, 1924 (repr. London, 1927); *The Collected Plays of W. B. Yeats*, London, 1934; New York, 1935; *The Collected Plays of W. B. Yeats*, London, 1952; New York, 1953 (repr. London, 1953, 1960, 1963, 1966).

For the cast in the first performance see Yeats's note, p. 86 above.

207　*Title*:

At the performance of the play described in Yeats's note above, on 4 April 1916, the programme gave the title as '*The Hawk's Well*, or *The Waters of Immortality*'.

Persons in the Play:

Nathan suggests (*TD* 183), that the distinction between those who wear masks and those whose faces are made up to resemble a mask indicates a distinction between those who are simplified 'to some essential and intense quality, defined by the fate that formulates itself in [the] tragic moment of choice', and those who mediate between the human and the supernatural – the musicians – and those who participate now in the human and now in the supernatural – the Guardian. That a distinction is to be made seems to be supported by Yeats's complaint to Lady Gregory that at the charity performance 'nobody seemed to know who was masked and who was not' (*L* 611).

SD   A drum and a gong and a zither: an adaptation of the traditional Noh instruments, the flute and different kinds of drum, Tsuzumi and Taiko (see Hiro Ishibashi, *Yeats and the Noh*, 1966, p. 190). 'In order to apply to the music the idea of great simplicity of execution underlying the whole spirit of the performance, it was necessary to use instruments that anyone with a fair idea of music could learn in a few days.' (*FPFD* 40) Yeats's use of music in the dance plays is much freer than in the Noh plays, where it was governed by strict conventions.

A well: the significance of this seems adequately explained in the   **208** play – see note on *Title* above, and **212**, lines 15–16 – but it has been variously interpreted. Henn (*LT* 280) associates it with sexual virility. Ure (*YTP* 71) claims that 'it is truer to what is in the play to see it as simply the one precious and mysterious gift that will release Cuchulain and the Old Man, the one from the toils of old age and the other from the bitter entanglements of the heroic fate, from the divided and thwarted life of the hero of *On Baile's Strand*'. For Wilson (*YI* 41), the well is primarily an archetypal symbol of life, though he makes a distinction between the full well, which is for him an image of Unity of Being, and the dry well, 'any ambition inimical to human happiness, any unattainable goal, spiritual or sexual' (*YI* 59). Bjersby's view is frankly autobiographical, that 'the dry well and the leafless tree are symbols of [Yeats's] love. It is like a well, long choked up and dry, or like a tree without its greenery. If the well water surges up, it is not for his benefit, and without the water the tree is dry and dead. In his love, he feels like the young Cuchulain, who imagines himself to be within reach of the miraculous water, when, on the contrary, it proves to be the very moment of deception.' (*ICL* 93) Vendler (*YV* 215) sees the empty well and the withered tree as the unpromising nature of any heroic undertaking.

Pallor of an ivory face: Vendler associates this with Aoife, comparing *On Baile's Strand*, **276**, line 3: 'She was an amorous woman – a proud, pale amorous woman'; Nathan (*TD* 175), with Cuchulain himself; so also Wilson (*YI* 61), though because he regards the play as basically an initiation grail-type quest, with a 'dissolute hero' who resembles Gawain rather than Parsifal, and who is bound to fail.

How little worth . . . birth: cf. 'Among School Children', *CP* 242, stanza V:

> What youthful mother, a shape upon her lap
> Honey of generation had betrayed,
> And that must sleep, shriek, struggle to escape
> As recollection or the drug decide,
> Would think her son, did she but see that shape
> With sixty or more winters on its head,
> A compensation for the pang of his birth,
> Or the uncertainty of his setting forth?

209   *hazel*: associated with wisdom and the Tree of Life, and with the axle-tree of the world.

The guardian of the well: Nathan (*TD* 178–9) distinguishes between the passive Guardian, whose 'simplicity of character appropriately represents the unity of Being possessed by immortals', which attracts Cuchulain to her, and the Guardian who, when possessed, emblemises in her dance the remote beauty and immediate power of the supernatural. See notes on *the hawk* on page 91.

210   *These fifty years*: Yeats was fifty when he wrote the play. See note on **213**.

Old Man's speech: for the change in the metrical pattern here, cf:

When I wrote in blank verse I was dissatisfied; my vaguely mediaeval *Countess Cathleen* fitted the measure, but our Heroic

Age went better, or so I fancied, in the ballad metre of *The Green Helmet*. There was something in what I felt about Deirdre, about Cuchulain, that rejected the Renaissance and its characteristic metres, and this was a principal reason why I created in dance plays the form that varies blank verse with lyric metres. ('A General Introduction for my Work', *E&I* 523–4)

For more than fifty years: 'It is not possible to forget that Yeats   **213**
had lived fifty years when he started to write the play' (Bloom, *Y* 297), and Wilson goes so far as to claim that 'Yeats's sympathies are obviously with the old man' (*YI* 63), on which Bloom's comment is: 'The Old Man is not Yeats, nor any part of him, but he is an image of what Yeats fears to become. The mask of age Yeats desires some day to wear is the ageless mask of Ahasuerus of *Hellas*, Old Rocky Face, oracle of secret wisdom, not the cowardly, degrading mask of the Old Man waiting endlessly by a dry well.'

SD   the hawk: has attracted varied interpretations. Bjersby (*ICL*   **214**
87–93) associates it mainly with the hawk-symbolism of the early story 'The Wisdom of the King', *On Baile's Strand*, and *Calvary*, and sees it as a composite image of nobility, bravery and proud defiance, a superhuman or divine power, dangerous – but also attractive – to mortals, the wisdom that it brings being associated with bitterness. Nathan (*TD* 183) cautions against taking the symbol out of its immediate context in the play, and interprets it as the appropriate embodiment of the supernatural. Ellmann (*Y:M&M* 218–19), building both on the autobiographical element in the play that Bjersby stresses and on Gogarty's report that Yeats called the well immortality and the hawk-woman intellect, associates the Old Man with Yeats's intellect and Cuchulain with his instinctive self, and interprets the hawk as logic and abstract thought. Vendler (*YV* 211) disagrees, since to her 'in Yeats's frame of reference abstract thought never is possessed, never cries out in supernatural voice, never dances'. She associates the hawk-woman with Attracta in *The Herne's Egg* and 'the other medium-like figures in the plays, while her aloofness, indifference and luring power link her with the women of Phase 14 of *A Vision* and consequently with the image in its despotic power over the mind' – though she does not interpret

the play in aesthetic terms. For Peter Ure (*YTP* 71), the 'guardian hawk that lulls and lures is deceit and illusion that destroy Cuchulain's unity of being, or confound his search for it. She is the "inhuman, bitter glory", "the persecution of the abstract". She resembles Fand and the Woman of the Sidhe in *The Only Jealousy of Emer* and Aoife in *The Death of Cuchulain*, with whom she is in some sort of league.' For Moore, writing from the standpoint of his general view that frequently in Yeats the hero's access to divinity is through the medium of a woman, the 'woman-figure represents a challenge to battle that combines a kind of religious commitment with sexual ardour' (*MLD* 46).

The Woman of the Sidhe: not precisely identified in the play, but probably the same Woman who is identified in *The Only Jealousy of Emer* as Fand. Cf. **292**, lines 4–10:

> I know you now, for long ago
> I met you on a cloudy hill
> Beside old thorn-trees and a well.
> A woman danced and a hawk flew,
> I held out arms and hands; but you
> That now seem friendly, fled away,
> Half woman and half bird of prey.

215   *That curse may be . . . children*: variously interpreted. Nathan (*TD* 280) sees the first curse, 'though not clearly applicable to Cuchulain', as 'applying to his ambiguous relationship with Eithne Inguba in *The Death of Cuchulain*: the second is realised with Aoife in the same play, the third in his fight with his son in *On Baile's Strand*.' Vendler (*YV* 210) thinks the first curse reflects 'Yeats's view of his own relation to Maud Gonne; the second Blake's maxim that sexual love is always accompanied by spiritual hate; and the final curse is the one encountered, of course, by Cuchulain – to kill his only son.'

217   *He might have lived . . . friends*: cf. 'An Acre of Grass', *CP* 346:

My temptation is quiet.
Here at life's end
Neither loose imagination,
Nor the mill of the mind
Consuming its rag and bone,
Can make the truth known.

Yeats had anticipated this stanza – and this situation – in an essay written in February 1917:

A poet, when he is growing old, will ask himself if he cannot keep his mask and his vision without new bitterness, new disappointment. Could he if he would, knowing how frail his vigour from youth up, copy Landor, who lived loving and hating, ridiculous and unconquered, into extreme old age, all lost but the favour of his Muses?

The Mother of the Muses, we are taught
Is Memory; she has left me; they remain,
And shake my shoulder, urging me to sing.

Surely, he may think, now that I have found vision and mask I need not suffer any longer. He will buy perhaps some small old house, where, like Ariosto, he can dig his garden, and think that in the return of birds and leaves, or moon and sun, and in the evening flight of the rooks he may discover rhythm and pattern like those in sleep and so never awake out of vision. Then he will remember Wordsworth withering into eighty years, honoured and empty-witted, and climb to some waste room and find, forgotten there by youth, some bitter crust. (*M* 342)

SD '*Aoife!*' '*Aoife!*': Yeats is drawing on the Red Branch cycle **218** of stories. After his betrothal to Emer, Cuchulain goes to Scotland, where he undergoes training in arms under Queen Scathach. She sends him to make war on Aoife, a neighbouring queen, whom he defeats. He makes love to her on the battlefield, begets a son on her and later kills him. See 'Cuchulain's Fight with the Sea' (*CP* 37).

The final lyric is a summing up, in equivocal terms, of the equi- **219** vocal themes of the play. Wilson (*YI* 59), supporting his view with the ending of the earliest draft:

Accursed the life of man, what he hopes for never comes.
Between passion and emptiness, what he hopes for never comes.

sees it in terms of 'consummate spiritual disillusion', a conclusion which in Nathan's view (*TD* 280) 'denies, in the face of reams of evidence, that Yeats cared anything about the subject of heroism'; Rajan (*YCl* 97), as the inevitability of failure, though he qualifies this view by suggesting that those who seek fulfilment will always seem fools by certain standards. Vendler (*YV* 215) comments: 'one finds one's own species of immortality at the well and tree. For Cuchulain it is battle and not the water, but he had to come to the well to find this out. The world counts praise of well and tree idiocy, and in those terms the last lyric criticizes Cuchulain – but such a criticism is actually praise.' She therefore disagrees with Bjersby's view, page 89, since it takes no account of Cuchulain's courage. For Peter Ure (*YTP* 70), it is precisely that courage 'without which there can be no heroic desire, but which is made the means to thwart it', that is the unifying theme of the play. Bloom (*Y* 296–7) also stresses the heroism, pointing out that Cuchulain shows no regret at the loss of his quest, only exultation at 'receiving his life's role, of incarnating the hero', in his true encounter, which is with Aoife – a view supported by Moore (*MLD* 204), who points out that 'Cuchulain is in full possession of his *arete*. He goes out to face these supernatural women of the hills with joyous abandon, "*no longer as if in a dream*", but fully conscious of his capacity to live up to the heroic part his successful initiation has proved that destiny has assigned him'.

If the last two stanzas of the lyric are taken as an objective comment by a chorus that 'has no part in the action' ('Certain Noble Plays of Japan', *E&I* 226), and thus represents ordinary life, regarding any form of commitment, heroic or otherwise, as a kind of idiocy or folly, then their praise is highly ambiguous, issuing as it does from an empty well and a leafless tree. Moore (*MLD* 204) agrees, and adds a final comment: 'The heroes of the earlier plays were exhibited in all their tragic glamour. In this play Yeats has done an extremely difficult thing: he has shown the young Cuchulain at the start of his career, impulsive and valiant, convincingly innocent of any self-doubt; he has given us a devastating picture of the horrors of the heroic vocation; he has been ironic at the expense of

both heroism and non-heroism, and at the same time he has
managed to convey a weird sense of tranquil beauty.'

I have found . . . unmoistened eyes: cf. **216**, lines 16–18:

> *She has felt your gaze and turned her eyes on us;*
> *I cannot bear her eyes, they are not of this world,*
> *Nor moist, nor faltering; they are no girl's eyes.*

Folly alone I cherish: cf. **212**, lines 24 ff:

> *O, folly of youth,*
> *Why should that hollow place fill up for you,*
> *That will not fill for me?*

a mouthful of air: the phrase was used by Yeats to describe faeries,
'nations of gay creatures, having no souls; nothing in their bright
bodies but a mouthful of sweet air' ('Tales from the Twilight', *SO*
(1 March 1890)). See *IY* 325. The phrase was used in 'Ganconagh's'
novel *John Sherman* (1891): for 'what have we in this life but a
mouthful of air' (see *PYP* 72) and in this lyric as well as in the play
The King of the Great Clock Tower, 'O, what is life but a mouthful of
air?' See note on **640**, p. 263.

The Green Helmet

This is a version, in verse, of the play originally written in prose and called *The Golden Helmet*. It is founded, Yeats tells us, 'upon an old Irish story, *The Feast of Bricriu*, given in Lady Gregory's *Cuchulain of Muirthemne* and is meant as an introduction to *On Baile's Strand*' (*CW*, IV). Saul (*PYPl* 50) points to an allied tale in the same volume, 'The Championship of Ulster', and also draws attention to the Middle English analogue, *Sir Gawain and the Green Knight*, though there is no evidence to suggest that Yeats knew this poem.

Bushrui (*YVP*) has made a study of the two versions. *The Golden Helmet* (prose) was produced at the Abbey Theatre on 19 March 1908, and *The Green Helmet* (verse) also at the Abbey on 10 February 1910. For a comment on the verse see page 90. The ballad metre was inspired by Wilfred Scawen Blunt's use of the alexandrine in his play *Fand*, which had been written at Yeats's request and performed at The Abbey Theatre in 1907.

The cast in the performance of 10 February 1910 was as follows: Cuchulain, J. M. Kerrigan; Conal, Arthur Sinclair; Laeghaire, Fred O'Donovan; Laeg, Sidney J. Morgan; Emer, Sara Allgood; Conal's Wife, Maire O'Neill; Laegaire's Wife, Eithne Magee; Red Man, Ambrose Power; Scullions, Horse Boys and Blackmen, Eric Gorman, J. A. O'Rourke, John Carrick, F. R. Harford, T. Moloney, T. Durkin, P. Byrne.

Yeats's note on the staging of *The Golden Helmet* is relevant:

In performance we left the black hands [see **241**, *SD*] to the imagination, and probably when there is so much noise and movement on the stage they would always fail to produce any effect. Our stage is too small to try the experiment, for they would be hidden by the figures of the players. We staged the play with a very pronounced colour-scheme, and I have noticed that the more obviously decorative is the scene and costuming of any play, the more it is lifted out of time and place, and the nearer to faeryland do we carry it. One also gets much more effect out of concerted movements – above all, if there are many players – when all the clothes are the same colour. No breadth of treatment gives monotony when there is movement and change of lighting. It concentrates attention on every new effect and makes every change of outline or of light and shadow surprising and delightful. Because of this one can use contrasts of colour, between clothes and background or in the background itself, the complementary colours for instance, which would be too obvious to keep the attention in a painting. One wishes to make the movement of the action as important as possible, and the simplicity which gives depth of colour does this, just as, for precisely similar reasons, the lack of colour in a statue fixes the attention upon the form. (*CW.* Appendix III)

The play was first printed in *The Green Helmet and Other Poems*, Dundrum, 1910, and subsequently in: *The Green Helmet and Other Poems*, New York, 1911; *The Forum*, September 1911; *The Green Helmet*, Stratford-upon-Avon, 1911; *Plays for an Irish Theatre*, London and Stratford-upon-Avon, 1911 (1913); *The Green Helmet and Other Poems*, New York and London, 1912; *Plays in Prose and Verse*, London, 1922; New York, 1924 (repr. London, 1922, 1926, 1931); *The Collected Plays of W. B. Yeats*, London 1934; New York, 1935; *Nine One-Act Plays*, London, 1937; *The Collected Plays of W. B. Yeats*, London, 1952; New York, 1953 (repr. London, 1953, 1960, 1963, 1966).

Connacht: one of the five ancient kingdoms in Ireland, in Cuchu-   **224**
lain's day ruled over by Ailill and his queen, Maeve.

rath: fort.   **228**

Manannan: the sea-God, son of Lir.   **231**

Irish: Bushrui (*YVP* 188) points out that this is one of the details,   **232**
not in the prose *Golden Helmet*, which Yeats introduced in this version in order to make clearer the identification of Conall's house with Ireland and to heighten the satiric view of its petty squabbling.

233 *the straw and the broken delf and the bits of dirty rag: The Golden Helmet* has 'withered leaves'. The previous note applies.

234 *SD ladles*: again, a detail added in the present version, as if to lower the heroic association with horns.

239 *Emer's song:* in *The Golden Helmet* all the wives sing. In the present version Yeats gives Emer greater prominence by having her alone sing and by raising her song, now a pure lyric, above the level of plot. She is a true mate for Cuchulain.

241 *SD three black hands*: see Yeats's note on the staging of *The Golden Helmet*, page 96.

242 *He played and paid . . . head*: in *The Golden Helmet*, the Red Man demands payment of the debt, otherwise 'no peace shall come to Ireland, and Ireland shall be weak before her enemies.' In offering his head Cuchulain states his motive: 'The quarrels of Ireland shall end'. But in this version, as Bushrui points out (*YVP* 194), he offers his head because a wrong has been done and someone has to right it, and to honour a guest. Cuchulain's gesture is an act of pure heroism, without thought of material gain, for himself or anyone else.

Moore, who thinks that this is the last play in which a hero receives unqualified approval, comments:

> Cuchulain is a match for the Red Man not because he could defeat him in an epic battle – he obviously could not – but because his confidence in his own destiny is so great that he can afford to be careless of his life . . . In Yeats's other plays about Cuchulain, the hero is in one way or another at odds with sovereign authority; he is, or seems, eccentric – an outlaw in conflict with the conventional wisdom of society. In *The Green Helmet*, he *is* the central authority, for a triumphant moment anyway. The uncrowned King is actually crowned; the hero in a public ceremony receives divine sanction. (*MLD* 158)

On Baile's Strand

On Baile's Strand was first performed on 27 December 1904 by the Irish National Theatre Society. The cast was: Cuchulain, Frank Fay; Conchubar, George Roberts; Daire [an old King, not included in later versions of the play], G. Macdonald; the Blind Man, Shamus O'Sullivan; the Fool, William Fay; the Young Man, P. MacShiubh-laigh; the old and young kings were played by R. Nash, N. Power, K. Wright, E. Kegan, Emma Vernon, Doreen Gunning and Sara Allgood. Owing to the small size of the company at the time, women played men's parts. Yeats later remarked, 'it were indefensible could we have helped it' (*A Selection from the Poetry of W. B. Yeats*, Leipzig, 1913; *Selected Poems*, New York, 1923). Yeats commented on it in his notes to *Poems* 1899–1905 (1906) which contained the text of this play and *The King's Threshold*:

It was revived by the National Theatre Society, Ltd., in a somewhat altered version at Oxford, Cambridge, and London a few months later. I then entirely rewrote it up to the entrance of the Young Man, and changed it a good deal from that on to the end, and this new version was played at the Abbey Theatre in April, 1906. It is now as right as I can make it with my present experience, but it must always be a little over-complicated when played by itself. It is one of a cycle of plays dealing with Cuchulain, with his friends and enemies. One of these plays will have Aoife as its central character, and the principal motive of another will be the power of the witches over Cuchulain's life. The present play is a kind of cross-road where too many interests meet and jostle for the hearer to take them in at a first hearing unless he listen carefully, or know something of the story of the other plays of the cycle. Mr. Herbert Hughes has written the music for the Fool's song in the opening dialogue, and another friend a little tune for the three women. These songs, like all other songs in our plays, are sung so as to preserve as far as possible the intonation and speed of ordinary passionate speech, for nothing can justify the degradation of an element of life even in the service of an art. Very little of the words of the song of the three women can be heard, for they must be for the most part a mere murmur under the voices of the men. It seemed right to take some trouble over them, just as it is right to finish off the statue where it is turned to the wall, and besides there is always the reader and one's own pleasure (*VPl* 526)

The play was first printed in *In the Seven Woods*, Dundrum, 1903; *In the Seven Woods*, New York and London, 1903; *The King's Threshold*: and *On Baile's Strand*, London, 1904; *On Baile's Strand*, Dublin, 1905 (see *VPl* 456 for wide differences between these and subsequent versions). It was included in *Poems*, 1899–1905, London and Dublin, 1906. There followed *On Baile's Strand*, London, 1907, and the play was included in *The Poetical Works of William B. Yeats*. Vol. ii, Dramatical Poems, New York and London, 1907 (1909, 1911; rev. and repr. New York and London, 1912, 1914, 1916, 1917, 1919 and 1921); in *The Collected Works in Verse and Prose of William Butler Yeats*, Vol. ii, Stratford-upon-Avon, 1908; in *Plays for an Irish Theatre*, London and Stratford-upon-Avon, 1911 (1913); in *A Selection from the Poetry of W. B. Yeats*, Leipzig, 1913 (1922); in *Selected Poems*, New York, 1921; in *Plays in Prose and Verse*, London, 1922; New York, 1924 (repr. London, 1922, 1926, 1931); in *The Collected Plays of W. B. Yeats*, London, 1934; New York, 1935; in *Nine One-Act Plays*, London, 1937; and in *The Collected Plays of W. B. Yeats*, London, 1952; New York, 1953 (repr. London, 1953, 1960, 1963, 1966); *Selected Plays*, Papermac edition, ed. A. Norman Jeffares, London, 1964; in *Eleven Plays of William Butler Yeats*, ed. A. Norman Jeffares, New York, 1964.

246   *William Fay*: W. G. Fay and his brother F. J. Fay were gifted amateur producers and actors who 'had been in the habit of playing little farces in coffee palaces and such like' (*OIT* 30). See *Samhain*, p. 91. Yeats was impressed by their work, gave them his *Cathleen ni Houlihan* and AE promised them his *Deirdre*. Lady Gregory, Yeats and AE joined or supported the Fays' society, which was reconstituted as the Irish National Dramatic Company. This almost immediately became the Irish National Theatre Society in 1902, and the Abbey Theatre followed in 1904. The Fays stayed with the Abbey till 1908, and W. G. Fay did much for Synge's plays in which he played the chief male parts, notably in *The Playboy of the Western World*. See Ernest Boyd, *Ireland's Literary Renaissance*, 1922, Chapter 2, p. 425, and Ellis-Fermor (*IDM* 40–6).

On Baile's Strand: Baile's Strand, near Dundealgan, modern **247** Dundalk.

Persons in the Play:

Cuchulain, King of Muirthemne: spelt Cuchullain in some versions. See *VPl* 527. Muirthemne, Cuchulain's residence in Dundalk, Co. Louth.

Conchubar, High King of Uladh: spelt Conchobar or Concobar in some versions; Uladh, Ulster, spelt Ulad or Ullad in some versions. See *VPl* 527.

SD   Dundealgan: Dundalk.

Boann: a goddess after whom the river Boyne is named. See **248** Lady Gregory, *CM* 28–9.

Fand: a goddess, wife of Mannanan MacLir, God of the Sea. Yeats wrote of her love for Cuchulain in his note on 'The Secret Rose', and see also the Woman of the Sidhe in *The Only Jealousy of Emer*.

I have imagined Cuchullain meeting Fand 'walking among flaming dew.' The story of their love is one of the most beautiful of our old tales. Two birds, bound one to another with a chain of gold, came to a lake side where Cuchullain and the host of Uladh was encamped, and sang so sweetly that all the host fell into a magic sleep. Presently they took the shape of two beautiful women, and cast a magical weakness upon Cuchullain, in which he lay for a year. At the year's end an Aengus, who was probably Aengus the master of love, one of the greatest of the children of the goddess Danu, came and sat upon his bedside, and sang how Fand, the wife of Mannannan, the master of the sea, and of the islands of the dead, loved him; and that if he would come into the country of the gods, where there was wine and gold and silver, Fand, and Laban her sister, would heal him of his magical weakness. [In 'Mortal

Help' Cuchullain 'won the goddess Fand for a while by helping her married sister and her sister's husband to overthrow another nation of the Land of Promise' (*M* 9).] Cuchullain went to the country of the gods, and, after being for a month the lover of Fand, made her a promise to meet her at a place called 'the Yew at the Strand's End', and came back to the earth. Emer, his mortal wife, won his love again, and Mannannan came to 'the Yew at the Strand's End', and carried Fand away. When Cuchullain saw her going, his love for her fell upon him again, and he went mad, and wandered among the mountains without food or drink, until he was at last cured by a Druid drink of forgetfulness. (*WR*)

249   *Cuchulain's master in earnest*: see **255**, lines 3–25.
    stone over you: erect a gravestone over you when you die.

250   *A young man*: Conlaech, Cuchulain's son by Aoife, the female warrior from whom he had learned warfare.
    Aoife's country: the Hebrides. See note on **218**.
    the High King: the Ard Rhi, the High King of Ireland, in this case Conchobar, King of Ulster.

251   *Banachas and Bonachas*: T. P. Cross, *Motif Index of Early Irish Literature*, Bloomington, Indiana, 1952, p. 251, describes them as white-faced and puck-faced goblins respectively. In some versions they are spelt Bananachs and Bocanachs or Bonochas (*VPl* 527).
    Fomor: Yeats described them in a note as 'Gods of night and death and cold . . . [they] were misshapen and had now the heads of goats and bulls, and now but one leg, and one arm that came out of the middle of their breasts'. They were the ancestors of the evil faeries and, according to one Gaelic writer, of all misshapen persons. *P* (1895), rev. 1899.

254   *forty years of age*: Yeats altered the tradition (in which Cuchulain is generally described as dying at twenty-seven). Cuchulain ages with the poet. See Bjersby, *ICL*.

Maeve of Cruachan: Maeve or Medb was Queen of Connaught **255** (Connacht) and her capital was Cruachan, now Rathcrogan, Co. Roscommon. The kingdom, one of the five in Ireland, was ruled by Ailill (Oilioll).

the northern pirates: a reference to the Norsemen who preyed on the Irish coasts and eventually set up trading posts which became towns – at Dublin, Waterford, Wexford and elsewhere.

Sorcha: Sorcha (Sorca) is part of the Celtic Otherworld. Cuchulain was given a cloak by the King of Sorcha (see Lady Gregory, *CM* 217).

figures/Upon the ashes: suggestive of an inactive man, brooding over the fire.

he burns the earth: cf. line 11, 'though your father came out of the **256** sun'. In one tradition Cuchulain was the son of Lugh, God of light.

like a burning cloud: cf. 'a thing once walked that seemed a burning cloud'. 'Fallen Majesty' (*CP* 138).

leave names upon the harp: e.g. their deeds will be celebrated by the **257** poets.

hawk . . . That, as men say, begot this body of mine: Cuchulain alludes to one of the stories about his begetting. He was called Setanta, son of Sualtim (son of Roig) and Dechtire. Lady Gregory gives a different version of his birth (*CM* 22–4).

Country-under-Wave: Tir-fa-tonn (Tir-fo-thoinn), part of the **258** Underworld. Cf. note on **28**, p. 15.

there was one/In Scotland: Aoife.

that high, laughing, turbulent head of hers: cf. various poems about Maud Gonne: 'Being high and solitary and most stern' ('No Second Troy', *CP* 101), 'Such a delicate high head' ('Peace', *CP* 103) and the passage in 'The Trembling of the Veil' where Yeats describes Maud Gonne's 'look of exultation as she walks with her laughing head thrown back' (*A* 368).

all's changed: the phrase appears in 'The Wild Swans at Coole' **261** (*CP* 147) with reference to Yeats's own ageing and twice in 'Easter

1916' (*CP* 202) and 'But all is changed' in 'Coole Park and Ballylee, 1931' (*CP* 275).

Shape-Changers: a reference to the frequent changes of shape in Gaelic mythology. Cf. *The Shadowy Waters* (*CP* 498), lines 3–4, where they are identified with 'the Ever-laughing ones/The Immortal Mockers'. See also *The Green Helmet*, **226**, line 4.

264   *to no man*: Saul (*PYPl* 55) remarks that this should be, more accurately, *to no unaccompanied inquirer* and he points out that Yeats follows Lady Gregory (*CM* 314) here.

266   *he that's in the sun*: Lugh.

268   *His head is like a woman's head/I had a fancy for*: cf. 'Your head a while seemed like a woman's head/That I loved once' ('Cuchulain's Fight with the Sea', *CP* 37).

269   *Laegaire*: Leary of Victories, a Red Branch warrior.
four provinces: of Ireland: Ulster, Leinster, Munster and Connaught.

271   *Ever-living*: see note on shape-changers, **261**.
ashes of the bowl: divination, akin to that of teacups?

273   *crubeen*: pig's foot.

274   *was I an eagle-cock*: Brendan Kennelly 'The Heroic Ideal in Yeats's Cuchulain' *Hermathena* (*CI*, autumn 1965), p. 14, remarks that there is an ironic and rather squalid parallel to the tension between Cuchulain's wildness and Conchubar's desire for stable government in the relationship between the Fool and the Blind Man.

Scathach: a warrior woman of Skye who taught Cuchulain war- **275**
fare. He crossed a magic bridge to get to her island (Skye), and
Uathach her daughter opened the door to him and told him, when
he asked for Scathach:

> where she was and what he had best do when he found her.
> So he went out to the place where she was teaching her two
> sons, Cuar and Cett, under the great yew-tree; and he took
> his sword and put its point between her breasts, and he
> threatened her with a dreadful death if she would not take him
> as her pupil, and if she would not teach him all her own skill
> in arms. So she promised him she would do that (*CM* 63)

Uathach: Scathach's daughter, who had an affair with Cuchulain.

Alba: old name for Scotland. **276**
Dubthach the Chafer: the Black Beetle of Ulster, or Dubtach
Chafertongue. In one version he went with Fergus to bring Deirdre
and the sons of Usna from Scotland. He afterwards joined Maeve
and Aileel after Conchubar's treacherous slaughter of the sons of
Usna.

The Only Jealousy of Emer

This play was first performed in Holland. It was produced by Albert van Dalsum in Amsterdam in 1922 and 1926 (see *IP* 68). It was performed at the Abbey Theatre on 13 August 1929. Yeats wrote to Olivia Shakespear about the production on 24 August 1929:

> My *Fighting the Waves* has been my greatest success on the stage since *Kathleen-ni-Houlihan* and its production was a great event here, the politician[s] and the governor general and the American minister present – the masks by the Dutchman Krop magnificent and Antheil's music. Every one here is as convinced as I am that I have discovered a new form by this combination of dance, speech and music. The dancing of the goddess in her abstract almost non-representative mask was extraordinarily exciting. The play begins with a dance which represents Cuchullan fighting the waves, then after some singing by the chorus comes the play which has for its central incident the dance of the goddess and of the ghost of Cuchullan, and then after more singing is the dance of the goddess mourning among the waves. The waves are of course dancers. I felt that the sea was eternity and that they were all upon its edge. (*L* 767)

The dances of the Woman of the Sidhe or Fand were danced by Ninette de Valois.

The first printing of *The Only Jealousy of Emer* was in a Cuala Press edition of January 1919; the play also appeared in *Poetry* (Chicago) in January 1919. The preface to the Cuala volume, entitled *Two Plays for Dancers*, was dated 11 October 1918. The play was subsequently included in *Four Plays for Dancers*, London 1921; New York 1921; in *Plays and Controversies*, London 1923; New York 1924; in *The Collected Plays of W. B. Yeats*, London 1934; New York 1935; in *The Collected Plays of W. B. Yeats*, London 1952; New York 1953 (repr. London 1953, 1960, 1963, 1966); in *Selected Plays*, Papermac edition, ed. A. Norman Jeffares, London, 1964; and in *Eleven Plays of William Butler Yeats*, ed. A. Norman Jeffares, New York, 1964.

Yeats wrote a note on his aim in writing the plays for dancers which was included in *Four Plays for Dancers* (1921):

While writing these plays, intended for some fifty people in a drawing-room or a studio, I have so rejoiced in my freedom from the stupidity of an ordinary audience that I have filled 'The Only Jealousy of Emer' with those little known convictions about the nature and history of a woman's beauty, which Robartes found in the *Speculum* of Gyraldus and in Arabia Deserta among the Judwalis. The soul through each cycle of its development is held to incarnate through twenty-eight typical incarnations, corresponding to the phases of the moon, the light part of the moon's disc symbolizing the subjective and the dark part the objective nature, the wholly dark moon (called Phase 1) and the wholly light (called Phase 15) symbolizing complete objectivity and complete subjectivity respectively. In a poem called, 'The Phases of the Moon' in *The Wild Swans at Coole* I have described certain aspects of this symbolism which, however, may take 100 pages or more of my edition of the Robartes papers, for, as expounded by him, it purports to be a complete classification and analysis of every possible type of human intellect, Phase 1 and Phase 15 symbolizing, however, two incarnations not visible to human eyes nor having human characteristics. The invisible fifteenth incarnation is that of the greatest possible bodily beauty, and the fourteenth and sixteenth those of the greatest beauty visible to human eyes. Much that Robartes has written might be a commentary on Castiglione's saying that the physical beauty of woman is the spoil or monument of the victory of the soul, for physical beauty, only possible to subjective natures, is described as the result of emotional toil in past lives. Objective natures are declared to be always ugly, hence the disagreeable appearance of politicians, reformers, philanthropists, and men of science. A saint or sage before his final deliverance has one incarnation as a woman of supreme beauty.

In writing these little plays I knew that I was creating something which could only fully succeed in a civilization very unlike ours. I think they should be written for some country where all classes share in a half-mythological, half-philosophical folk-belief which the writer and his small audience lift into a new subtlety. All my life I have longed for such a country, and always found it quite impossible to write without having as much belief in its real existence as a child has in that of the wooden birds, beasts, and persons of his toy Noah's Ark. I have now found all the mythology and philosophy I need in the papers of my old friend and rival, Robartes. (*VPl* 566)

The first, second and seventh sections of the Introduction to *Fighting the Waves*, included in *Wheels and Butterflies* (1934), illustrate further some of Yeats's objectives:

I

I wrote *The Only Jealousy of Emer* for performance in a private house or studio, considering it, for reasons which I have explained, unsuited to a public stage. Then somebody put it on a public stage in Holland and Hildo van Krop made his powerful masks. Because the dramatist who can collaborate with a great sculptor is lucky, I rewrote the play not only to fit it for such a stage but to free it from abstraction and confusion. I have retold the story in prose which I have tried to make very simple, and left imaginative suggestion to dancers, singers, musicians. I have left the words of the opening and closing lyrics unchanged, for sung to modern music in the modern way they suggest strange patterns to the ear without obtruding upon it their difficult, irrelevant words. The masks get much of their power from enclosing the whole head; this makes the head out of proportion to the body, and I found some difference of opinion as to whether this was a disadvantage or not in an art so distant from reality; that it was not a disadvantage in the case of the Woman of the Sidhe all were agreed. She was a strange, noble, unforgettable figure.

I do not say that it is always necessary when one writes for a general audience to make the words of the dialogue so simple and so matter-of-fact; but it is necessary where the appeal is mainly to the eye and to the ear through songs and music. *Fighting the Waves* is in itself nothing, a mere occasion for sculptor and dancer, for the exciting dramatic music of George Antheil. (*W&B* 69–70; *VPl* 567)

II

'It is that famous man Cuchulain ...' In the eighties of the last century Standish O'Grady, his mind full of Homer, retold the story of Cuchulain that he might bring back an heroic ideal. His work, which founded modern Irish literature, was hasty and ill-constructed, his style marred by imitation of Carlyle; twenty years later Lady Gregory translated the whole body of Irish heroic legend into the dialect of the cottages in those great books *Cuchulain of Muirthemne* and *Gods and Fighting Men*, her eye too upon life. In later years she often quoted the saying of Aristotle: 'To think like a wise man, but express oneself like the common people,' and always her wise man was heroic man. Synge wrote his *Deirdre of the Sorrows* in peasant dialect, but died before he had put the final touches to anything but the last act, the most poignant and noble in Irish drama. I wrote in blank verse, which I tried to bring as close to common speech as the subject permitted, a number of connected plays – *Deirdre, At the Hawk's Well, The Green Helmet, On Baile's Strand, The Only Jealousy of Emer*. I would have attempted the Battle of the Ford and the Death of Cuchulain, had not the mood of Ireland changed. (*W&B* 70–1; *VPl* 567–8)

VII

'Everything he loves must fly,' everything he desires; Emer too must renounce desire, but there is another love, that which is like the man-at-arms in the Anglo-Saxon poem, 'doom eager.' Young, we discover an opposite through our love; old we discover our love through some opposite neither hate nor despair can destroy, because it is another self, a self that we have fled in vain. (*W&B* 79; *VPl* 571)

Part of an earlier Introduction to *Fighting the Waves* gives further insight into his aims:

I have written a series of plays upon certain events of the Irish heroic age, set out in their chronological order. In *Deirdre* the hero Naoise, who holds what the translators call the 'championship of the Red Branch,' dies, making way for his successor in the championship, Cuchullain, to whom I have given four plays: 'The Hawk's Well', 'The Green Helmet', 'On Baile's Strand' and the present play, or my verse play on the same theme 'The Only Jealousy of Emer'. If the first phase of our dramatic movement had lasted I would have dramatised other episodes from his life. Lady Gregory, John Synge and I, Standish O'Grady before us, James Stephens after us, planned a literature, comic or tragic, founded upon the inventions and habits of Gaelic-speaking Ireland. O'Grady started us off by re-creating Cuchullain in the image of Achilles, and when Lady Gregory wrote her 'Folk History Plays' and I my plays in verse, we thought them like Greek plays; the simple fable, the logically constructed plot, the chorus of the people, their words full of vague suggestion, a preoccupation with what is unchanging and therefore without topical or practical interest. (*Dublin University Magazine*, April–June, 1932; *VPl* 572)

The play's text was revised in small points of detail in *Four Plays for Dancers*, the major revisions occurring in *The Collected Plays* (1934).

A prose version, *Fighting the Waves*, was printed in *Wheels and Butterflies*, London 1934; New York, 1935. Yeats wrote to Lady Gregory on 10 February 1928: 'A few days ago I dictated to George [his wife] a vigorous new version in prose of 'The Only Jealousy' arranged for stage dancing' (*ICL* 50).

In these Emer gives up Cuchulain's love before he wakes and associates himself with Eithne Inguba.

The play is founded on an Irish saga called *The Sickbed of Cuchulain and the Only Jealousy of Emer*. There is some confusion in the saga: in the first part Eithne Inguba is Cuchulain's wife, and in the second Emer. (Bjersby, *ICL* 45, points out that two parallel stories are conflated, one from the ninth century, the other from the eleventh.) Yeats may have known Eugene O'Curry's 'The Sleeping Sickness of Cuchulain', *Atlantis*, 1865; he knew Sigerson's *Bards of the Gael and Gall*, 1897, pp. 391–5 of which supply plots of the legend; and he obviously drew upon Lady Gregory's version in *Cuchulain of Muirthemne*, pp. 276–93, and omitted the first half of the saga, since he envisaged the action of *The Only Jealousy of Emer* as succeeding upon the death of Cuchulain in *On Baile's Strand*. Bjersby has supplied an account of the saga:

At Samhain – 1st Nov. – the Ulstermen had gathered for their usual great festival, when suddenly a great flock of wonderful birds settled on the lake in front of them. All the women, and above all, Eithne Inguba, Cuchulain's wife, wanted these birds to be given to them. Cuchulain was asked to go and catch the birds. One woman alone did not get any bird at all, Cuchulain's wife. Proudly she declared that this negligence meant nothing to her, because, whilst all the other wives were in love with Cuchulain, she alone loved her own husband, Cuchulain.

After a while there came two beautiful birds, linked together by a golden chain. In spite of his wife's warning not to disturb these birds, Cuchulain could not be prevented from going out hunting them. For the first time in his life Cucuhlain, so noted for his skilfulness with the sling, missed the mark. Down-hearted he leaned against a stone pillar and fell asleep. In a

dream he saw two women, one in a green, the other in a purple
cloak, who, both smiling, beat him hard with their horsewhips.
He felt as if half dead, and when he woke up, he could not tell
what had happened, but he forbade the Ulstermen to carry him
to Dundealgen, where Emer, his wife, was. He remained ill for
a whole year.

The day before next Samhain, when the chief Ulster heroes
and Eithne Inguba were sitting there round his bed, a man
came and sat beside his bed, singing about Fand and her world.
After having revealed that he was Aengus Mac Aeda Abrot
and that Fand, the Queen of the Sidhe, intended to send her
sister to Cuchulain as a messenger, he disappeared, a being from
the Otherworld. The whole thing ended by Cuchulain's going
to the Otherworld, where he spent a month with Fand. When
he left, they agreed to meet again after some time. Then
Cuchulain sent Laeg, his charioteer, who had been with him, to
Emer his wife, to tell her that the fairies had put their spell
on him.

Emer came with fifty women to Fand's and Cuchulain's
meeting-place armed with knives to kill Fand. Cuchulain told
Fand that he would defend her, and then he and Emer started
a battle of words in which Emer blamed Cuchulain for slighting
her. Cuchulain answered that he would always love her. but
he did not understand why she could not let him for some
time enjoy the company of a woman that had so many advan-
tages as Fand.

Then Fand became just as much afraid of losing Cuchulain
as Emer was, and she bade him go with his wife. Fand's
deserted husband Manannan Mac Lir came and saved her out
of her plight. Cuchulain fell ill for a whole year. Then a drink
of forgetfulness was given to him as well as to Emer. For
additional security, Manannan also shook his cloak between
Fand and Cuchulain, to make them never meet again. (*ICL* 45-6)

Persons in the Play: 281
Cuchulain: see note, pp. 101, 301-6.
Emer: see note, p. 102.
Eithne Inguba: Cuchulain's mistress. See notes on **295-6,** pp. 118-
23.
The Sidhe: see note, pp. 11-15.
SD   At the Hawk's Well: Yeats's play, see notes pp. 81-95.
A woman's beauty: the first twenty-eight lines of the play were

printed as an untitled poem in *Poetry* (Chicago) January 1919. It also appeared with the title 'A Woman's Beauty is like a white frail bird' in *Selected Poems* (1929) and subsequent printing of this edition in the Golden Treasury Series (1951, 1952).

How many centuries: Saul (*PYPl* 58) compares these lines with 'The Phases of the Moon', *CP* 183: 'All dreams of the soul/End in a beautiful man's or woman's body'.

The preceding lines:

> All thought becomes an image and the soul
> Becomes a body: that body and that soul
> Too perfect at the full to lie in a cradle,
> Too lonely for the traffic of the world:
> Body and soul cast out and cast away
> Beyond the visible world. (*CP* 185)

suggest that Yeats may have in mind the fifteenth phase of *A Vision*:

The being has selected, moulded and remoulded, narrowed its circle of living, been more and more the artist, grown more and more 'distinguished' in all preference. Now contemplation and desire, united into one, inhabit a world where every beloved image has bodily form, and every bodily form is loved. This love knows nothing of desire, for desire implies effort, and though there is still separation from the loved object, love accepts the separation as necessary to its own existence. *Fate* is known for the boundary that gives our *Destiny* its form, and – as we can desire nothing outside that form – as an expression of our freedom. Chance and Choice have become interchangeable without losing their identity. As all effort has ceased, all thought has become image, because no thought could exist if it were not carried towards its own extinction, amid fear or in contemplation; and every image is separate from every other, for if image were linked to image, the soul would awake from its immovable trance. All that the being has experienced as thought is visible to its eyes as a whole, and in this way it perceives, not as they are to others, but according to its own perception, all orders of existence. Its own body possesses the greatest possible beauty, being indeed that body which the soul will permanently inhabit, when all its phases have been repeated according to the number allotted: that which we call the clarified or Celestial Body. Where the being has lived out of phase, seeking to live through *antithetical* phases as though they had been *primary*, there is now terror of solitude, its forced, painful and slow acceptance, and a life haunted by terrible dreams. Even for the most perfect, there is a time of pain, a passage through a vision, where evil reveals itself in its final meaning. In this passage Christ, it is said, mourned over the length of time and the unworthiness of man's lot to man, whereas his forerunner mourned and his successor will mourn over the shortness of time and the unworthiness of man to his lot; but this cannot yet be understood. (*AV*(B) 135–7)

toils of measurement: cf. 'the Statues' with 'the lineaments of a   **282**
plummet-measured face' and

> Pythagoras planned it. Why did the people stare?
> His numbers, though they moved or seemed to move
> In marble or in bronze, lacked character.
> But boys and girls, pale from the imagined love
> Of solitary beds, knew what they were,
> That passion could bring character enough,
> And pressed at midnight in some public place
> Live lips upon a plummet-measured face. (*CP* 375)

Archimedes: Greek mathematician of the third century B.C.
A fragile, exquisite, pale shell,
That the vast troubled waters bring: cf. 'Ancestral Houses' ('Meditations in Time of Civil War,' I, *CP* 225):

> though now it seems
> As if some marvellous empty sea-shell flung
> Out of the obscure dark of the rich streams,
> And not a fountain, were the symbol which
> Shadows the inherited play of the rich.

The image may derive from Shelley's *The Revolt of Islam* (Canto Fourth, I)

> Upon whose floor the spangling sands were strown
> And rarest sea-shells, which the eternal flood,
> Slave to the mother of the months, had thrown
> Within the walls of that grey tower.

The labyrinth of the mind, cf. 'the labyrinth of her [Maud Gonne's]   **282**
days' ('Against unworthy Praise', *CP* 103); 'the labyrinth of

another's being' and 'a great labyrinth' [of Maud Gonne's personality] in 'The Tower', II (*CP* 218), 'to die into the labyrinth of itself' ('The Phases of the Moon', *CP* 185), 'the labyrinth that he has made/In art and politics' ('Nineteen Hundred and Nineteen', III, *CP* 235) and the 'labyrinth of the wind' in the same poem, VI, *CP* 237; and 'the unconquerable labyrinth of the birds' ('Blood and the Moon', II, *CP* 268).

283   *that amorous man*: Cuchulain's affairs were numerous and Eithne Inguba was his latest love.

284   *at Baile's tree*: Cuchulain fought the sea at Baile's Strand, after killing his son nearby. Cf. the poem 'Cuchulain's Fight with the Sea' (*CP* 37).
    his own son: Conlaech.
    some wild woman: Aoife.

285   *Manannan, Son of the Sea*: Manannan MacLir, God of the sea. He brought up Deirdre's children in Emhain of the Apple Trees; he taught Cuchulain the use of his sword, the Gae Bulg, and aided Conchubar in many ways. He also taught Diarmuid of the Fianna the use of arms. In some legends he took many shapes; he may have been Culain the smith who gave his name to Cuchulain. See Lady Gregory, *Gods and Fighting Men*, 1904, pp. 100–35 for legends about him and his islands in the Land of the Ever-living. He is described as 'an old juggler' in *The Green Helmet*, **231**.
    All that are taken from our sight . . . loiter . . . For certain hours or days: cf. 'The Cold Heaven' (*CP* 140):

> Ah! when the ghost begins to quicken,
> Confusion of the death-bed over, is it sent
> Out naked on the roads, as the books say, and stricken
> By the injustice of the skies for punishment?

This refers to beliefs that there is a period after death before the soul finds its habitat. There is an interesting item in *AL* I, 224–5, which Yeats had read:

In the Islands, when a person is dying, they place twelve lighted rushes round the bed. This, they say, is to prevent the devil coming for the soul; for nothing evil can pass a circle of fire. They also forbid crying for the dead until three hours have passed by, lest the wail of the mourners should waken the dogs who are waiting to devour the souls of men before they can reach the throne of God.

There may be echoes of Neo-Platonic ideas on the journeying of the soul after death in Yeats's description of Cuchulain's 'loitering' after apparent death. (See W. F. Jackson Knight, *Elysion: Ancient Greek and Roman Beliefs Concerning Life after Death*, 1970, pp. 159–72.) The 'loitering' is expanded later in the play:

> He heard no sound, heard no articulate sound;
> They could but banish rest, and make him dream,
> And in that dream, as do all dreaming shades
> Before they are accustomed to their freedom,
> He has taken his familiar form; and yet
> He crouches there not knowing where he is
> Or at whose side he is crouched.

Old Manannan's unbridled horses: the horses of the sea.   **286**
   the dreaming foam: cf. 'that forgetfulness/Of dreamy foam', *The Wanderings of Oisin*, 1 (*CP* 421).
   struggling with the sea: the lure of the heroic life?

Sidhe: fairy people.   **287**
   Bricriu: a Red Branch warrior, Bricriu of the Bitter Tongue, who had a capacity for intrigue, for setting people against each other. See Lady Gregory's account of his treachery at the feast he gave Conchubar and the chief men of Ulster, *CM* 48–61.

people of the wind: the Sidhe.   **288**

Country-under-Wave: Tir-fa-tonn, see note on **28**, p. 15.   **290**

the fifteenth night: a reference to the thought of *A Vision*. See   **291**
previous quotation of this p. 112. Cf. also 'The Phases of the
Moon' (*CP* 183):

> *Aherne*   The song will have it
> That those that we have loved got their long fingers
> From death, and wounds, or on Sinai's top,
> Or from some bloody whip in their own hands.
> They ran from cradle to cradle till at last
> Their beauty dropped out of the loneliness
> Of body and soul.
> *Robartes.*   The lover's heart knows that.
> *Aherne.*   It must be that the terror in their eyes
> Is memory or foreknowledge of the hour
> When all is fed with light and heaven is bare.
> *Robartes.*   When the moon's full those creatures of
>   the full
> Are met on the waste hills by countrymen
> Who shudder and hurry by: body and soul
> Estranged amid the strangeness of themselves,
> Caught up in contemplation, the mind's eye
> Fixed upon images that once were thought;
> For separate, perfect, and immovable
> Images can break the solitude
> Of lovely, satisfied, indifferent eyes.

A Woman danced and a hawk flew: a reference to Yeats's play *At the*   **292**
Hawk's Well. See note on *the hawk*, p. 91.

And there shall be oblivion: this corresponds to the *True Mask*,   **293**
oblivion, of *A Vision*'s Phase 28:

The natural man, the Fool desiring his *Mask*, grows malignant,
not as the Hunchback, who is jealous of those that can still feel,
but through terror and out of jealousy of all that can act with
intelligence and effect. It is his true business to become his own
opposite, to pass from a semblance of Phase 14 to the reality of
Phase 28, and this he does under the influence of his own mind
and body – he is his own *Body of Fate* – for having no active
intelligence he owns nothing of the exterior world but his mind

and body. He is but a straw blown by the wind, with no mind
but the wind and no act but a nameless drifting and turning, and
is sometimes called 'The Child of God'. At his worst his hands
and feet and eyes, his will and his feelings, obey subconscious
fantasies, while at his best he would know all wisdom if he
could know anything. The physical world suggests to his mind
pictures and events that have no relation to his needs or even
to his desires; his thoughts are an aimless reverie; his acts are
aimless like his thoughts; and it is in this aimlessness that he
finds his joy. His importance will become clear as the system
elaborates itself, yet for the moment no more need be said but
that one finds his many shapes on passing from the village fool
to the Fool of Shakespeare.

> Out of the pool,
> Where love the slain with love the slayer lies,
> Bubbles the wan mirth of the mirthless fool.
>
> (*AV* (B) 182)

Cf. also 'The Phases of the Moon' (*CP* 183):

> *Aherne.*   And what of those
> That the last servile crescent has set free?
> *Robartes.* Because all dark, like those that are all light,
> They are cast beyond the verge, and in a cloud,
> Crying to one another like the bats;
> And having no desire they cannot tell
> What's good or bad, or what it is to triumph
> At the perfection of one's own obedience;
> And yet they speak what's blown into the mind;
> Deformed beyond deformity, unformed,
> Insipid as the dough before it is baked,
> They change their bodies at a word.
> *Aherne.*   And then?
> *Robartes.* When all the dough has been so kneaded up
> That it can take what form cook Nature fancies,
> The first thin crescent is wheeled round once more.

Fand's enemy: Fand was the wife of Manannan MacLir; there   **294**
may be some confusion here between Fand and the Hawk woman
of **292.** It may be that shape-changing is at work?

I renounce . . . for ever: Peter Ure comments on Emer's renunciation:

Emer's heroic deed, like Cuchulain's in *At the Hawk's Well*, is an assertion of her identity, of her name as loving wife, and her only reward, like Deirdre's, is that the long-remembering harpers shall have matter for their song.

But Emer here has a dimension which is absent from the Cuchulain of *At the Hawk's Well*. Her act is of such a character that it knows its consequence, and this is necessitated by the conditions under which it is performed. She does not find, after she has asserted her nature, that her destiny is in consequence to suffer its frustration; she chooses this destiny. She does not, as Cuchulain in the previous play does, dare the curse as part of the adventure, but chooses to be cursed. For she is fulfilling her side of the bargain with Bricriu and knows what is bound to follow:

> He'll never sit beside you at the hearth,
> Or make old bones, but die of wounds and toil
> On some far shore or mountain, a strange woman
> Beside his mattress

Her assent to the bargain is deliberate, and the nature of the bargain, as not in *The Golden Helmet*, is that neither side is pretending, so that the bargain cannot be comically evaded. Nothing Emer does is founded on a mistaking. She is more the heroine of the moral choice than any of Yeats's earlier protagonists, much more so than the Countess Cathleen, who, as we have seen, was never really given a chance to 'choose', and whose bargain is eventually annulled by heavenly justice. The difference shows Yeats's progress in the bleaker ironies. (*YTP* 74–5)

SD   The heroic mask: see stage directions on **282** and **286**.

295–6   *Why does your heart beat so . . . A passing word*: comments on this final lyric can be found in Nathan (*TD* 238–40), who argues that earlier versions of the musicians' final song seemed merely an extension of the concern with Fand's frustration that occupied the last half of the play:

> With Fand's role cut so that Emer's part dominates the action, the last song can be seen for what it was meant to be, antistrophe, so to speak, to the play's opening song, which was devoted to

introducing the beautiful Eithne Inguba, comparing her to a frail sea bird, useless product of untold suffering, cast upon the shore of human life. As Eithne Inguba, one extreme form of woman, receives the musicians' first tribute, so Fand, the other extreme, receives their last. (238)

Helen Hennessy Vendler draws on a manuscript draft (at Harvard University) of the lyric to support her interpretation, which runs:

The final lyric shows Yeats at his most maddening, and here I must differ with Wilson, with whom I agree in general on *Emer*. The first two stanzas are common ground, but on the third, and on the refrain, we part company. Before I say more, I will print the lyric as I conceive it divided into voices:

Emer to Fand: Why does your heart beat thus?
Emer to us: Plain to be understood,
                I have met in a man's house
                A statue of solitude,
                Moving there and walking;
                Its strange heart beating fast
                For all our talking.
Emer to Fand: O still that heart at last.
Emer to us: O bitter reward
                Of many a tragic tomb!
                And we though astonished are dumb
                Or give but a sigh and a word,
                A passing word.
Emer to Fand: Although the door be shut
                And all seem well enough,
                Although wide world hold not
                A man but will give you his love
                The moment he has looked at you,
                He that has loved the best
                May turn from a statue
                His too human breast.
Fand to us: O bitter reward
                Of many a tragic tomb!
                And we though astonished are dumb
                Or give but a sigh and a word,
                A passing word.
Emer to Fand: What makes your heart so beat?
                What man is at your side?

Fand to Emer: When beauty is complete
　　　　　　　Your own thought will have died
　　　　　　　And danger not be diminished;
　　　　　　　Dimmed at three-quarter light,
　　　　　　　When moon's round is finished
　　　　　　　The stars are out of sight.
Emer to us: 　O bitter reward, etc.

This arrangement of the poem is open to charges of over-ingenuity, but so is any other reading, given the inherent difficulty of the stanzas. It will be seen that in my reading Emer taunts Fand, then Fand taunts Emer, each claiming a victory of sorts. I am led to this reading partly by earlier versions of the closing lyric. In a manuscript draft at Harvard the play ends with a song bearing only a slight resemblance to the present lyric; in it, we can clearly see that Yeats's sympathies are equally divided between Fand and Emer:

How may that woman find
Being born to ill luck as it seems
And groping her way half blind
In labyrinths of his dreams
A little friendship and love
(For all the delight of the chase)
(A passionate man [*unrecoverable word*] enough)
(When he finds her not of his race)
(A lover his courtship done)
(Will weary likely enough)
(Of the alien thing he has won)
For all its chase and its jest
Passion soon has enough
Of an alien thing on its breast.

O bitter reward
Of many a tragic tomb!
And we though astonished are dumb
Or give but a look and a word
A passing word.

And how could I dream that this wife
Busied at her hearthstone
And a mere part of our life
Could speak with a gentle tongue
And give him the hand of a friend?

Could she not see in (his) that eye
That (she) it must endure to the end
Reproach of jealousy?

O bitter reward
Of many a tragic tomb!
And we though astonished are dumb
Or give but a look or a word
A passing word.

The first stanza is one of commiseration for Fand for the
faithlessness of earthly lovers, and in reading it we must recall
that in the early version which ends with this lyric Cuchulain
eventually turns on Fand with recriminations: 'That face,
though fine enough, is a fool's face.' He deserts Fand for
Emer: not simply plucked back, he makes a deliberate choice
against the alien, in favor of the familiar. And the refrain, too,
seen in this light, is sympathetic to Fand: Cuchulain's tragic
tomb has brought her only a bitter reward of momentary hope
eventually frustrated. But the second stanza changes the
perspective: Emer's unexpected nobility of behavior touches
the narrator too. Far from being a mindless drudge, Emer has
revealed depths of generosity and forgiveness: but she too has
won bitter rewards from Cuchulain's sojourn among the dead –
the loveless continuation of her marriage, reproaches for her
jealousy. In short, the bewitchment has yielded only bitter
fruit in all directions, and the play ends on a stalemate.

This is, I think, the mood in which the final version ends as
well. We may glance for a moment at an intermediate draft.
Dissatisfied with the version I have just quoted, Yeats wrote
the lyric as we now have it, substantially the same except for
the closing stanza:

> What makes (her) your heart so beat?
> Some one should stay at her side
> When beauty is complete
> Her own thoughts will have died
> And danger not be diminished;
> Dimmed at three-quarter light
> When moon's round is finished
> The stars are out of sight.

It is clear that the first question is addressed to Fand, whose
beating heart is mentioned in the otherworld scene. We must
then account for the woman in the second line, and it seems

most probable that it is Emer, who will fade into insignificance beside the full moon. In her danger of extinction she needs a protector, a companion, a husband; powerless to help herself (because 'her own thoughts will have died') she should not be left alone. Fand, though to be pitied perhaps, is an inhuman creature hardly in need of a guardian or comforter.

We may now return to the final version of the lyric. The speaker of the first manuscript version is clearly a spectator whom for convenience we may call Yeats. The second version is less clearly objective, lacking as it does the reflective tone ('And how could I dream,' etc.) of the first. By the time we arrive at the final version, I am not sure whether any objective speaker is intended. The last stanza seems to be so clearly a dialogue of two warring positions that I am inclined to see the entire lyric in that way, but I may be mistaken.

To recapitulate: a speaker, sharing Emer's view, asks of Fand, 'Why does your heart beat thus?' implying that Fand's heartbeat is somehow strange or excited, being so close to the otherworld of death. Then the speaker explains the question by describing the unwonted appearance of 'a statue of solitude', as Fand is described, in Cuchulain's house. Emer's fear of the Sidhe is reflected in the speaker's language, and since Cuchulain's time among the Sidhe is a tragic death in Emer's eyes, the refrain embodies her reaction to the bitter reward of her renunciation – a loveless life. The impotence in the refrain echoes Emer's earlier speech of frustration, in which she says that after men are bewitched by the Sidhe their wives cannot penetrate their abstraction:

> Our men awake in ignorance of it all,
> But when we take them in our arms at night
> We cannot break their solitude.

'And we though astonished are dumb' – the reaction is Emer's.

In the second stanza, Emer momentarily asserts her victory over the 'statue of solitude': though Fand may have supreme beauty, and can lure whom she will, still men may find themselves too human to be permanently happy with a Woman of the Sidhe. This is not true, and Emer knows it: Cuchulain did not return of his own accord – he was plucked away. But it is the perennial human hope, and it is Emer's dramatic function to voice the claims of human attachment. Her refrain, however, once again repeated, immediately negates her vaunted power. Fand replies victoriously in the third stanza, comparing humanly beautiful women like Emer and Eithne to stars which vanish in the light of the full moon. Cuchulain has no choice, she says: all human attraction is eclipsed when the Muse displays her sovereignty. Though human beauty may have temporary victories, in reality these are ephemeral, and the danger of losing Cuchulain to the otherworld is not diminished by this temporary setback. The hapless human residue doomed to extinction at Phase 15 ('your own thought will have died,' says Fand) can only look on and sigh, murmuring perhaps a protest which is unheard and vanishes as soon as it is uttered. Officially, Emer has Cuchulain back; officially, Eithne has his love; but we notice that Yeats has not given Cuchulain the drink of forgetfulness mentioned in the source. His Cuchulain will not forget the Woman of the Sidhe. (*YV* 230–4)

Harold Bloom remarks (*Y* 298–306) that the play ends with a difficult song that expresses Fand's bitter grief and Yeats's acute sense of his vision's limitation:

Fand, the woman of the Sidhe, is the 'statue of solitude,/ Moving there and walking,' a phantom with a beating heart, like the Christ of *The Resurrection*. That heart cannot be stilled at last, despite the bitter reward it has received, which is the loss of Cuchulain. For the Muse's lovers are faithless: 'He that has loved the best/May turn from a statue/His too human breast.' Cuchulain too was human, all too human; the forerunner is not always a Zarathustra. We are asked to attend to the suffering of the bereft Muse, and while it is difficult to feel sympathy for an occult grief, Yeats is unique enough among the poets almost to compel it in us. Even the Sidhe may be betrayed; the Belle Dame wither, in spite of her beauty, on the cold hill's side. (*Y* 305–6)

The Hour Glass

The play first took shape in Yeats's mind in 1902, and continued to nag at it off and on until 1922, when the two final versions, one in prose and the other in prose and verse, were published. It is based on a story, 'The Priest's Soul', recorded by Lady Wilde in *AL* 1, in which a priest, the cleverest in Ireland, denies the existence of the soul, of Heaven, of Purgatory and Hell. He is visited by an angel who tells him that he may either live on earth for a hundred years enjoying every pleasure and then be cast into Hell for ever, or die in twenty-four hours in the most horrible torments, and pass through Purgatory, there to remain till the Day of Judgement, unless he can find someone who believes, through whose mercy his soul can be saved. Finally he is saved by a child 'from a far country' who convinces him of the existence of the soul. The priest then retracts his blasphemy and bids the child kill him and call his pupils to watch his soul escaping, which becomes 'the first butterfly that was ever seen in Ireland'.

The figure of the Fool (not in the Wilde tale) was always present in Yeats's imagination, from the first version, a prose play called *The Fool and the Wise Man*, which under the title *The Hour-Glass* was first performed, with great success, on 14 March 1903 at the Molesworth Hall, Dublin, and published in the September issue of the *North American Review*. Although he reprinted it in 1904, and again in 1911 after a new production undertaken in collaboration with Gordon Craig, Yeats was not satisfied with it. (See note on *The Player Queen*, p. 142.) He revised it drastically in 1912, a 'new version' – in prose and verse – being performed at the Abbey Theatre on 21 November 1912, and published in Gordon Craig's magazine *The Mask* in April 1913, with the following preface:

> I took the plot of 'The Hour Glass' from an Irish Folk Tale but tried to put my own philosophy into the words. An action on the stage, however, is so much stronger than a word that

when the Wise Man abused himself before the Fool I was
always ashamed. My own meanings had vanished and I saw
before me a cowardly person who seemed to cry out 'the
wisdom of this world is foolishness' and to understand the words
not as may a scholar and a gentleman but as do ignorant
preachers.

I began a revision of the words from the moment when the
play converted a music hall singer and sent him to mass and
to confession; but no revision of words could change the effect
of the Wise Man down on his knees before the Fool; so last
year I changed action and all.

I made a new play of it and when I had finished discovered
how I might have taken the offence out of the old by a change
of action so slight that a reader would hardly have noticed it. I
shall let our 'second company' go on playing the old version
thus amended in Irish provincial towns but think the new one
better for myself and my friends.

He printed yet another version, containing some important
revisions, in 1914, in *RPP*, a text with only minor revisions was
issued again in 1922 and is substantially that given in *CPl*.

He kept the prose version in print when he published both
versions – the prose (with some important changes from 1911),
and the verse-and-prose – in *PPV*.

The 1922 edition carried the following note – itself a re-working
of the Preface to the 1913 version – which represents Yeats's final
attitude towards the play:

... The early version of the Play, which was only too effective,
converting a music-hall singer and sending him to Mass for six
weeks, made me ashamed, but I did not know until very
lately how to remedy it. I had made my Wise Man humble
himself to the Fool and receive salvation as a reward, but now
I have given it a new end which is closer to my own thought
as well as more effective theatrically. The Fool too, when it is
now played at the Abbey Theatre, wears a mask designed by
Mr. Gordon Craig which makes him seem less a human being
than a principle of the mind.

One sometimes has need of a few words for the Pupils
to sing at their first or second entrance, and I have put
into English rhyme three of the many verses of a Gaelic
Ballad.

> I was going the road one day
> (O the brown and the yellow beer),
> And I met with a man that was no right man
> (O my dear, O my dear).
>
> 'Give me your wife,' said he
> (O the brown and the yellow beer),
> 'Till the sun goes down and an hour of the clock'
> (O my dear, O my dear).
>
> 'Good-bye, good-bye, my husband
> (O the brown and the yellow beer),
> 'For a year and a day by the clock of the sun'
> (O my dear, O my dear).

A note in the 1914 edition makes clearer what Yeats meant by giving it 'a new end which is closer to my own thought as well as more effective theatrically': 'Now I have made my philosopher accept God's will, whatever it is, and find his courage again, and helped by the elaboration of verse, have so changed the fable that it is not false to my own thoughts of the world.'

Both Teigue and the Wise Man become more complex figures in the course of these changes, the latter approaching the Yeatsian 'heroic man'. For a full discussion of the versions, see Bushrui, 'The Hour Glass: Yeats's Revisions, 1903–1922', *YCE.*

The play was first printed in *The Mask,* Florence, April 1913 and subsequently in *The Hour-Glass,* Dundrum, 1914; *Responsibilities: Poems and a Play,* Dundrum, 1914; *Responsibilities and Other Poems,* London, 1916; New York, 1916 (repr. London, 1922, 1926, 1931); *The Collected Plays of W. B. Yeats,* London, 1934; New York, 1935; *The Collected Plays of W. B. Yeats,* London, 1952; New York, 1953 (repr. London, 1953, 1960, 1963, 1966).

The cast of the 1903 performance was as follows: The Wise Man, J. Dudley Digges; Bridget, Maire T. Quinn; Children, Eithne and Padragan Nic Shiubhlaigh; Pupils, P. J. Kelly, Seamus O'Sullivan, P. Columb, P. MacShiubhlaigh; The Angel, Maire Nic Shiubhlaigh; The Fool, F. J. Fay.

299 *Title:*
   The 1903 prose version was subtitled A Morality.

SD   *the books*: either 'books' or 'the Book'.   **301**

'*There are two . . . there*': in the 1903 prose version these words are said to be written by a beggar on the walls of Babylon (see lines 20–2). In *PASL* Yeats added a footnote in 1924 to the sentence 'There are two realities, the terrestial and the conditions of fire':

> When writing this essay I did not see how complete must be the antithesis between man and Daimon. The repose of man is the choice of the Daimon, and the repose of the Daimon the choice of man; and what I have called man's terrestial state the Daimon's condition of fire. I might have seen this, as it all follows from the words written by the beggar in *The Hour-Glass* upon the walls of Babylon. (*M* 356)

Diem . . . labuntur: 'I argue day and night, but those whom I have chosen, whom I have loved, are being brought to trial.' In a note to the 1922 edition, *PPV*, Yeats wrote that he 'got Mr. Alan Porter to put into mediaeval Latin certain passages, as I found that in performance verbal repetitions which did not get on the nerves in the prose version, did so when all the first half of the play was in verse. We listen more intently to verse than to prose, and therefore notice verbal repetition more quickly. Nothing said in Latin, necessary to the understanding of the play, cannot be inferred from who speaks and who is spoken to.'

Virgas . . . nugas: 'the birds bind twigs together that they may   **302** nurture the young, the mind of man gathers trifles.'

Were it but true . . . twice: for this change to verse cf. Yeats's letter to Lady Gregory, 3 January 1903: 'I have got to think this necessary to lift the "Wise man's" part out of a slight element of platitude.' (*L* 391). Certainly it differentiates the perceptions of the Wise Man from those of both his pupils and the Fool. Except for the three-line snatch of verse at the end of the play, the Fool speaks in prose throughout. The Wise Man comes to occupy a point between the blind reason of the Pupils and the inarticulate vision of the Fool – see note on **310**, *SD*.

I have dreamed it twice: the Wise Man's dream provokes or is   **303** corroborated by the fact, just as his dream of the Angel (**308**, line 7) provokes or is corroborated by the Angel's entry. It is the dream that bears witness to the 'invisible order of imagination and spiritual being', which is opposed to the 'visible world of nature and other people'. (Moore, *MLD* 83.)

Frenzy will beat his drum: cf. 'A Prayer for my Daughter', *CP* 211, second stanza:

> I have walked and prayed for this young child an hour
> And heard the sea-wind scream upon the tower,
> And under the arches of the bridge, and scream
> In the elms above the flooded stream:
> Imagining in excited reverie
> That the future years had come,
> Dancing to a frenzied drum,
> Out of the murderous innocence of the sea.

and 'What Magic Drum?', Supernatural Songs, VII, *CP* 331, second stanza;

> Through light-obliterating garden foliage what magic drum?
> Down limb and breast or down that glimmering belly
>   move his mouth and sinewy tongue.
> What from the forest came? What beast has licked its young?

a hawk: not the usual symbolism of logic or subjectivity, but conveying by its swiftness, accuracy and power, a sense of supernatural conviction. See **314**, lines 6–8.

307 *SD   An Angel has come in . . . with the right voice . . .*: cf: '. . . when one wishes to make the voice immortal and passionless, as in the Angel's part in my *Hour-Glass*, one finds it desirable for the player to speak always upon pure musical notes, written out beforehand and carefully rehearsed. On the one occasion when I heard the Angel's part spoken in this way with entire success, the contrast between the crystalline quality of the pure notes and the more confused and passionate speaking of the Wise Man was a new dramatic effect of great value.' *Samhain*, 1904, *E* 174.

308 *I think . . . dreams*: see note on **303**.

Pardon me: in the corresponding passage in the 1903 prose version   **309**
the Wise Man humbles himself here by kneeling to the Angel. In
this version he retains his self-sufficiency; conviction of the spiritual
world comes from his own vision.

SD   Enter other Pupils with Fool: it is worth noting, for the dramatic   **310**
effect, that the Fool is on stage from here until his exit with the
Pupils at the top of **317**, and that after his second demand for a
penny, **311**, he says nothing.

Nullum esse . . . mater: 'I have asserted God and the Mother of   **311**
God to be nothing: but I have lied: both God and the Mother of
God exist for the truly wise man.'

Argumentis . . . particeps: 'Now prove by arguments; for he who   **312**
is a companion of reason demands arguments.'
    Pro certo . . . vidisse: 'I know for certain that one of you has
remained firm in his faith, that one has seen higher than I.'
    Quae destruxi . . . reaedificem: 'It is necessary that all I have
destroyed be rebuilt.'
    Haec . . . incunbula: 'These things did not enter our childish minds:
but now we have grown up: we have laid aside swaddling-clothes.'

Non iam . . . est: 'We are not now boys; only the body is conceived   **313**
from the mother.'
    Docuisti . . . persuadetur: 'You have taught, and we are convinced.'
    Mendaciis . . . simulacris: 'I have filled you with lies, and your
minds with shadows.'
    Nulli . . . persuasisti: 'There is no-one you have not convinced.'
    Nulli . . . nulli: 'No-one, no-one, no-one.'
    Babylonian moon: with the usual association of scientific rationalism.
Cf. 'The Dawn', *CP* 164, with its reference to what Yeats called
'the Babylonian mathematical starlight' in *AV*(B) 268:

> I would be ignorant as the dawn
> That has looked down
> On that old queen measuring a town
> With the pin of a brooch,
> Or on the withered men that saw
> From their pedantic Babylon
> The careless planets in their courses,
> The stars fade out where the moon comes,
> And took their tablets and did sums . . .

314   *those three in the furnace*: a reference to the story of Shadrack, Meshack and Abednego, who were cast into the fiery furnace by King Nebuchadnezzar. When the king looked into it he saw not only the three unscathed, but also a fourth figure: 'and the form of the fourth is like the Son of God'. *Daniel* III, 1–25.

   hawk: see note on **303**, line 13.

   Argumentum . . . profer: 'Produce the proof, O teacher.'

315   *Credo . . . sanctum*: 'I believe in the Father, the Son, and the Holy Ghost.'

316   *a mustard-grain of faith*: with the obvious biblical echo of *Matthew* XIII, 31: Another parable put he forth unto them, saying, The kingdom of heaven is like to a grain of mustard seed, which a man took, and sowed in his field: Which indeed is the least of all seeds: but when it is grown, it is the greatest among herbs, and becometh a tree, so that the birds of the air come and lodge in the branches thereof.

317   *SD He drives them out*: Teigue must go out with the pupils, since he has to re-enter on p. **319**. The 1903 prose version has *All go out*.

321   *Speak, speak*: in the 1903 prose version the Wise Man kneels here. See note on **309**, line 6.

bodach: beggar, tramp, churl.   **322**

Be silent . . . He dies: Bushrui shows that the moment and manner   **323**
of the Wise Man's death represent a major alteration. In the 1911
version the Wise Man receives salvation from the Fool *before* he
dies, when the Fool confesses to his belief in Angels, and after the
Wise Man has actually knelt before him and begged for pity. In
the 1913 version, the Wise Man still kneels before the Fool, but the
Fool says nothing about his belief until after the Wise Man's death.
The Wise Man dies in resignation. In the 1914 revision – substantially the text of *CPl* – resignation comes close to heroic dignity by
the addition of the lines:

> *Be silent. May God's will prevail on the instant,*
> *Although his will be my eternal pain.*
> *I have no question . . .*

The Unicorn from the Stars

This is a reworking of an earlier play, *Where There is Nothing*, written by Yeats, Lady Gregory and Douglas Hyde, 'in a fortnight' as he told A. H. Bullen, 'to keep George Moore from stealing the plot' (*L* 503). The earlier play was first published as a supplement to *The United Irishman*, 1 November 1902, and performed at the Royal Court Theatre, London, 26 June 1904. Yeats withdrew it from circulation. It is reprinted in *VPl*.

About the new play, *The Unicorn from the Stars*, Yeats wrote in a letter to A. H. Bullen: 'Though *The Unicorn* is almost altogether Lady Gregory's writing, it has far more of my spirit in it than *Where There is Nothing* . . . I planned out *The Unicorn* to carry to a more complete realization the central idea of the stories of *The Secret Rose* and I believe it has more natural affinities with those stories than has *Where There is Nothing* . . .' (*L* 503).

In his note to *PPV*, Yeats wrote:

I wrote in 1902, with the help of Lady Gregory and another friend, a play called *Where There is Nothing*, but had to write at great speed to meet a sudden emergency. Five acts had to be finished, in, I think, a fortnight, instead of the five years that would have been somewhat nearer my natural pace. It became hateful to me because, in desperation, I had caught up from a near table a pamphlet of Tolstoy's on the Sermon on the Mount, and made out of it a satirical scene that became the pivot of the play. The scene seemed amusing on the stage, but its crude speculative commonplaces filled me with shame and I withdrew the play from circulation. That I might free myself from what seemed a contamination, I asked Lady Gregory to help me turn my old plot into *The Unicorn from the Stars*. I began to dictate, but since I had last worked with her, her mastery of the stage and her knowledge of dialect had so increased that my imagination could not go neck and neck with hers. I found myself, too, stopped by an old difficulty, that my words never flow freely but when people speak in verse; and so after an

attempt to work alone I gave up my scheme to her. The result
is a play almost wholly hers in handiwork, which is so much
mine in thought that she does not wish to include it in her own
works. I can indeed read it after the stories in *The Secret Rose*
and recognize thoughts, points of view, and artistic aims which
seem a part of my world. Her greatest difficulty was that I had
given her in my re-shaping of the plot – swept as I hoped of
dogmatism and rhetorical arrogance – for chief character, a
man so plunged in trance that he could not be otherwise than all
but still and silent, though perhaps with the stillness and silence
of a lamp; and the movement of the play as a whole, if we were
to listen, if we were to understand what he said, had to be
without hurry or violence. The strange characters, her handiwork, on whom he sheds his light, delight me. She has enabled
me to carry out an old thought for which my own knowledge is
insufficient, and to commingle the ancient phantasies of poetry
with the rough, vivid, ever-contemporaneous tumult of the
roadside; to share in the creation of a form that otherwise I
could but dream of, though I do that always, an art that mur-
mured, though with worn and failing voice, of the day when
Quixote and Sancho, long estranged, may once again go out
gaily into the bleak air. Ever since I began to write I have
awaited with impatience a linking all Europe over of the
hereditary knowledge of the countryside, now becoming known
to us through the work of wanderers and men of learning, with
our old lyricism so full of ancient frenzies and hereditary wisdom; a yoking of antiquities; a Marriage of Heaven and Hell.

He had put much the same point in 1908:

I feel indeed that my best share in it [*The Unicorn from the Stars*]
is that idea, which I have been capable of expressing in criticism alone, of bringing together the rough life of the road and
the frenzy that the poets have found in their ancient cellar, –
a prophecy, as it were, of the time when it will be once again
possible for a Dickens and a Shelley to be born in the one body.
    The chief person of the earlier Play was very dominating,
and I have grown to look upon this as a fault, though it in-
creases the dramatic effect in a superficial way. We cannot
sympathise with the man who sets his anger at once lightly and
confidently to overthrow the order of the world, for such a
man will seem to us alike insane and arrogant. But our hearts
can go with him, as I think, if he speak with some humility, so
far as his daily self carry him, out of a cloudy light of vision;

for whether he understand or not, it may be that voices of angels and archangels have spoken in the cloud, and whatever wildness came upon his life, feet of theirs may well have trod the clusters. But a man so plunged in trance is of necessity somewhat still and silent, though it be perhaps the silence and the stillness of a lamp; and the movement of the Play as a whole, if we are to have time to hear him, must be without hurry or violence. (*US*)

The first performance of *The Unicorn from the Stars* was given at the Abbey Theatre, 23 November 1907. For accounts of the differences between *Where There is Nothing* and *The Unicorn from the Stars*, see Ure, *YTP* 131-4, Nathan, *TD* 146-51 and Ellis-Fermor, *IDM* 104-7. The cast was as follows: Father John, Ernest Vaughan; Thomas Hearne, a coachbuilder, Arthur Sinclair; Andrew Hearne, brother of Thomas, J. A. O'Rourke; Martin Hearne, nephew of Thomas, F. J. Fay; Johnny Bachach, a beggar, W. G. Fay; Paudeen, J. M. Kerrigan; Biddy Lally, Maire O'Neill; Nanny, Brigit O'Dempsey.

The play was first printed in *The Unicorn from the Stars*, New York, January 1908 and again in *The Unicorn from the Stars and Other Plays*, New York, May 1908; and subsequently in *The Collected Works in Verse and Prose of William Butler Yeats*, Vol. III, Stratford-upon-Avon, 1908; *Plays in Prose and Verse*, London, 1922; New York, 1924 (repr. London, 1922, 1926, 1931); *The Collected Plays of W. B. Yeats*, London, 1934; New York, 1935; *The Collected Plays of W. B. Yeats*, London, 1952; New York, 1953 (repr. London, 1953, 1960, 1963, 1966).

327   *Title*:

The Unicorn: in a letter to his sister Elizabeth, Yeats said that the unicorn was 'a private symbol belonging to my mystical order' and that it was the soul. (*L* 662) Cf., however, *CPl* **338**, lines 14-16. Melchiori, in his discussion of the Unicorn image (*WMA* 35-71), points out that this explanation is only partial. In *Where There is Nothing* Paul Ruttledge, the prototype of Martin Hearne, has a vision of an apocalyptic beast 'with iron teeth and brazen claws that can root up spires and towers', defined as 'Laughter, the mightiest of the enemies of God.' But this symbol is uneasily combined with another for the same concept – 'white angels on white unicorns'. The visual origins of the unicorn symbol can be found in Gustave Moreau's painting *Ladies and Unicorns*, and in the design drawn by U. L. Brockman for the endpapers of the magazine *The Dome*, to which Yeats contributed regularly between 1897 and 1900. This depicted a unicorn, rampant, on a mosaic background, its head encircled by a solar disc.

The visual impact of the unicorn image, already confirmed in *The King's Threshold* (see **112**, lines 19–20) and in *Deirdre* (**175**, line 16), was reinforced for him by its symbolic significance. The title for the third grade of the Order of the Golden Dawn, which Yeats held for some time in the early nineties, was that of *Monocris* (or *Monoceros*) *de Astris*, the Unicorn from the Stars.

In *The Unicorn from the Stars* Martin takes over from the earlier play the image of the unicorn as the Apocalyptic Beast, reinforced now by Biblical associations from the Book of Revelations and Isaiah, though all references to the image of the wild beast of laughter are discarded.

The spiritual significance is also a development of Paul Ruttledge's transformation of the physical revolution on to the mental plane: 'We cannot destroy the world with armies, it is inside our minds that it must be destroyed, it must be consumed in a moment inside our minds.' The unicorn becomes, in effect, a symbol for a divine force working within the soul and manifested in the moment of inspiration, of joyous vision, that will bring renewal with destruction.

He is fallen into a trance: for this concept cf. 'The Host of the Air',   **328**
CP 63, and Yeats's long note (dated 1889) on the poem quoted on
p. 12.

calash: a light, low-wheeled carriage with a folding hood.   **330**

If you wanted . . . for that: the clue to Father John, who recognizes   **334**
the force of Martin's vision because he has experienced it himself
and paid the penalty for his unorthodoxy. See **350**, 13–16.

335   *Leave thinking . . . Andrew*: for Andrew the unicorn is sensual self-indulgence.

337   *There were . . . the wind*: see note on pp. 11–15.

Then I saw . . . I could not: cf. *Revelation*, XIV, 20: 'And then the winepress of the wrath of God was trodden without the city, and blood came out of the winepress, even into the horse-bridles, by the space of a thousand and six hundred furlongs.'

338   *Et calix . . . est*: 'And how splendid is the cup of my drunkenness.'

339   *I will go out . . . again*: For the commanding authority of vision cf. 'The Song of Wandering Aengus', last stanza, *CP* 66.

340   *They are the same . . . mouth*: cf. 'There', *CP* 329:

> There all the barrel-hoops are knit,
> There all the serpent-tails are bit,
> There all the gyres converge in one,
> There all the planets drop in the Sun.

'There' is perfection, the 'sphere' of *A Vision*'s thirteenth cone:

> The *Thirteenth Cone* is a sphere because sufficient to itself; but as seen by man it is a cone. It becomes even conscious of itself, as so seen, like some great dancer, the perfect flower of modern culture, dancing some primitive dance and conscious of his or her own life and of the dance. There is a mediaeval story of a man persecuted by his Guardian Angel because it was jealous of his sweetheart, and such stories seem closer to reality than our abstract theology. All imaginable relations may arise between a man and his God. I only speak of the *Thirteenth Cone* as a sphere and yet I might say that the gyre or cone of the *Principles* is in reality a sphere, though to Man, bound to birth and death, it can never seem so, and that it is the antinomies that force us to find it a cone. Only one symbol exists, though the reflecting mirrors make many appear and all different. (*AV*(B) 240)

Whitaker (*S&S* 118) remarks that solar apocalypse, which Yeats terms the 'Sphere' in *A Vision*, Ribh calls 'There' – the term by which (in the MacKenna translation) Plotinus refers to the Divine Sphere: 'the sun, There, is all the stars; and every star, again, is all the stars and sun.' There, as Boehme said 'life windeth itself *Inwards* to the Sun.'

Cf. a passage in *Discoveries*, 'On the Serpent's Mouth':

> If it be true that God is a circle whose centre is everywhere, the saint goes to the centre, the poet and artist to the ring where everything comes round again. The poet must not seek for what is still and fixed, for that has no life for him; and if he did, his style would become cold and monotonous, and his sense of beauty faint and sickly, as are both style and beauty to my imagination in the prose and poetry of Newman, but be content to find his pleasure in all that is for ever passing away that it may come again, in the beauty of woman, in the fragile flowers of spring, in momentary heroic passion, in whatever is most fleeting, most impassioned as it were, for its own perfection, most eager to return in its glory. Yet perhaps he must endure the impermanent a little, for these things return, but not wholly, for no two faces are alike, and, it may be, had we more learned eyes, no two flowers. It is that all things are made by the struggle of the individual and the world, of the unchanging and the returning, and that the saint and the poet are over all, and that the poet has made his home in the serpent's mouth? (*E&I* 287–8)

'For hundreds of years, and over an area shifting from Ireland to China, the most vital expression of order was an imaginary animal biting its own tail'. Clark, K., *The Nude*, Penguin ed., London, 1970, p. 4.

The Munster poet: Aodhagan O'Rathaille (Egan O'Rahilly, 1670–   **341**
1726) a Kerry poet, one of the last of the Irish aristocratic poets. His *Poems*, ed. Rev. P. S. Dineen and Tadhg O'Donoghue (with translations) were published by the Irish Texts Society.

a shining vessel: Melchiori relates the vessel to the 'golden bowl'   **345**
of *Ecclesiastes*, XII, 6.

350   *Saint Ciaran*: sixth-century founder of the school at Clonmacnois. Saul, *PYPl* 65.

353   *the day of the recognition of tricks*: Judgement Day.
SD Nanny grabs at it: Saul, *PYPl* 65, points out that in view of Nanny's next speech, it seems more logical that Biddy should grab the tobacco.

354   *Van Diemen's Land*: Tasmania, whither criminals were deported.

356   *That sounds . . . heard of before*: all the groups mentioned were agrarian secret or semi-secret societies. They flourished especially from the second half of the eighteenth century onwards into the nineteenth century. The Rightboys and Peep o'Day boys were Protestant, often acting against landlords about rents and also to keep out Catholic tenants who might outbid the Protestants for land. The Ribbonmen of the nineteenth century were very much a Catholic protection group flourishing in Ulster border counties. The Whiteboys groups flourished in the late eighteenth century, though the name was carried over into the nineteenth and became almost a general description for all kinds of violent agrarian conspiracies. As Johnny's next speech makes clear, for the Beggars the Unicorn is political-social revolution, effected by violence.

357   *Columcille*: the sixth-century prince and missionary to Britain.

362   *that happy townland*: cf. in general, 'The Happy Townland', *CP* 94.
SD giving banner to Paudeen: impossible on stage: Paudeen is in the next room – see **360**, *SD*.

364   *the lion*: of England.
the harp: of Ireland.

the Gael to be as high as the Gall: the Gael are the Irish and the Gall   **369**
the English in Ireland.

That music . . . clashing of swords: cf. the music heard at the death   **376**
of Hanrahan in 'The Death of Hanrahan', *M* 258:

> One morning he heard music somewhere outside the door,
> and as the day passed it grew louder and louder until it drowned
> the faint joyful voices, and even Winny's cry upon the hillside
> at the fall of evening. About midnight and in a moment, the
> walls seemed to melt away and to leave his bed floating on a
> pale misty light that shone on every side as far as the eye could
> see; and after the first blinding of his eyes he saw that it was
> full of great shadowy figures rushing here and there.
> And at the same time the music came very clearly to him,
> and he knew that it was but the continual clashing of swords.
> 'I am after my death,' he said, 'and in the very heart of the
> music of Heaven. O Cherubim and Seraphim, receive my soul!'

Where there is nothing . . . there is God!: cf. the passage in the story   **382**
'Where There is Nothing, There is God', *The Secret Rose*, *M* 184,
in which the young child Olioll questions the assembled Brothers:

> . . . He turned presently to the Brother who wrote in the big
> book, and whose duty was to teach the children, and said,
> 'Brother Dove, to what are the stars fastened?' The Brother,
> rejoicing to see so much curiosity in the stupidest of his
> scholars, laid down the pen and said, 'There are nine crystal-
> line spheres, and on the first the Moon is fastened, on the
> second the planet Mercury, on the third the planet Venus,
> on the fourth the Sun, on the fifth the planet Mars, on the sixth
> the planet Jupiter, on the seventh the planet Saturn; these are
> the wandering stars; and on the eighth are fastened the fixed
> stars; but the ninth sphere is a sphere of the substance on which
> the breath of God moved in the beginning.'
> 'What is beyond that?' said the child.
> 'There is nothing beyond that; there is God.'

> And then the child's eyes strayed to the jewelled box, where
> one great ruby was gleaming in the light of the fire and he
> said, 'Why has Brother Peter put a great ruby on the side of
> the box?'

'The ruby is a symbol of the love of God.'

'Why is the ruby a symbol of the love of God'?

'Because it is red, like fire, and fire burns up everything, and where there is nothing, there is God.'

The Mountain of Abiegnos: Ellmann (*Y:M&M* 191), 'For the members of the Golden Dawn . . . the Mountain of Abiegnos was the mountain of spiritual struggle, to be ascended only by those who had sufficiently purified themselves', and he quotes a meditation which Yeats wrote in July 1909 in which he refers to the concept of the central mountain of the world on which is Eden, and which ends: 'Think of the soul as ascending into a world of light & knowledge where the meaning of life will become clear. Rise into the supernal Eden.'

In September 1908 Yeats wrote to Florence Farr that he was in the worst stages – the dreadful opening work on the scenario in prose – of a new play, *The Player Queen*. He continued working at it in 1909, and by September 1914 it was almost finished. In May 1916 he was still working on it, especially the first half of the second act, and about a year later was revising it. When he published it in *PPV* he wrote this note:

> I began in, I think, 1907 [an error for 1908], a verse tragedy, but at that time the thought I have set forth in *Per Amica Silentia Lunae* was coming into my head, and I found examples of it everywhere. I wasted the best working months of several years in an attempt to write a poetical play where every character became an example of the finding or the not finding of what I have called The Antithetical Self; and because passion and not thought makes tragedy, what I had made had neither simplicity nor life. I knew precisely what was wrong and yet could neither escape from thought nor give up my play. At last it came into my head all of a sudden that I could get rid of the play if I turned it into a farce; and never did I do anything so easily, for I think that I wrote the present play in about a month; and when it was performed at the Stage Society in 1919 I forgot that it was my own work, so completely that I discovered from the surprise of a neighbour, that, indignant with a house that seemed cold to my second act (since much reformed), I was applauding. If it could only have come into my head three years earlier. Since then the play has been revived twice at the Abbey Theatre.
>
> It is the only play of mine which has not its scene laid in Ireland. While at work at the Abbey Theatre I had made many experiments with Mr. Gordon Craig's screens (see The Tragic Theatre in *The Cutting of an Agate*), and both the tragedy I first planned, and the farce I wrote, were intended to be played in front of those screens. My *dramatis personae* have no nationality because Mr. Craig's screens, where every line must suggest

some mathematical proportion, where all is phantastic, incredible, and luminous, have no nationality.

The screens in question were the product of Gordon Craig's work on *Hamlet*, which he was invited to produce for Stanislavsky's Moscow Art Theatre. They were made from unpainted canvas mounted on light wooden frames, of varying height and width, ivory-coloured, able to stand by themselves and dispensing with the braces, struts, pulleys, ropes and counterweights of conventional 'scenery'. In 1910 Craig made four drawings for Yeats's *PAIT*: one for *Deirdre*, two for *The Hour Glass* and another for *On Baile's Strand*. He gave to Yeats and Lady Gregory a set of model screens from which they made a full-sized set, and which remained in use at the Abbey (see note on *KGCT*, **634**). A note on the programme for the Abbey for January 1911 says:

The method of decoration in . . . *The Hour Glass* was invented by Mr. Gordon Craig and will be used by the Art Theatre of Moscow, where it will make possible the performance of the full *Hamlet*, with a different decoration for every little scene, so rapidly can the scenes be changed. Thursday night will, however, be its first public use. It does not aim at effects of realism, but at a decoration of the stage almost infinite in the variety of its expression and suggestion, and for the first time makes possible effects of lights and shadows various, powerful, and delicate. Mr. Craig has given us the right to make use of his patent in Ireland, with the generosity of a great artist, and because he respects our work and ambition.

In a letter to the *Evening Telegraph*, written on 9 January 1911, just before the production of *The Hour Glass* in which these screens had been used for the first time, Yeats declared what importance they had for him:

The primary value of Mr. Craig's invention is that it enables one to use light in a more natural and more beautiful way than ever before. We get rid of all the top hamper of the stage, all the hanging ropes and scenes which prevent the free play of light. It is now possible to substitute in the shading of one scene real light and shadow for painted light and shadow. Continually in the contemporary theatre, the painted shadow is out of relation to the direction of the light, and what is more to the point, one loses the extraordinary beauty of delicate light and shade. This means, however, an abolition of realism, for it makes scene-painting which is, of course, a matter of painted light and shade, impossible. One enters into a world of decorative effect which gives the actor a renewed importance. There is less to compete against him, for there is less detail, though there is more beauty. (D. Bablet, *Edward Gordon Craig*, London, 1966, p. 130)

Craig himself wrote more elaborately about these screens in *The Mask*, Vol. VII, no. 2, May 1915: 'Screens. The Thousand scenes in One Scene – Some notes and facts relative to the "Scene" invented and patented by Edward Gordon Craig.'

The most immediately relevant passages from *PASL* are the following:

Some years ago I began to believe that our culture, with its doctrine of sincerity and self-realisation, made us gentle and passive, and that the Middle Ages and the Renaissance were right to found theirs upon the imitation of Christ or of some classic hero. Saint Francis and Caesar Borgia made themselves overmastering, creative persons by turning from the mirror to meditation upon a mask. When I had this thought I could see nothing else in life. I could not write the play I had planned, for all became allegorical, and though I tore up hundreds of pages in my endeavour to escape from allegory, my imagination became sterile for nearly five years and I only escaped at last when I had mocked in a comedy my own thought . . .

I think all happiness depends on the energy to assume the mask of some other life, on a re-birth as something not oneself, something created in a moment and perpetually renewed; in playing a game like that of a child where one loses the infinite pain of self-realisation, in a grotesque or solemn painted face put on that one may hide from the terror of judgement . . . Perhaps all the sins and energies of the world are but the world's flight from an infinite blinding beam; . . .

If we cannot imagine ourselves as different from what we are, and try to assume that second self, we cannot impose a discipline upon ourselves though we may accept one from others. Active virtue, as distinguished from the passive acceptance of a code, is therefore theatrical, consciously dramatic, the wearing of a mask . . . (*M* 333–4)

Yeats's attempts to escape from allegory have not, however, prevented critics, puzzled by the play's mixture of mockery and seriousness, from offering quasi-allegorical interpretations. Both Wilson (*Y&T*) and Melchiori (*WMA*) relate it to the early story 'The Adoration of the Magi' (1897), in the 1925 version of which a Parisian prostitute gives birth to a 'cold, hard, and virginal unicorn', the emblem of the new – anti-Christian – era. Wilson claims that 'it is certainly suggested that the Harlot/Decima is to copulate with the unicorn and so, a new cycle arriving, propagate a new race.' Vendler, though she finds the play private, chaotic and allegorical, also concentrates on the timing of the play at 'a moment of revolution', but admits that 'an ironic manner of vision is trained on the prospect of cataclysm.' This revolution, therefore, issues not in a second Deluge, but in a 'rather commonplace reversal of fashion' in which Decima, the focal point of the play, and her commoner-husband inaugurate the new dispensation. She accepts Wilson's view that the play moves towards the putative copulation of the Unicorn and Decima, but takes him to task for not perceiving that the conjunction is symbolic of the poetic process. For her, Decima combines woman, image and Muse. The Unicorn is beast, image and the divine mystery of an overpowering inspiration. Septimus is a man and a poet under the spell of the terrible despotism of the image, who has to learn, however, that in the new dispensation that follows from the union of Decima and the Unicorn, or in other words in the creation of new images for poetry, the old cannot be saved from destruction, and further that those that are lost – the mask of Noah's sister drowned in the flood – are restored, and the sovereignty of the image reasserted.

Peter Ure had already objected to this putative mating of Decima and the Unicorn by pointing out that the new dispensation is inaugurated not by this act but as a result of the comic intrigue in which Decima marries the Prime Minister, and secondly that the unicorn is not an objective creature but the creation of Septimus's imagination, who disappears from the play with Septimus's departure. Bloom agrees with Ure and also objects to Vendler's reading of the play as an aesthetic allegory, since Decima is too human to be The Muse itself, though she may be the muse of Septimus. He distinguishes between Decima as Yeats's private symbol for the Harlot/Helen of a new dispensation, who does not appear in the play, and her vitality as the dramatic *persona* who does. In this view he is following Ure, who links the theme of the finding of the Mask to the miraculous end of an era and the coming of a new dispensation, but concludes that the play leaves Decima's role as the Harlot/Leda of the new annunciation impenetrably obscure.

Henn, *The Harvest of Tragedy*, London, 1956, p. 208, while recognising the mixed tone of the play, with its 'sardonic levity, esoteric symbolism and passionate pleading for the place of the Poet in society', nevertheless sees it in terms of tragedy, unique in that 'it represents the triumph of pure evil, and the destruction by woman (who takes her sexual revenge upon him), and by society, of the inspired poet.'

The account which is the least allegorical and discovers the most coherence in the play is that by Becker ('The Mask Mocked', *Sewanee Review*, 61, 1953), who analyses it in terms of the two linked stories of which it is constituted – one concerning the Prime Minister, the Queen, and the impending revolution, and the other concerning Septimus, Decima and Nona. Within this framework he discovers three areas of speculation: the first centring on Decima and Woman, in which three different types of womanhood are revealed in Decima, Nona and the Queen; the second on Septimus and the theme of Poetry; the third on the Prime Minister and Politics (a view developed by Newton, *Essays in Criticism*, VIII, 1938). What unites all three areas is the central idea, the doctrine of the Mask, by which 'wholeness is achieved in opposition'. Moore's concern (*MLD* 164–92), with what he calls 'the kaleidoscopic shifts in the colour of an idea as it twists this way and that' rather than 'a dialectical working-out of fundamental opposites', makes it impossible to do justice to his view of the play in summary. He concludes: 'The play ['a negative inversion of the heroic design', 'a comedy of anti-romance', in which Septimus and Decima, hero and heroine who are lowered into the mire of life, learn to fall out of love in order to realise their separate subjectivities], *does* suggest a certain cynicism about the tricks of human imagination, but the remarkable detachment Yeats has achieved here does not entirely conceal the indignation beneath the surface. For if *Player Queen* is in some sense a parable of the fragmentation, deception, unreliability, even disintegration of modern life, Yeats clearly does not approve of what is going on. If the world has reduced Septimus and Decima to actors who can only play at heroism, their virtues rejected by the sceptical and their vices encouraged by the gullible, so much the worse for the world. We may be amused at the spectacle, and Yeats intends us to be, but we should realize the implications of his comedy. In such a world tragedy is no longer possible.'

The play received its first performance by the Stage Society on 25 May 1919 at the King's Hall, Covent Garden. It was repeated at the Abbey Theatre on 9 December, for which the cast was as follows: 1st Old Man, Barry Fitzgerald; 2nd Old Man, Philip Guiry; Septimus, Arthur Shields; 3rd Old Man, R. C. Murray; Old Woman, Maureen Delany; Happy Tom, Peter Nolan; Peter of the Purple Pelican, T. Quinn; Citizens, Bryan Herbert, J. J. Lynch, R. C. Murray, Philip Guiry, etc.; Tapster, F. J. McCormick; Countrymen, Hugh Nagle, J. G. St. John, P. J. McDonnell, etc.; Big Countryman, Ambrose Power; Old Beggar, Michael J. Dolan; Prime Minister, Eric Gorman; Nona, May Craig; Players, Margaret Nicholls, Barry Fitzgerald, Bryan Herbert, J. J. Lynch, P. J. McDonnell, etc.; Queen, Shena Tyreconnell; Decima, Christine Hayden; Stage Manager, Philip Guiry; Bishop, Peter Nolan.

The play was first published in *The Dial*, November 1922, and subsequently in *Plays in Prose and Verse*, London, 1922; New York, 1924 (repr. London, 1922, 1926, 1931); *The Player Queen*, London, 1922; *The Collected Plays of W. B. Yeats*, London, 1934; New York, 1935; *The Collected Plays of W. B. Yeats*, London, 1952; New York, 1953 (repr. London, 1953, 1960, 1963, 1966); *Selected Plays* (Papermac edition, ed. A. Norman Jeffares), London, 1964; and *Eleven Plays of William Butler Yeats*, edited A. Norman Jeffares, New York, 1964.

389 *SD He is very drunk*: cf. 'The Blessed', *CP* 75:

> I see the blessedest soul in the world
> And he nods a drunken head.

Ure (*YTP* 137) suggests that his drunkenness is 'a literalized and comical version of the spiritual intoxication of Paul Ruttledge [in *Where There is Nothing*] and Martin Hearne [in *The Unicorn from the Stars*], drunk with the grapes of wrath.'

The characteristic tone of Septimus's speeches is a mixture of romantic self-pity and grandiose rhetoric. He is a parody of the Romantic Poet *par excellence*, as Becker points out, an amalgam of Yeats's friends of the Rhymers Club, the drunkard Johnson and the whoremonger Dowson, but also a focal point of the central theme of self and anti-self.

Kubla Khan: literally the thirteenth century founder of the Mongol **390** dynasty, but used here to suggest the extravagance of Septimus's romantic imagination.

Adonis: never, in point of fact, promoted to the status of a planet. **391** Septimus is drunk. Cf. Yeats's memory of:

an intoxicated man coming on Derby Day to apologise for some madness by some young men who had not recognised us, and his looking at us all, hesitating, and then saying, 'No, no, I will not. I care for nobody now but Venus and Adonis and the other planets of heaven'. (*Memoirs*, p. 111).

The Bible says: Exodus XXII, 18: 'Thou shalt not suffer a witch to **393** live.' For the ignorant and brutal populace, religion sanctions its brutal impulses.

He saw her coupling . . . unicorn: the unicorn never appears itself, **396** but seems to have different significations for different characters. To the Tapster and the mob, incapable of vision, it is a real animal and its coupling with the Queen an act of bestialism; to the romantic poet Septimus it is an image of nobility, beauty and chastity; to the Queen an image of her own self-mortification, timidity and prudery. Melchiori points out that the play is full of seminal ideas treated in later works. See also the note on *The Unicorn from the Stars, Title*, p. 134.

my breast-feathers . . . divinity: for a moment Septimus sees himself **397** as a divine swan, and cf. Decima's act, **415**.

flighty: the use of this adjective to describe both the Unicorn and **398** his wife (see **423**, line 15) indicates that the two are united in his imagination. Both Decima and the Unicorn are inspirational sources of the poet's creative power.

399 *seven years ago*: i.e. on the last occasion when the crown changed hands – see **393**, line 12. This is objective testimony to the truth of the beggar's prophecies.

he brayed like a donkey: cf. 'Solomon and the Witch', *CP* 199, lines 8–18:

> Who understood,
> Whatever has been said, signed, sung,
> Howled, miau-d, barked, brayed, belled, yelled,
>   cried, crowed.
> Thereon replied: 'A cockerel
> Crew from a blossoming apple bough
> Three hundred years before the Fall,
> And never crew again till now,
> And would not now but that he thought,
> Chance being at one with Choice at last,
> All that the brigand apple brought
> And this foul world were dead at last.
> He that crowed out eternity
> Thought to have crowed it in again.

The noise announces a change of dispensation. See **401**, line 16. This idea is developed in *The Herne's Egg*, which Yeats recognised was a development of *The Player Queen*: 'I have a three-act tragi-comedy in my head ... as wild a play as *The Player Queen*, as amusing but more tragedy and philosophic depth' (*L* 843). For comments on 'Chance' and 'Choice', see Yeats's note on *Calvary*, **456**, p. 170 and *Comm* 218.

They say ... sovereign: cf. *Matthew* XXI, 2–10.

400 *SD An Old Beggar*: it is characteristic of the play's patterning that the prophet should appear as a filthy beggar. He is a grotesque parody of the Evangelist.

401 *Then we are indeed brothers*: i.e. the union of poet and prophet.
Asphodels!: the immortal flower of Elysium, the classical paradise.

'*The Tragical History of Noah's Deluge*': probably a reference to **403**
the Chester miracle play, which deals with both destruction and
regeneration, and also in slapstick comedy.

the Old Man in the Sky: God. Cf. the '*old man in the skies*' in 'The **404**
Wild Old Wicked Man', *CP* 356. The 'prank' is the creation of Eve
from Adam's rib, the reference being to *Genesis* 11, 21: 'And the
Lord God caused a deep sleep to fall upon Adam and he slept.'

Saint Octema: an invented character, who completes the sequence **405**
Septimus, Octema, Nona, Decima. Becker is unable to find any
particular significance in this sequence; Moore, 181, suggests that
Yeats puts his two idealists, seven and eight, below his two pragma-
tists, nine and ten.

I have a plan to settle that: in point of fact the plan does not work
out as the Prime Minister had hoped. Instead of marrying the pliant
Queen, he is forced to accept the dominant Decima.

eagle look: associated with the proud aristocratic manner, the **406**
antithesis of her description in the *SD*, **404** as 'timid'. See in general,
'Upon a House Shaken by the Land Agitation', *CP* 106; 'To a
Wealthy Man . . .', *CP* 119, 'Friends', *CP* 139 and 'His Phoenix',
CP 170. There is an echo here of Maud Gonne. The eagle symbolises
nobility, activity, greatness, objectivity.

Sleep of Adam!: Wilson (*Y&T* 183) refers to Rossetti's *Eden
Bower*: 'then the bridesleep fell upon Adam.' See also **687**, line 21.

a seamew: see also *The King of the Great Clock Tower*, **637**, line 2. **407**
In both cases the seamew appears to announce the event which the
cyclical movement of history brings to pass.

to put all summer in a look: cf. 'The Folly of Being Comforted', **408**
CP 86, lines 11–12:

> *O she had not these ways*
> *When all the wild summer was in her gaze*

409   *Little do you . . . man is*: cf. note on **162**.

411   *Put off . . . not cold*: the first verse of the poem published as 'The Mask', *CP* 106. See *Comm* 109:

> What I have called 'the Mask' is an emotional antithesis to all that comes out of their [subjective men] internal nature (*A* 189).

412   *O would . . . head*: appears, rewritten, as the second of 'Two Songs Rewritten for the Tune's Sake', *CP* 325.

415   *SD   She begins cutting . . . the Swan*: see **397**, lines 29–30 and note.
     Dance: the dance with the players as animals suggests promiscuous sexual union with the bestial, parallel to the mating of the Queen and the Unicorn. Wilson (*Y&T* 182), sees the dance as a 'sexual invitation to Godhead', the miraculous union of woman and fabulous animal (as in 'Leda and the Swan') which can herald 'the end of an era and the advent of a New Dispensation' – Melchiori (*WMA* 67). But, as Ure points out (*YTP* 141), 'the change of crowns itself is effected not by miracle but by the development of the story of Decima as a personage in a comic intrigue, and that Decima does not marry the Unicorn but the Prime Minister.'
     stretch and yawn: see note on **622**, line 22.

416   *Queen Pasiphae*: in mythology the daughter of Helios, married to Minos of Crete who, in order to receive the throne, prayed to Poseidon to send him a bull from the sea to sacrifice. The bull was so beautiful that Minos would not kill it, whereupon Pasiphae fell in love with it, disguised herself as a cow, and bore the Minotaur, half-man, half-bull, which lived in the labyrinth of Crete.
     Leda: the mother of the Dioscuri (Castor and Pollux), Helen and Clytemnestra. Zeus raped her in the shape of a swan and begat Helen.
     These myths are used by Yeats to express the notion that the destruction of the old dispensation and the birth of the new are generated at the point of union of the temporal and the extra-temporal, the divine and the bestial. Hence Septimus's next speech. As yet, however, the Unicorn is not coupled to its opposite.

Cato: Marcus Porcius Cato Uticensis (95–46 B.C.), a Roman **417** stoic who supported Pompey and, after his defeat, joined the Pompeians in Africa. After Caesar's victory at Thapsus, he committed suicide at Pharsalia.

Cicero: Marcius Tullius Cicero (106–43 B.C.), Roman orator, author and politician, led the opposition to Mark Antony and faced death bravely after Octavius took Rome.

Demosthenes: Athenian orator (384–322 B.C.), who, while in exile, tried to organise combined action against Macedon after the death of Alexander. He returned to Athens, which was subsequently occupied by a Macedonian garrison, and a decree for his execution was passed. He took refuge in a temple. Being pursued there, he sucked poison concealed in his pen and died.

Petronius Arbiter: the Roman author of *Cena Trimalchius*, a former pro-consul and Nero's *arbiter elegentiae*, who, when Nero was turned against him, committed suicide, writing a document denouncing Nero and his accomplices.

Agamemnon: husband of Clytemnestra, leader of the Greek **418** expedition against Troy. He sacrificed his daughter Iphigeneia at Aulis, was murdered on his return to Argos by his wife with the help of her lover, Aegistheus.

cleft of the rocks: associated with prophetic utterance, as in 'The **419** Man and The Echo', *CP* 393, line 1: '*In a cleft that's christened Alt*'. Alt was a rocky fissure on Ben Bulben, perhaps chosen because of its rocky nature, as an Irish equivalent to Delphi.

Man is nothing . . . image: see, in general, 'Ego Dominus Tuus', **420** *CP* 180 and p. 143 above for further references to the doctrine of the Mask (see also *Comm* 197–8). Ellmann (*IY* 108–9) glosses:

> That is, must man have a dream of what he might be in order to become it. The next remark is less clear: 'Now the Unicorn is both an image and a beast; that is why he alone can be the new Adam.' The unicorn is both symbol and body; when the self attains this unity it is reborn. Yeats sees all human beings

engaged in a great struggle to become united to their image of themselves. At the moment of unification the temporal and the permanent are one. As the heroine of *The Player Queen* remarks in a 1915 draft of the play, 'Septimus told me once that no one finds their genius [until] they have found some role, some image, that gives them a pose towards life, that liberates something within them, that had else been deaf and numb. Only by images, he said, do we make the eternal life become a part of our ephemeral life.' In a letter written about 1910 to his father, Yeats said the theme of his play was 'that the world being illusive one must be deluded in some way if one is to triumph in it.'

Becker (*Sewanee Review*, Vol. 61, 98), suggests that Septimus is the, prophet of this idea, Decima its exemplification. Moore (*MLD* 176) glosses: 'Here Septimus is projecting in fantasy the true marriage of flesh and spirit, idea and reality, which is mocked by the counterfeit marriages of the play.'

Ionian music . . . Dorian scale: Yeats is making the normal distinction between these modes of Greek music: the Ionian soft and effeminate, the Dorian simple and solemn.

Delphi: the seat of the temple of Apollo and of his oracle.

422   *The Christian era has come to an end*: cf. 'Each age unwinds the thread another age has wound, and it amuses one to remember that before Phidias, and his westward-moving art, Persia fell, and that when full moon came round again, amid eastward-moving thought, and brought Byzantine glory, Rome fell; and that at the outset of our westward-moving Renaissance Byzantium fell; all things dying each other's life, living each other's death.' (*AV*(B) 270–1)

In the Introduction to *Four Plays for Dancers* Yeats wrote that:

The conception of the play is derived from the world-wide belief that the dead dream back, for a certain time, through the more personal thoughts and deeds of life. The wicked, according to Cornelius Agrippa, dream themselves to be consumed by flames and persecuted by demons; and there is precisely the same thought in a Japanese 'Noh' play, where a spirit, advised by a Buddhist priest she has met upon the road, seeks to escape from the flames by ceasing to believe in the dream. The lovers in my play have lost themselves in a different but still self-created winding of the labyrinth of conscience. The Judwalis [a fictitious Arab tribe invented by Yeats] distinguish between the Shade which dreams back through events in the order of their intensity, becoming happier as the more painful and, therefore, more intense wear themselves away, and the Spiritual Being, which lives back through events in the order of their occurrence, this living back being an exploration of their moral and intellectual origin.

All solar natures, to use the Arabian terms, during life move towards a more objective form of experience, the lunar towards a more subjective. After death a lunar man, reversing the intellectual order, grows always closer to objective experience, which in the spiritual world is wisdom, while a solar man mounts gradually towards the most extreme subjective experience possible to him. In the spiritual world subjectivity is innocence, and innocence, in life an accident of nature, is now the highest achievement of the intellect. I have already put the thought in verse.

> He grows younger every second
> That were all his birthdays reckoned
> Much too solemn seemed;
> Because of what he had dreamed,
> Or the ambitions that he served,
> Much too solemn and reserved.
> Jaunting, journeying
> To his own dayspring,

> He unpacks the loaded pern
> Of all 'twas pain or joy to learn,
> Of all that he had made.
> The outrageous war shall fade;
> At some winding whitethorn root
> He'll practise on the shepherd's flute,
> Or on the close-cropped grass
> Court his shepherd lass,
> Or run where lads reform our daytime
> Till that is their long shouting playtime;
> Knowledge he shall unwind
> Through victories of the mind,
> Till, clambering at the cradle side,
> He dreams himself his mother's pride,
> All knowledge lost in trance
> Of sweeter ignorance.

[Lines 17 and 18 of this extract from 'Shepherd and Goatherd' run as follows in *CP* 159:

> Or put his heart into some game
> Till daytime, playtime seem the same;]

The Shade is said to fade out at last, but the Spiritual Being does not fade, passing on to other states of existence after it has attained a spiritual state, of which the surroundings and aptitudes of early life are a correspondence. When, as in my poem, I speak of events while describing the ascent of the Spiritual Being, I but use them as correspondence or symbol. Robartes writes to John Aherne, under the date of May 1917, a curious letter on this subject: 'There is an analogy between the dreaming back of the Body of Passion' (I have used instead of this term the more usual term Shade), 'and our ordinary dreams – and between the life of Spirit and Celestial Body taken together' (I have substituted for both terms the less technical, though, I fear, vague term Spiritual Being), 'and those coherent thoughts of dreamless sleep, which, as I know on my personal knowledge, coincide with dreams. These dreams are at one time their symbols, and at another live with an independent life. I have several times been present while my friend, an Arab doctor in Bagdad, carried on long conversations with a sleeping man. I do not say a hypnotized man, or even a somnambulist, for the sleep seemed natural sleep produced by fatigue, though sometimes with a curious suddenness. The sleeper would discuss the most profound truths and yet while doing so make, now and again, some movement that suggested dreaming, although the part that spoke remained entirely unconscious of the dream. On waking he would often describe a long dream, sometimes a symbolic reflection of the conversation, but more often produced by some external stimulus – a fall in temperature in the rooms, or some condition of body perhaps. Now and again these dreams would interrupt the conversation, as when he dreamed he had feathers in his mouth and began to blow. Seeing, therefore, that I have observed a separation between two parts of the nature during life, I find no difficulty in believing in a more complete separation, affirmed by my teachers, and supported by so much tradition, when the body is no longer there to hold the two parts together.'

I wrote my play before the Robartes papers came into my hands, and in making the penance of Dermot and Dervorgilla last so many centuries, I have done something for which I had no warrant in these papers, but warrant there certainly is in the folk-lore of all countries. At certain moments the Spiritual Being, or rather that part of it which Robartes calls 'the Spirit', is said to enter into the Shade, and during those moments it can converse with living men, though but within the narrow limits of its dream. (*FPFD*, 1921)

Yeats explains this 'dreaming-back process' again in *PASL*, and even more fully in Book III of *AV*(B), 'The Soul in Judgement'.

Spiritism, whether of folk-lore or of the séance-room, the visions of Swedenborg, and the speculation of the Platonists and Japanese plays, will have it that we may see at certain roads and in certain houses old murders acted over again, and in certain fields dead huntsmen riding with horse and hound, or ancient armies fighting above bones or ashes. We carry to *Anima Mundi* our memory, and that memory is for a time our external world; and all passionate moments recur again and again, for passion desires its own recurrence more than any event, and whatever there is of corresponding complacency or remorse is our beginning of judgement. . . .

The dead, as the passionate necessity wears out, come into a measure of freedom and may turn the impulse of events, started while living, in some new direction, but they cannot originate except through the living. (*PASL*, M 354–6)

The close parallelism of the play to the Noh 'play of spirits', and especially to *Nishikigi*, which Yeats read in the Pound-Fenollosa translation, has been frequently noted. Here are the typical adventure which is 'often the meeting with ghost, god or goddess at some holy place or much legended tomb', which 'reminds me at times of our own Irish legends and beliefs'; the sense of location, 'the sense of awe that our Gaelic-speaking countrypeople will sometimes show when you speak to them of Castle Hackett or of some holy well', which is parallel to that emotion that 'Japanese poets, too, feel for tomb and wood'; here, too, the 'playing upon a single metaphor'. ('Certain Noble Plays of Japan', *E&I* 232–4)

The extent of his debt to Nishikigi can be seen from Yeats's account of the play, first given in *Visions and Beliefs*:

In a play still more rich in lyric poetry a priest is wandering in a certain ancient village. He describes the journey and the scene, and from time to time the chorus sitting at the side of the stage sings its comment. He meets with two ghosts, the one holding a red stick, the other a piece of coarse cloth, and both dressed in the fashion of a past age, but as he is a stranger he supposes them villagers wearing the village fashion. They sing as if muttering, 'We are entangled up – whose fault was it, dear? Tangled up as the grass patterns are tangled up in this coarse cloth, or that insect which lives and chirrups in dried seaweed. We do not know where are today our tears in the undergrowth of this eternal wilderness. We neither wake nor sleep and passing our nights in sorrow, which is in the end a vision, what are these scenes of spring to us? This thinking in sleep for someone who has no thought for you, is it more than a dream? And yet surely it is the natural way of love. In our hearts there is much, and in our bodies nothing, and we do nothing at all, and only the waters of the river of tears flow quickly.' To the priest they seem two married people, but he cannot understand why they carry the red stick and the coarse cloth. They ask him to listen to a story. The two young people had lived in that village long ago and night after night for three years the young man had offered a charmed red stick, the token of love, at the young girl's window, but she pretended not to see and went on weaving. So the young man died and was buried in a cave with his charmed red sticks and presently the girl died too, and now because they were never married in life they were unmarried in their death. The priest, who does not yet understand that it is their own tale, asks to be shown the cave, and says it will be a fine tale to tell when he goes home. The chorus describes the journey to the cave. The lovers go in front, the priest follows.

They are all day pushing through long grasses that hide the
narrow paths. They ask the way of a farmer who is mowing.
Then night falls and it is cold and frosty. It is stormy and the
leaves are falling and their feet sink into the muddy places made
by the autumn showers; there is a long shadow on the slope of
the mountain, and an owl in the ivy of the pine tree. They have
found the cave and it is dyed with red sticks of love to the
colour of 'the orchids and chrysanthemums which hide the
mouth of a fox's hole': and now the two lovers have 'slipped
into the shadows of the cave'. Left alone and too cold to sleep
the priest decides to spend the night in prayer. He prays that
the lovers may at last be one. Presently he sees to his wonder
that the cave is lighted up 'where people are talking and setting
up looms for spinning and painted red sticks'. The ghosts
creep out and thank him for his prayer and say that through
his pity 'the love promises of long past incarnations' find
fulfilment in a dream. Then he sees the love story unfolded in a
vision and the chorus compares the sound of weaving to the
clicking of crickets. A little later he is shown the bridal room
and the lovers drinking from the bridal cup. The dawn is
coming. It is reflected in the bridal cup and now singers, cloth,
and stick break and dissolve like a dream, and there is nothing
but 'a deserted grave on a hill where morning winds are blowing through the pine'. (*E* 67–8)

In giving this story an Irish setting by the identification of the
lovers of the Japanese play with the historical Dermot and Dervorgilla, Yeats also weaves into it a contemporary political reference
which he feared might be 'too powerful' (*L* 626). This he achieves
by turning the priest into a young man who had been involved in
the 1916 Rising.

Dermot and Dervorgilla had already appeared in the 1897 story,
Hanrahan's Vision, in which their 'sin [that] brought the Norman in'
is punished with the torment of 'the battles we brought into Ireland',
and in which echoes from Dante's story of Paolo and Francesca can
be clearly heard. Wilson, *YI* 209, suggests that the theme of the
absolution of guilt, not present in the early story, and denied to the
lovers by the young revolutionary in the play, may have been
suggested by Lady Gregory's play, *Dervorgilla* (1911).

Historically, Diarmuid MacMurrough, king of Leinster, had
carried off in 1152 Dervorgilla, daughter of the King of Meath, and
wife of Tegernan O'Rourke. He appealed for help to Henry II of

England, who gave him an army under Strongbow (Richard Fitz-gilbert de Clare, Earl of Pembroke, *c* 1130–1176) in order to regain the kingdom of Leinster, from which he had been banished. Dervorgilla, having outlived O'Rourke, Diarmuid, Henry and Strongbow, is said to have died at the abbey of Mellefont, near Drogheda in 1193, aged eighty-five.

For the first performance at the Abbey Theatre on 6 December 1931, the cast was as follows: Young Man, W. O'Gorman; Stranger, J. Stephenson; Girl, Nesta Brooking; Singer, Joseph O'Neill; Flautist, T. Browne; Zither, Julie Grey; Drum, Doreen Cuthbert.

The play was first published in *The Little Review*, January 1919 and subsequently in *Two Plays for Dancers*, Dundrum, 1919; *Four Plays for Dancers*, London, 1921; New York, 1921; *Plays and Controversies*, London, 1923; New York, 1924 (repr. London, 1927); *The Collected Plays of W. B. Yeats*, London, 1934; New York, 1935; *The Collected Plays of W. B. Yeats*, London, 1952; New York, 1953 (repr. London, 1953, 1960, 1963, 1966).

433 *old writers*: Wilson (*YI* 226 ff.), identifies this with such writers in the occult tradition as Agrippa, Henry More and Swedenborg.

434 *Like wine . . . cup of jade*: for a possible source of this image, see Yeats's account of *Nishikigi* given above. This is one of the binding or group metaphors of the play. For Nathan it implies sexual fulfilment or sexual power' (*TD* 211), which 'is augmented by the repeated image of the red cock crowing in the potent and fulfilling month of March.' Clark (*YTDR* 52) sees it as a rather arbitrary sign for the coming of the spirits that 'fill waste mountains with the invisible tumult/Of the fantastic conscience', adducing the association of wine and the spirits of the dead in 'All Souls Night', *CP* 256:

> And it is All Soul's Night,
> And two long glasses brimmed with muscatel
> Bubble upon the table. A ghost may come;
> For it is a ghost's right,
> His element is so fine
> Being sharpened by his death,
> To drink from the wine-breath
> While our gross palates drink from the whole wine.

and *A Drunken Man's Praise of Sobriety, CP* 359:

> A drunkard is a dead man,
> And all dead men are drunk.

He suggests, however, that the filling of the cup is analogous to the direction the action takes as the characters climb to the summit of the mountain and to its climax.

The hour . . . covered up: both the darkest hour, and, in Yeats's system, a phase of complete objectivity. The lovers are from an earlier, subjective, phase.

Abbey of Corcomroe: in the northern corner of Co. Clare, and associated with the treachery of Donough O'Brien. See note on **439**, line 9.

bawneen: the traditional jacket of the West of Ireland, made of home-spun flannel and without lapels or pockets.

SD   They wear heroic masks: see note on **442**, line 22.

I was in the Post Office: the General Post Office, Dublin, a centre of **435** fighting during the Easter 1916 Rising. Cf. 'The Statues', *CP* 375:

> When Pearse summoned Cuchulain to his side,
> What stalked through the Post Office?

'Cuchulain is in the last stanza because Pearse and some of his followers had a cult of him. The Government has put a statue of Cuchulain in the rebuilt post office to commemorate this.' (*L* 911) Yeats sees Pearse (who was in the General Post Office in the Easter Rising of 1916) as summoning intellectual and aesthetic forces into being, as well as those skills of measuring and numbering, so that the Irish can return to the Pythagorean philosophy, cf. Ure, *RES* (1949) xv, 254–7 and Yeats (*E* 451), 'art must again accept the Greek proportions'.

Muckanish . . . Finvara: the first an island off the Connemara coast, and the second a village in Co. Clare. These place names help to establish the objective reality of the scene compared with the subjective reality suggested in the opening lyric of the play.

the pathways that the sheep tread out: cf. 'Shepherd and Goatherd', *CP* 159, especially lines 79–91:

Shepherd. They say that on your barren mountain ridge
  You have measured out the road that the soul treads
  When it has vanished from our natural eyes:
  That you have talked with apparitions.
Goatherd,   Indeed
  My daily thoughts since the first stupor of youth
  Have found the path my goats' feet cannot find.
Shepherd. Sing, for it may be that your thoughts have
  plucked
  Some medicable herb to make our grief
  Less bitter.
Goatherd. They have brought me from that ridge
  Seed-pods and flowers that are not all wild poppy.
               [Sings]

 'He grows younger every second
 That were all his birthdays reckoned
 Much too solemn seemed;

The paths are those traced by the souls of the dead in the 'dreaming-back' process. This is developed in the main theme of the poem, that Major Robert Gregory will grow younger and live his life backwards, an idea dealt with in the Introduction to *WWP* in terms of Indian belief, where the unpurified dead

> examine their past if undisturbed by our importunity, tracing events to their source, and as they take the form their thought suggests, seem to live backward through time; or if incapable of such examination, creatures not of thought but of feeling, renew as shades certain detached events of their past lives, taking the greater excitements first. (*E* 366)

This is a later version of the idea. In an essay on 'Swedenborg, Mediums and Desolate Places' of 1914 Yeats reported country people in the west of Ireland as saying that

> after death every man grows upward or downward to the likeness of thirty years, perhaps because at that age Christ began His ministry, and stays always in that likeness; and these angels move always towards the 'springtime of their life' and grow more and more beautiful, 'the more thousand years they live' ... 'for to grow old in heaven is to grow young.' (*E* 39)

Wilson (*Y&T* 201) traces the idea to Thomas Taylor's *A Dissertation* (1790) quoting a passage dealing with the Orphic theology which stated that souls under the government of Saturn, who is pure intellect, instead of progressing from youth to age advance from age to youth. In the Orphic mysteries the soul in heaven was represented as a child. Wilson goes on to quote Plato's myth of two cycles, of Jupiter and Saturn. The latter was the intellectual world, a prenatal condition from which the soul descended and to which it returned after death. In the Saturnian kingdom man was no longer seen advancing to old age but became younger and more delicate. But in the previous cycle Plato described the world as a paradise resembling the intellectual condition, and Wilson quotes this passage from Taylor's *Plato*, IV 123; 'The white hairs of those more advanced in years became black, and the cheeks of those that had beards became smooth, and thus each was restored to the past flower of his age.' Wilson regards Yeats's commentary on a passage in Shelley's *Prometheus Unbound* as evidence that Yeats knew the Platonic myth because, he argues, Shelley drew on this myth of Plato for Asia's song in *Prometheus Unbound*, and Yeats saw in Asia's voyage a movement against the current from age to youth, from youth to infancy, and so to the prenatal condition, 'peopled by Shapes too bright to see'.

Red bird . . . crow: for Wilson, *YI* 234–40, the red March cock is a   **437** 'clinching symbol, a device which will weld together aesthetically . . . Yeats's two themes of politics and ghosts'. He interprets it on several planes: its 'central function is to establish a simple day-night antithesis'; it is an 'emblem of consciousness and sanity' and also, being a cock of the springtime, 'a more powerful defence against the supernatural than any other'; it is also a reincarnation emblem; and 'the red symbolic bird of Mars, regent of war and in Yeats's system . . . of the first bloody phases of a new historical cycle. We know from many poems and plays that Yeats expected the "cycle of freedom" to begin with world-wide wars – involving among other things the liberation of Ireland – at a full moon in March, the month of Mars . . . the Easter Rising of 1916 came almost exactly at this time.' It is finally 'the symbol of heroic martial endeavour and of that universal anarchy that he thought would usher in the collapse of the present "objective" age; which the Dublin rebellion seemed to him at this time to presage.'

Clark (*YTDR* 56) substantially agrees, suggesting that 'dawn defeats the ghosts and releases the Young Man. 'The subjectivity of the ghosts has been presented through the darkness, the calls of night birds, the blinding of clouds, the wind . . . blowing out the lantern, the dim path to the ruined abbey and on up to the ridge where the grave of the lovers is. All these are symbols of the dizzy dreams that spring from the dry bones of the dead, the consciousness of tragic guilt in the past.

On the other hand, the Young Man's objectivity is presented 'through the dawn and sunlight, the crowing of the cocks and the panorama of the landscape ruined by civil war.'

Vendler (*YV* 186 ff), in spite of the overt political references in the play, both historical and contemporary, sees it in terms of 'mental travel' – an occasion in which the mind cannot cast out remorse for some reason or other, cannot come to terms with the events in its own memory – and interprets these lines as 'an impatient protest against the night and the powers that inhabit it, those powers that make us remember, relive and consider the past in all its mixed emotions. The musician cries out for a discarding of the past (as March always symbolizes a new phase) and urges the morning to break and dispel the ghosts.'

438   *cloud*: the element in which the lovers move. See **444**, lines 12–13.
cat-headed birds: Wilson, *YI* 230–1, associates them with 'the man-headed birds of *The Shadowy Waters*', which are the spirits of the dead, and 'with many such apparitions in Celtic folk-lore and heroic myth'. The function of the image is 'purely atmospheric', to point the atmosphere of dark expectancy against which [the] action is played out.'

439   *Donough O'Brien*: was one of a group of nobles who invited the Scots to invade Thomond and take it from the King. After their defeat Donough escaped from the battlefield of Athenry but fell in 1317 near the Abbey of Corcomroe. Wilson, *YI* 206, suggests that his and his followers' penance is less than Dermot and Dervogilla's because either they did not bring in the alien English – the Scots and the Irish being thought kindred – or because it is doubtful if he sponsored the Scottish invasion at all.

Helen: the Young Girl sees the crime of Dermot and Dervogilla   **442**
primarily, though not exclusively, in terms of private passion; the
Young Man in terms of political betrayal, the consequences of
which include Easter 1916 and his own situation.

O never . . . be forgiven: For Nathan (*TD* 210–11), who sees the
subject of the play as the 'spiritual life of Ireland as a nation', this
refusal to forgive his own past is a refusal to give modern objective
Ireland its heroic mask, its fullness of being – it is the ghosts who
wear heroic masks, not the Young Man. The result is a horror that
'returns the spirit lovers to their terrible fate and leaves the young
Revolutionist unchanged, full of a cruel bitterness that is his fruitless answer to a seven-hundred-year-old cruel bitterness.'

Clark (*YTDR* 55 ff), who also sees the characters not as individuals but as 'symbolic embodiments of directions in Irish history
and in the history of modern civilization' and who places the action
at the end of an antithetical or subjective era and just before a new
primary or objective civilisation, sees this refusal as a rejection of
the temptation to forgive 'the ghosts of Ireland's own guilt, which
has been more formidable in ruining the country than English
armies have. The subjective and interior peril is seen as greater
than the objective peril.' 'No longer caught in its subjective consciousness of guilt, Ireland starts objectively, and, one must admit,
somewhat unimaginatively, into its new day.'

Wilson sees in it an echo of the 'swift, unflinching, terrible
judgement of the young' which is taken from Lady Gregory's play,
Dervogilla (Irish Folk History Plays, 1912).

Vendler (*YV* 192) sees it in terms of 'an image of the mind's
refusal to accept as its own some past action; until such an action is
admitted, measured, and forgiven it is a destructive force in the
mind and unavailable for creative use . . . The young man is
unwilling to make himself part of the history of all Ireland by a
yielding to human sympathy – he turns irritably from the elusive
demands of night to the grosser realities of day, and the Musician's
final song embodies his refusal of experience . . .'

For Bloom (*Y* 308), the refusal is 'a failure of vision. When the
lovers dance before him, they offer the soldier the supreme chance
to cast out fanaticism and hatred, but though he almost yields, he
ends in an ugly obduracy, cursing the temptation. To forgive would
be to cast out remorse, for hatred is a kind of inverted remorse,

and is the soldier's own "dark idolatry of self". Yeats had seen that hatred disfigure Maud Gonne, and other women of surpassing excellence, and in his more visionary and redemptive moods he understood such hatred as a blight upon Ireland.

The final song of the play makes clear that the blight withers imagination.'

Ure (*YTP* 95–6) says: 'The antique story is tied to the present moments of flight and disaster because they proceed from it; the lovers inhabit a landscape of ruin which they made themselves; they address their hopeless appeal to the traveller whom, as revolutionary and fugitive, they fathered . . . There is, as it were, no room for a peripeteia. The soldier himself is caught inside this tight circle: he is one of the consequences of their transgression and cannot forgive the authors of the evil which he fights and curses.'

443 *any old admired Italian town*: cf. in general, 'The People', *CP* 169. Wade included a fragment of a letter in his selection, which described a rehearsal at the Gaiety Theatre, Dublin, probably in October 1901, in which Yeats described his longing to get away from his work for an audience which he regarded as unsuitable:

> The kid Benson is to carry in his arms was wandering in and out among the artificial ivy. I was saying to myself 'Here are we a lot of intelligent people, who might have been doing some sort of work that leads to some fun. Yet here we are going through all sorts of trouble and annoyance for a mob that knows neither literature nor art. I might have been away in the country, in Italy, perhaps writing poems for my equals and betters. That kid is the only sensible creature on the stage. He knows his business and keeps to it.' At that very moment one of the actors called out 'Look at the goat eating the property ivy.' (*L* 356)

444 *the final lyric*: see, in general, notes on **442**, line 22. Ure (*YTP* 91) notes the repetition of the image-cluster associated with the night, and its contrast with the 'longed-for crowing of the cock that heralds the coming of the day.' For Nathan (*TD* 211), the 'musicians end the play with images that suggest a sort of primal sexual power meant to foil the impotence of the lovers who, tortured by fruitless proximity, cannot consummate their love.' But against this view there is nothing in the play to suggest that the lovers have not consummated their love. What tortures them is that their sin has not been forgiven. For the views of Bloom and Vendler see notes on 442.

music of a lost kingdom: probably to be associated with the supernatural music of the Irish faery-world, and also with the music made by the spirits of the dead in their form of 'the airy people', about which Yeats wrote in *Swedenborg, Mediums, Desolate Places*, quoting Henry More's account in his treatise *The Immortality of the Soul*, of 'their comely carriage . . . their graceful dancing, their melodious singing and playing with an accent so sweet and soft as if we should imagine air itself to compose lessons and send forth musical sounds without the help of any terrestial instrument . . .' (*E* 64)

Calvary

The play was first published in *Four Plays for Dancers*, London, 1921; New York, 1921; and subsequently in *Plays and Controversies*, London, 1923; New York, 1924 (repr. London, 1927); *The Collected Plays of W. B. Yeats*, London, 1934; New York, 1935; *The Collected Plays of W. B. Yeats*, London, 1952; New York, 1953 (repr. London, 1953, 1960, 1963, 1966).

When Yeats published this play in *FPFD*, he appended the following note:

I have written the little songs of the chorus to please myself, confident that singer and composer, when the time came for performance, would certainly make it impossible for the audience to know what the words were. I used to think that singers should sing a recipe for a good dish, or a list of local trains, or something else they want to get by heart, but I have changed my mind and now I prefer to give him some mystery or secret. A reader can always solve the mystery and learn the secret by turning to a note, which need not be as long as those Dante put to several of the Odes in the *Convito*. I use birds as symbols of subjective life, and my reason for this, and for certain other things, cannot be explained fully till I have published some part at any rate of those papers of Michael Robartes, over which I have now spent several years. The following passage in a letter written by Robartes to Aherne in the spring of 1917 must suffice. 'At present I rather pride myself on believing all the superstitions of the Judwalis, or rather in believing that there is not one amongst them that may not be true, but at first my West European mind rebelled. Once in the early morning, when I was living in a horse-hair tent among other similar tents, a young Arab woke me and told me to come with him if I would see a great wonder. He brought me to a level place in the sand, just outside the tent of a certain Arab, who had arrived the night before and had, as I knew, a reputation as a wonder-worker, and showed me certain marks on the sand. I said they were the marks of a jackal, but he would

not have this. When he had passed by a little after sunrise there
was not a mark, and a few minutes later the marks were there.
No beast could have come and gone unseen. When I asked his
explanation he said they were made by the wonder-worker's
"Daimon" or "Angel". "What", I said, "has it a beast's
form?" "'He goes much about the world," he said; "he has been
in Persia and Afghanistan, and as far west as Tripoli. He is
interested in things, in places, he likes to be with many people,
and that is why his Daimon has the form of a beast, but your
Daimon would have a bird's shape because you are a solitary
man." Later on, when I mastered their philosophy, I came to
learn that the boy had but classified the wonder-worker and
myself according to their division of all mankind into those
who are dominated by objects and those who are dominated
by the self or *Zat*, or, as we would say, into objective and subjective natures. Certain birds, especially as I see things, such
lonely birds as the heron, hawk, eagle, and swan, are the
natural symbols of subjectivity, especially when floating upon
the wind alone or alighting upon some pool or river, while the
beasts that run upon the ground, especially those that run in
packs, are the natural symbols of objective man. Objective
men, however personally alone, are never alone in their thought,
which is always developed in agreement or in conflict with the
thought of others and always seeks the welfare of some cause
or institution, while subjective men are the more lonely the
more they are true to type, seeking always that which is unique
or personal.

I have used my bird-symbolism in these songs to increase
the objective loneliness of Christ by contrasting it with a loneliness, opposite in kind, that unlike His can be, whether joyous
or sorrowful, sufficient to itself. I have surrounded Him with the
images of those He cannot save, not only with the birds, who
have served neither God nor Caesar, and await for none or for
a different saviour, but with Lazarus and Judas and the Roman
soldiers for whom He has died in vain. "Christ", writes Robartes, "only pitied those whose suffering is rooted in death, in
poverty, or in sickness, or in sin, in some shape of the common
lot, and he came especially to the poor who are most subject
to exterior vicissitude". I have therefore represented in Lazarus
and Judas types of that intellectual despair that lay beyond His
sympathy, while in the Roman soldiers I suggest a form of objectivity that lay beyond His help . . .'

The source of the play is Oscar Wilde's story, told to Yeats by an actor, which impressed him by its 'terrible beauty', though he regretted the 'verbal decoration' that Wilde gave to its later form, when he published it as *The Doer of Good*:

> Christ came from a white plain to a purple city, and as He passed through the first street He heard voices overhead, and saw a young man lying drunk upon a window-sill. 'Why do you waste your soul in drunkenness?' He said. 'Lord, I was a leper and You healed me, what else can I do?' A little further through the town He saw a young man following a harlot, and said, 'Why do you dissolve your soul in debauchery?' and the young man answered, 'Lord, I was blind, and You healed me, what else can I do?' At last in the middle of the city He saw an old man crouching, weeping upon the ground and when He asked why he wept, the old man answered, 'Lord I was dead, and You raised me into life, what else can I do but weep?' (*A* 286)

Vendler (*YV* 172) comments: 'The types of "intellectual despair" and of "objectivity" which the play sets in opposition to Christ are not, then, simply contrasts to Him: they have been made what they are by Christ. The play is concerned with the interaction of objective and subjective life, the double interlocking gyres.' In other words, Judas cannot get free of Christ, nor can the soldiers' indifference release them from Him; nor can He escape the consequences of His own actions.

It is essential to bear in mind the double nature of Christ, as man and as God. As God Christ is primary. ('At the birth of Christ religious life becomes *primary*, secular life *antithetical* – man gives to Caesar the things that are Caesar's. A *primary* dispensation looking beyond itself towards a transcendant power is dogmatic, levelling, unifying, feminine, humane, peace its means and end . . .' (*AV*(B) 263) As man Christ is antithetical, 'We say of him because His sacrifice was voluntary that He was love itself, and yet that part of Him which made Christendom was not love but pity, and not pity for intellectual despair, though the man in Him, being *antithetical* like His age, knew it in the Garden, but *primary* pity, that for the common lot, man's death, seeing that He raised Lazarus, sickness, seeing that He healed many, sin, seeing that He died.' (*AV*(B) 275)

Christ's agony in the play is the agony of the man forced to re-live, in the act of 'dreaming his Passion through', the consequences of His incarnation, which includes his involvement in a world that is opposed to Him. In Yeats's terminology He is 'out of phase', thrust into an hostile world which, though he has created it, he cannot affect. Moore (*MLD* 236) comments: 'Christ's calvary consists in the discovery of the limits of His power, even when that power is conceived as universal love. The Saviour is impotent to impose his unity on the recalcitrant duality of the world.'

heron: Yeats's note above establishes the heron as a type of subjectivity. **449**

But that . . . soon: Christ's birth, at Phase 15, the full moon, initiates the objective Christian age, which supplants the previous subjective one, and only the certainty of the renewal of the cycle can support the subjective heron. His only salvation is his self-absorption. **450**

O, but the . . . played: Vendler (*YV* 174) compares the flute music in *The Herne's Egg* played to summon Attracta, which announces a new dispensation. **451**
Lazarus: the Biblical story is given in *John* xi, 1–46.

Martha, and those three Marys: they are so completely caught up in Christ's objective pity that they have no individuality at all, and are given nothing to speak. By contrast Judas and Lazarus are both individualised. The three Marys are Mary the mother of Christ, Mary His mother's sister, and Mary Magdalene, who came to Him on the cross. **453**
Take but . . . the full: when the objective era is over, at Christ's death, and the subjective returns, deprived of His love, which gives meaning to their lives, they would become mere fragments of subjectivity.
eagle, swan or gull: see Yeats's note above, p. 167.
Judas: see Yeats's note above. He resists absorption in the will of God by the assertion of self in an extreme act of choice. In *A Vision*

Judas is an example of the Hunchback, 'who commits crimes . . . because he wants to feel certain that he can', whose 'greatest temptation may be to defy God, to become a Judas, who betrays, not for thirty pieces of silver, but that he may call himself creator.' *AV*(B) 178.

455 *SD Roman soldiers*: see Yeats's note above, p. 167.
SD Judas holds up the cross: Judas supporting the cross indicates visually that he has not won his freedom from Christ. Moore, on the other hand (*MLD* 238), suggests that Judas asserts his freedom by creating the Crucifixion.

456 *The dance of the dice-throwers*: see Yeats's note in *FPFD*:

> . . . Kusta ben Luki has taught us to divide all things into Chance and Choice; one can think about the world and about man, or anything else until all has vanished but these two things, for they are indeed the first cause of the animate and inanimate world. They exist in God, for if they did not He would not have freedom, He would be bound by His own Choice. In God alone, indeed, can they be united, yet each be perfect and without limit or hindrance. If I should throw from the dice-box there would be but six possible sides on each of the dice, but when God throws He uses dice that have all numbers and sides. Some worship His Choice; that is easy; to know that He has willed for some unknown purpose all that happens is pleasant; but I have spent my life in worshipping His Chance, and that moment when I understand the immensity of His Chance is the moment when I am nearest Him.

Vendler (*YV* 176) comments: 'Those who worship God's chance, like the soldiers, stand outside the cycles of objectivity and subjectivity, and can regard them with indifferent eyes, needing neither support nor consolation. It is irrelevant to them which cycle is in the ascendant, and therefore they lie totally outside the scope of Christ's powers.' But Bloom (*Y* 212), counters that 'to be indifferent is not to be self-sufficient, it is only not to know that one is dependent.' See also note on **399**, p. 148.

SD   They dance: visually the tableau of Christ crucified on the cross supported by Judas and the soldiers dancing round it suggests the inescapability of the cycles. Judas's act has not freed him, and the soldiers' indifference to Christ can only circle round him. Christ's despair is that of Him as man, deprived of his own completion, but it is itself part of His design as God.

In blue deep . . . air: Wilson (*YI* 173) traces this back to the early   **457** story *The Tables of the Law*. See *M* 299.

But where . . . empty: cf. the closing stanza of 'The Wild Swans at Coole', *CP*. An early draft read

> Where have last year's cygnets gone?
> Coole lake's empty.

The Cat and the Moon

This play, written shortly before his marriage in 1917, was first published in 1924, and performed at the Abbey Theatre on 21 September 1931 (though Yeats gives the date as 9 May 1926), with the following cast: Blind Man, Michael J. Dolan; Lame Man, W. O'Gorman; Singer, Joseph O'Neill; Flautist, T. Browne; Zither, Julie Gray; Drum, Muriel Kelly. The play was printed in *The Criterion*, July 1924, and in *The Dial*, July 1924; subsequently in *The Cat and the Moon and Certain Poems*, Dublin, 1924; *Wheels and Butterflies*, London, 1934; New York, 1935; *The Collected Plays of W. B. Yeats*, London, 1934; New York, 1935; *The Collected Plays of W. B. Yeats*, London, 1952; New York, 1953 (repr. London, 1953, 1960, 1963, 1966).

When Yeats included it in *The Cat and the Moon and Certain Poems*, he gave it this note:

I wrote this play with the intention of including it in 'Four Plays for Dancers', but did not do so as it was in a different mood. I published the musicians' song however in 'The Wild Swans at Coole' [as 'The Cat and the Moon', *CP* 188]. I have amused myself by imagining incidents and metaphors that are related to certain beliefs of mine as are the patterns upon a Persian carpet to some ancient faith or philosophy. It has pleased me to think that the half of me that feels can sometimes forget all that belongs to the more intellectual half but a few images. The night's dream takes up and plays in the same forgetful fashion with our waking thoughts. Minnaloushe and the Moon were perhaps – it all grows faint to me – an exposition of man's relation to what I called the Antithetical Tincture, and when the Saint mounts upon the back of the Lame Beggar he personifies a certain great spiritual event which may take place when Primary Tincture, as I have called it, supersedes Antithetical – 'The burning bow ... is drawn between deformity of body and mind.' I have altogether forgotten whether other parts of the fable have, as is very likely, a precise meaning, and that is natural, for I generally forget in contemplating my copy of an old Persian carpet that its winding and wandering vine had once that philosophical meaning, which has made it very interesting to Josef Stryzgowski and was part of the religion of Zoraster. The Well itself is within a couple of miles of my Galway house, Thoor Ballylee, and is sacred to St. Colman, and began a few years ago to work miracles again, rejuvenated by a Gaelic League procession in its honour. There is some story, which I have half forgotten, of a lame man and a blind man's arrival at it, though not of their quarrel there. I intended my play to be what the Japanese call a 'Kiogen' [brief farces in colloquial language, introduced early in the development of Noh drama as interludes between the more serious ritualistic plays], and to come as a relaxation between, let us say, 'The Hawk's Well' and 'The Dreaming of the Bones', & as the Musicians would be already in their places, I have not written any verses to be sung at the unfolding and the folding of a cloth. It is all the slighter because probably unfinished, and must remain unfinished until it has been performed and I know how the Lame Man is to move. Is he to remain, after he comes from the other's back, upon one knee, or crouching till he can pick up, as I have no doubt he does, the Blind Man's stick? Or is he but to walk stiffly, or limp as if a leg were paralysed? Whatever his movements are they must be artificial and formal, like the movement upon a puppet stage, or in a dance, & I may have to give him more words here and there to explain these movements. But it may never be played, never seem worth the trouble of making those two masks, or of writing the music and so I let it go as it is.

When he included it in *Wheels and Butterflies*, his note was more elaborate:

These plays, which substitute speech and music for painted scenery, should suit Cellars and Garrets, though I do not recommend *The Resurrection* to the more pious Communist or Republican cellars; it may not be as orthodox as I think; I recommend *The Cat and the Moon*, for no audience could discover its dark, mythical secrets. Myth is not, as Vico perhaps thought, a rudimentary form superseded by reflection. Belief is the spring of all action; we assent to the conclusions of reflection but believe what myth presents; belief is love, and the concrete alone is loved; nor is it true that myth has no purpose but to bring round some discovery of a principle or a fact.

The saint may touch through myth the utmost reach of human faculty and pass not to reflection but to unity with the source of his being . . .

A couple of miles as the crow flies from my Galway house is a blessed well. Some thirty years ago the Gaelic League organised some kind of procession or 'pattern' there, somebody else put a roof over it, somebody else was cured of a lame leg or a blind eye or the falling sickness. There are many offerings at the well-side left by sufferers; I seem to remember bits of cloth torn perhaps from a dress, hairpins, and little pious pictures. The tradition is that centuries ago a blind man and a lame man dreamed that somewhere in Ireland a well would cure them and set out to find it, the lame man on the blind man's back. I wanted to give the Gaelic League, or some like body, a model for little plays, commemorations of known places and events, and wanted some light entertainment to join a couple of dance plays or *The Resurrection* and a dance play, and chose for theme the lame man, the blind man and the well. It seemed I could be true to the associations of such places if I kept in mind, while only putting the vaguest suggestion of it into the play, that the blind man was the body, the lame man was the soul. When I had finished I found them in some medieval Irish sermon as a simile of soul and body, and then that they had some like meaning in a Buddhist Sutra. But as the populace might well alter out of all recognition, deprive of all apparent meaning, some philosophical thought or verse, I wrote a little poem where a cat is disturbed by the moon, ['The Cat and the Moon', *CP* 188] and in the changing pupils of its eyes seems to repeat the movement of the moon's changes, and allowed myself as I wrote to think of the cat as the normal man and of the moon as the opposite he seeks perpetually, or as having any meaning I have conferred upon the moon elsewhere. Doubtless, too, when the lame man takes the saint upon his back, the normal man has become one with that opposite, but I had to bear in mind that I was among dreams and proverbs, that though I might discover what had been and what might be again an abstract idea, no abstract idea must be present. The spectator should come away thinking the meaning as much his own manufacture as that of the blind man and the lame man had seemed mine. Perhaps some early Christian – Bardaisan had speculations about the sun and moon nobody seems to have investigated – thought as I do, saw in the changes of the moon all the cycles; the soul realising its separate being in the full moon, then, as the moon seems to approach the sun and dwindle away, all but realising its absorption in God, only to whirl away once more: the mind of a man, separating itself from the common matrix, through childish imaginations, through struggle – Vico's heroic age – to roundness, completeness, and then externalising, intellectualising, systematising, until at last it lies dead, a spider smothered in its own web: the choice offered by the sages, either with the soul from the myth to union with the source of all, the breaking of the circle, or from the myth to reflection and the circle renewed for better or worse. For better or worse according to one's life, but never progress as we understand it, never the straight line, always a necessity to break away and destroy, or to sink in and forget . . .'

SD   St. Colman's Wall: see Yeats's notes above, and note on *The*   **461**
King's Threshold, **119** (p. 52). St Colman was the patron saint of the now ruined Cathedral Church of Kilmacduagh, near Coole. Saul, *PYPl* 76.
SD   Two beggars: cf. in general Synge's *The Well of the Saints*.

One thousand and six: Wilson, in his extensive commentary (*YI cap* 4), interprets these distances in terms of the pilgrimage of history between two points of highest civilisation, though such an interpretation relies on evidence external to the text. 'Each pace Blind Beggar takes represents a year's progress towards the millenium, and he has already taken over a thousand.' For him Blind Man is the type of peasant wisdom, and Lame Man the aristocrat, the Blind Man primitive intuition, the Lame Man soaring imagination. Calling it one of the most concentrated pieces of symbolism in Yeats's work, he interprets it primarily in terms of Yeats's cyclical theory of history, but also of the life-cycle of man as it is expressed in the relation of Soul and Body, and reincarnation. For Moore (*MLD* 244), the play is 'a little parable of the mixed nature of humanity. Blind Man and Lame Man, bound together in a symbiotic relationship like body and soul, have discovered their irreconcilable differences and gone their separate ways. St Colman has allowed them to fulfil themselves by giving them the power of realising their inmost desires. The Blind Man chooses to be cured (and thereby surrenders the inner vision he has had) and the Lame Man chooses to be blessed (which means giving up physical lameness.)' The consequences are that the Blind Man has his eyes opened to the viciousness of the world and the Lame Beggar learns that sainthood involves the role of a scapegoat and physical purgatory (*MLD* 246).

465   *since I went blind . . . world*: cf. 'In primitive times the blind man became a poet, as he became a fiddler in our villages, because he had to be driven out of activities all his nature cried for, before he could be contented with the praise of life.' (*E&I* 277–8)

the holy man in the big house at Laban: 'The holy man in the big house' . . . and his friend from Mayo were meant for Edward Martyn and George Moore, both of whom were living when the play was written. I think the audience understood the reference, but when the play is performed where the reference is not understood it might be best to cut out all from 'Do you mind what the beggar told you' down to 'will you answer me that now?' and put into the Blind Beggar's mouth instead the words 'He would soonest'. (*W&B* 141)

468   *I see it all . . . sight*: cf. Martin Doul's speech in *The Well of the Saints*, Act III: 'I'll say it's ourselves have finer sight than the lot of you, and we sitting abroad in the sweetness of the warmth of night, hearing a late thrush, maybe, and the swift crying things do be racing in the air, till we do be looking up in our own minds into a grand sky, and seeing lakes, and broadening rivers, and hills are waiting for the spade and plough.'

470   *I'm up now*: it is important for the reader to remember that there is no one at all on the Lame Man's back.

Sophocles' King Oedipus

Yeats began to write his version of Sophocles' *Oedipus Rex* about 1904. Ulick O'Connor remarks:

> It is generally thought that Yeats didn't begin his first attempt at Sophocles' *Oedipus* until 1908, owing to Gilbert Murray's refusal to make a literal translation for him in 1904. But a note from Gogarty to an Oxford acquaintance shows that the poet turned to his young friend instead and asked him to give him a version which he could turn into English verse. To G. K. A. Bell Gogarty wrote in February 1904, 'I am preparing a trans. (verse) of Oedipus Rex for Yeats.' *Oedipus* in fact was to be Yeats's finest dramatic work. Later, as he completed the play in the 'twenties, he made Gogarty chant passages to him in Greek so that he could capture in English some of the assonances of the original. (*Oliver St John Gogarty: A Poet and his Times*, 1965, p. 45)

He wrote to Professor Grierson on 12 October 1909 that 'we are going to produce *Oedipus the King* early in the New Year with Murray Carson in chief part, as a further precedent of our freedom from the Lord Chamberlain who has forbidden the play.' (*L* 537). In the winter of 1911–12, according to Joseph Hone (*WBY* 256), Dr Rynd of the Norwich Cathedral Chapter who was visiting Dublin stood over Yeats with the Greek text while he turned R. C. Jebb's translation into 'speakable English with rough unrhymed verse for Chorus'.

Gordon Craig was involved in design work in January 1910 which Yeats thought might have been used for *Oedipus* (*L* 546). A note by Yeats entitled 'Plain Man's *Oedipus*' was published by the *New York Times* on 15 January 1933 which ran:

> When I first lectured in America thirty years ago, I heard at the University of Notre Dame that they had played *Oedipus the King*. That play was forbidden by the English censorship on the ground of its immorality; Oedipus commits incest; but if a

Catholic university could perform it in America my own theatre could perform it in Ireland. Ireland had no censorship, and a successful performance might make her proud of her freedom say even, perhaps, 'I have an old historical religion moulded to the body of man like an old suit of clothes, and am therefore free.'

A friend of mine used to say that it was all a toss-up whether she seemed good or bad, for a decision firmly made before breakfast lasted three months. When I got back to Dublin I found a young Greek scholar who, unlike myself, had not forgotten his Greek, took out of a pigeonhole at the theatre a manuscript translation of *Oedipus* too complicated in its syntax for the stage, bought Jebb's translation and a translation published at a few pence for dishonest schoolboys. Whenever I could not understand the precise thoughts behind the translators' half Latin, half Victorian dignity, I got a bald translation from my Greek scholar. I spoke out every sentence, very often from the stage, with one sole object, that the words should sound natural and fall in their natural order, that every sentence should be a spoken, not a written sentence. Then when I had finished the dialogue in the rough and was still shrinking at the greater labour of the choruses, the English censor withdrew his ban and I lost interest.

About five years ago my wife found the manuscript and set me to work again, and when the dialogue was revised and the choruses written, Lady Gregory and I went through it all, altering every sentence that might not be intelligible on the Blasket Islands. Have I made a plain man's *Oedipus*? The pit and gallery of the Abbey Theatre think so. When I say intelligible on the Blasket Islands I mean that, being an ignorant man, I may not have gone to Greece through a Latin mist. Greek literature, like old Irish literature, was founded upon belief, not like Latin literature upon documents. No man has ever prayed to or dreaded one of Vergil's nymphs, but when Oedipus at Colonus went into the Wood of the Furies he felt the same creeping in his flesh that an Irish countryman feels in certain haunted woods in Galway and in Sligo. At the Abbey Theatre we play both *Oedipus the King* and *Oedipus at Colonus*, and they seem at home there.

The 'young Greek scholar' was Gogarty, in whose house 'Fairfield', in Co. Dublin, Yeats wrote some of his version. On 16 January 1910 he wrote to a friend (in an unpublished letter written from

Fairfield) that he was rehearsing '[indecipherable] and will start the Oedipus after that. We shall play Oedipus against a great purple curtain and take away the front rows of the stalls to make room for chorus.' The play was not proceeded with, and Yeats, who did not know Greek, was dissatisfied with R. C. Jebb's translation, *Sophocles, The Plays and Fragments*, Part 1, 2nd ed., 1887, which he had used as the main basis for his own work. Later he used the translation by Paul Masqueray, *Sophocle*, Tome 1, Paris 1900 (quotations in this commentary are from the second edition of 1929) for his second attempt. (See David R. Clark and James B. McGuire, 'Yeats's Versions of Sophocles: two typescripts', *Yeats Studies*, 3, 1974.) This was first printed in *Sophocles' King Oedipus*, London, 1928; New York, 1928; subsequently it was included in *The Collected Plays of W. B. Yeats*, London, 1934; New York, 1935; *The Collected Plays of W. B. Yeats*, London, 1952; New York, 1953 (repr. London 1953, 1960, 1963, 1966). It was first produced at the Abbey Theatre, Dublin on 7 December 1926. The cast was: Oedipus, F. J. McCormick; Jocasta, Eileen Crowe; Creon, Barry Fitzgerald; Priest, Eric Gorman; Tiresias, Michael J. Dolan; Boy, D. Breen; First Messenger, Arthur Shields; Herdsman, Gabriel J. Fallon; Second Messenger, P. J. Carolan; Nurse, May Craig; Children, Raymond and Edna Fardy; Servants, Tony Quinn, Michael Scott, C. Haughton; Leader of the Chorus, J. Stevenson; Chorus, Peter Nolan, Walter Dillon, T. Moran, M. Finn, D. Williams. The play was produced by Lennox Robinson. Yeats wrote on 7 December 1926 to Olivia Shakespear before the production:

My version of *Oedipus* comes on to-night. I think my shaping of the speech will prove powerful on the stage, for I have made it bare, hard and natural like a saga, and that it will be well, though not greatly, acted – it is all too new to our people. I am more anxious about the audience, who will have to sustain an hour and a half of tension. The actor who plays Oedipus felt the strain at dress rehearsal so much that he could hardly act in the last great moments – a good audience will give him life, but how will the Catholics take it? In rehearsal I had but one over-whelming emotion, a sense as of the actual presence in a terrible sacrament of the god. But I have got that always, though never before so strongly, from Greek Drama.

Yours   W B YEATS

[*On the envelope*] *Oedipus* great success. Critics and audience enthusiastic. (*L* 719)

Yeats wrote a Preface, dated 1 June, for the first printing of the play which ran:

> This version of Sophocles' play was written for Dublin players, for Dublin liturgical singers, for a small auditorium, for a chorus that must stand stock still where the orchestra are accustomed to put their chairs, for an audience where nobody comes for self-improvement or for anything but emotion. In other words, I put readers and scholars out of my mind and wrote to be sung and spoken. The one thing that I kept in mind was that a word unfitted for living speech, out of its natural order, or unnecessary to our modern technique, would check emotion and tire attention.
>
> Years ago I persuaded Florence Farr to so train the chorus for a Greek play that the sung words were almost as intelligible and dramatic as the spoken; and I have commended that art of hers in *Speaking to the Psaltery*. I asked my Dublin producer Lennox Robinson to disregard that essay, partly because liturgical singers were there to his hand, but mainly because if a chorus stands stock still in half shadow music and singing should, perhaps, possess a variety of rhythm and pitch incompatible with dramatic intelligible words. The main purpose of the chorus is to preserve the mood while it rests the mind by change of attention. A producer who has a space below the level of the stage, where a chorus can move about an altar, may do well to experiment with that old thought of mine and keep his singers as much in the range of the speaking voice as if they sang 'The west's awake,' or sang round a binnacle. However, he has his own singers to think of and must be content with what comes to hand. (*Sophocles' King Oedipus*, London, 1928; New York, 1928; *VPl* 851).

475   *Cadmus*: according to legend, Cadmus was the son of Agenor, King of Tyre. When his sister Europa disappeared (after Zeus had turned himself into, or sent a bull which brought her to Crete) Cadmus and his brothers Cilix and Phoenix were sent to find her. Cadmus went to Delphi and was advised to settle where a cow (which he would find on leaving the temple) lay down. The cow led him to the site of Thebes where he built the citadel, the Cadmea.

He killed a dragon, the offspring of Ares, god of War, and had to make compensation for this act by a term of servitude. He sowed the dragon's teeth – on Athene's advice – and when they came up as a harvest of armed men he set them fighting each other. Five survived; they were the ancestors of the Theban nobility. He married Harmonia, the daughter of Ares and Aphrodite, and was the great-grandfather of Laius.

Zeus: the only certain Greek god of Indo-European origin. The word means sky; his residence was on Mount Olympus. The title of 'Father' was not due to his begetting gods and men but was to be understood in the sense of a protector and ruler of a family. He stood for the maintenance of laws, such as a respect for guests: he was a God of the household. Zeus dethroned Kronos and fought against the Titans (possibly pre-Greek gods) with the Olympian gods, Kronos himself having dethroned his father Uranus.

fruitful blossoms of the land: the same phrase is used in Jebb's translation.

riddling Sphinx: a mythological monster, with lion body and a   **476** human head. It was female in Greek literature. In an early version of the legend the Sphinx was sent to Thebes by Hera, and asked the Thebans the riddle about the three ages of man. They failed to solve it and after each attempt of theirs the Sphinx carried off one of them. Finally Oedipus solved the riddle. The Sphinx committed suicide or was killed by Oedipus.

son of Menoeceus, Creon, my own wife's brother: Creon, Jocasta's brother, offered her hand and the kingdom to anyone who could rid Thebes of the Sphinx. His own son Haemon had been carried off by her. Another legend has it that Menoecus (the name of Creon's son as well as of his father) killed himself over the dragon's lair when Tiresias revealed that Thebes could not survive the assault of the Seven (see note on **481**) unless atonement were made for the killing of the dragon by Cadmus.

Pythian house of Phoebus: Phoebus Apollo was a prophetic god from earliest times; his other functions covered music, archery, medicine, and the care of herds and flocks. He approved codes of law and philosophy, and his oracles were regarded as the supreme authority in matters of purification. Delphi was his chief oracular shrine. There the female medium was filled with the god or his inspiration. The oracle's site was supposed to be the centre of the earth and the sacred navel-stone (*omphalos*) marked this. Apollo was a latecomer to the site, his priestess was called the Pythia.

477   *Our lord Phoebus*: Phoebus Apollo.
he was journeying to Delphi: to ask Apollo whether the child (Oedipus), formerly exposed by the God's command, had died.

479   *Chorus*: this consisted of Theban elders, men of noble birth.
the Golden House: Delphi was wealthy in its dedicated adornments, and also because the treasury of the temple acted as a bank in which gold and silver could be deposited.
Zeus: because Zeus is speaking by the mouth of his son. Cf. Paul Masqueray's note in his translation, p. 146, 'Tous les oracles sont inspirés par Zeus et Loxias, en particulier, est l'interprète de son père.'
the Delian God's reply: Delos is a small island in the Cylades, sacred to Apollo (whose birth place it was in legend) who was honoured by a festival held there as early as the eighth century B.C.
the God of Death: in the original Ares, who is not merely a war god in Sophocles but a destroyer – here connected with the plague, because he 'bears no rattling shield and yet consumes this form with pain'.
that God-trodden western shore: cf. Jebb's version: '. . . grant that . . . may turn his back in speedy flight . . . borne by a fair wind to the great deep of Amphitrite, or to those waters in which none find haven, even to the Thracian wave' (p. 37) and Masqueray's 'qu'il tourne le dos, soit vers le lit immense d'Amphitrite, soit vers le flot inhospitalier de la mer de Thrace' (p. 148). The 'great deep' of Amphitrite was the Atlantic.

480   *Master of the thunder-cloud*: Zeus.
God-hated God: probably taken from the end of the chorus and a rendering of ἀπότιμον, without honour. Jebb renders this 'the God unhonoured among Gods' (p. 41).

Artemis: Apollo's sister, a daughter of Zeus, and a huntress who also brought fertility to man and beast, and was a helper of women in childbirth.

Maenads: women inspired to frenzy by Dionysus. They celebrated his power in song, dance and music, and had superhuman force, uprooting trees, killing wild animals and eating their raw flesh. The women of Thebes followed Dionysus, became Maenads and destroyed his enemies, Pentheus and Orpheus.

Lysian King: Apollo as God of light (λύξ).

Bacchus' wine ensanguined face: Bacchus was another name for Dionysus (a Lydian word), and was probably the god, primarily of vegetation, in Asia Minor.

the Pythian God: see note on **476**.   **481**

Tiresias: a legendary blind and wise seer of Thebes who according to one legend saw Athene bathing. Because his mother was her friend she blinded him instead of killing him, and gave him prophetic gifts in compensation. According to another legend he struck a pair of coupling snakes with a stick and turned into a woman. He did the same thing again and turned into a man. He was asked to settle a dispute between Zeus and Hera as to which sex got more pleasure in love and plumped for the female. Hera then blinded him but Zeus gave him long life and the gift of prophecy.

the voice of birds nor any other sort of wisdom: cf. **486**, lines 4 and 7,   **482**
502, line 8. Tiresias may resort to divination by fire if the voices of birds fail him (as in the *Antigone*, 1005).

Your words are strange and unkind to the State: in other words   **483**
Tiresias is not conforming to normal usage as the State's μάντις or seer.

Loxias: a surname of Apollo in his oracular guise, generally   **486**
connected with λοξός or oblique, a reference to the oblique nature of some of Apollo's oracles.

487   *an alien*: because Oedipus was reputed to be a Corinthian.

488   *the Delphian rock*: Delphi's town and temple stood in an amphi-theatre-like recess on a high platform of rock, sloping out from the south face of the cliff.

Cloudy Parnassus: snowy is the adjective used by Sophocles, and so translated by Jebb and Masqueray.

the Fates: the avenging spirits, the Κῆρες.

the navel of the world: the white stone in the Delphian temple, hence the oracle.

491   *Pythian Oracle*: see note on **476**.

the Soothsayer: Tiresias. See note on **481**.

493   *God's love*: the Greek is plural, and so translated by Jebb and Masqueray.

Helios, by the first of all the Gods: Helios, the sun god. In the fifth century B.C. he was at times identified with Apollo.

495   *bound its feet together*: the Greek is more brutal, and can be trans-lated as fastened its feet together by driving a pin through them.

in Phocis, where the road . . . Delphi . . . Daulia: Jebb's note (pp. 101–2) reads:

> In going from Thebes to Delphi, the traveller passes by these 'Branching Roads' – still known as the τρίοδοι, but better as the στενό: from Daulia it is a leisurely ride of about an hour and a half along the side of Parnassus. The following is from my notes taken on the spot: – 'A bare isolated hillock of grey stone stands at the point where our path from Daulia meets the road to Delphi and a third road that stretches to the south. There, in front, we are looking up the road down which Oedipus came [from Delphi]; we are moving in the steps of the man whom he met and slew; the road runs up a wild and frowning pass between Parnassus on the right hand and on the left the spurs of the Helican range, which here approach it. Away to the south a wild and lonely valley opens, running up

among the waste places of Helicon, a vista of naked cliffs or slopes clothed with scanty herbage, a scene of inexpressible grandeur and dissolution'.

the Dorian Merope: she was of ancient stock, claiming descent   **497**
from Dorus, son of Helen, who settled in the area between Parnassus and Oeta.

a herald: heralds were sacred, and were known by their carrying a herald's staff ($\kappa\eta\rho\acute{\upsilon}\kappa\epsilon\iota o\nu$).

Olympian Zeus . . . Empyrean: Olympian in the Greek text; it is   **499**
not a reference to the mountain, but to the supernal bright dwelling place of the gods and hence the sky itself.

the holy images, Delphian Sibyl's trance . . . navel-stone: the holy images (cf. the 'ancient image made of olive wood', 'Nineteen Hundred and Nineteen', *CP* 232) are those placed in temple or holy place as objects of worship. Cf. notes on **476** for 'Delphian Sibyl's trance' and 'navel stone'.

Lysian Apollo: cf. Lysian king, **480**.

Cithaeron: Mount Cithaeron is described by Jebb as having   **504**
'winding glens', and he comments that the phrase 'becomes vivid to anyone who traverses Cithaeron by the road ascending from Eleusis and winding upwards to the pass of Dryoscephalae whence it descends into the plain of Thebes' (p. 136).

the cords left their marks upon your ankles . . . the spancel . . . marks from the cradle . . . the name you bear. See note on **495**.

Good Luck: $\tau\acute{\upsilon}\chi\eta$, or beneficent fortune.   **506**

Helicon: the largest mountain in Boeotia: a little way below its   **507**
summit is the spring Hippocrene, struck by Pegasus's foot from the rock, and the inspiration of poets.

Lord Pan: Pan, a god native to Areadia, where the goat was the characteristic animal. He was usually regarded as the son of Hermes, and was an amorous god, who made the flocks fertile. He was half goatish in shape, human to the loins, but with goat's ears, legs and horns.

the mountain Lord: the god of Bacchic frenzy.

508   *the love of God*: plural in the Greek (πρὸς θεῶν).

510   *the woman-breasted fate*: the Sphinx, who according to Apollodorus threw herself from a rock when her riddle was solved.

511   *Time*: here, according to Jebb (p. 158), is 'invested with the attributes of the divine omniscience and justice'. Masqueray (p. 185) remarks 'Le Temps est confondu ici avec la justice, dont il a la perspicacité divine, car il éntend tout, il dévoile tout'. (*Sophocle, Fragments*, p. 280)

House of Labdacus: it was an old family, tracing its descent to Cadmus and Agenor, a point made in the original Greek, where Oedipus says (see Jebb, p. 47) he seeks the murderer 'for the honour of the son of Labdacus and of Polydorus and Elder Cadmus and Agenor who was of old' (line 267).

Ister . . . Phasis: Ister, the Thracian name for the lower reaches of the Danube; the Phasis divided Colchis from Asia Minor and flowed into the Euxine, or Black Sea.

Sophocles' Oedipus at Colonus

This play was being written at the same time as *Oedipus the King* (*L* 720, note 4; 721). Work on the former play made Yeats 'bolder', he thought, and in working on *Oedipus at Colonus* he wanted to be 'less literal and more idiomatic and modern.' (*L* 721) See pp. 176–8. It was first printed in *The Collected Plays of W. B. Yeats*, London, 1934; New York, 1935, and in *The Collected Plays of W. B. Yeats*, London, 1952; New York, 1953 (repr. London, 1953, 1960, 1963, and 1966). The play was first staged by the National Theatre Society Ltd, at the Abbey Theatre, Dublin on 12 September 1927. The cast was: Oedipus, F. J. McCormick; his daughters: Antigone, Shelah Richards; Ismene, K. Curling; Polyneices, his son, Gabriel J. Fallon; Theseus, King of Athens, Michael J. Dolan; Creon, King of Thebes (brother-in-law of Oedipus), Barry Fitzgerald; a Stranger, Arthur Shields; a Messenger, P. J. Carolan; Leader of the Chorus, J. Stephenson; Chorus, Peter Nolan, Walter Dillon, T. Moran, M. Finn, M. Scott; Servants and Soldiers, V. Wright, C. Culhane, G. Green, J. Breen, P. Raymond, W. J. Scott, The play was produced by Lennox Robinson.

towers: according to R. C. Jebb, *Sophocles, The Plays & Fragments*, **521** II, 1889, p. 14, Sophocles was suggesting the Acropolis and the line of city-walls with their towers.

this place
... when I prepared 'Oedipus at Colonus' for the Abbey stage I saw that the wood of the Furies in the opening scene was any Irish haunted wood. No passing beggar or fiddler or benighted countryman has ever trembled or been awe-struck by nymph-haunted or Fury-haunted wood described in Roman poetry. Roman poetry is founded upon documents, not upon belief. (*VPl* 899)

522   *SD   Colonus*: Κολωνὸς ἵππιος, Colonus of the Horses, an attic
deme or district, the birth place of Sophocles (495–406 B.C.),
a hill little more than a mile north of Athens.

Dreadful Goddesses, daughters of the earth and of darkness: The Furies
called themselves the children of Night (as mother) in Aeschylus;
in Hesiod their mother was Earth, impregnated by the blood of
Uranus. In another legend they were children of Earth and the Sea.

the Furies . . . pleasanter names: the Eumenides, sometimes known
as the Maniai, or Poinai, or Semnai, or Potniai, or Arai. The distinction being made is between the Erinyes, or Furies, and the Eumenides, or kindly ones.

523   *Poseidon . . . Prometheus the Firebringer*: Poseidon was god of horses
and the sea, patron saint of Colonus (see **551**, line 20). Prometheus
was a Titan, the son of the Titan Capetus; he rebelled against Zeus,
giving fire to men when Zeus had hidden it from them. In another
legend Zeus punished him by chaining him up and sending an
eagle to eat his liver. As he was immortal his liver grew as fast at
night as the eagle could eat it by day. Heracles eventually rescued
him from this punishment. He was a craftsman, and worshipped as
such by craftsmen. He was not attached to Colonus but to the
academy, and is mentioned as one of the neighbouring gods.

the Brazen Threshold: near the grove of the Eumenides was a rift
or cavern in the rock called the threshold of Hades. The region
around this rift (which had some brazen steps) was known as the
Brazen Threshold, and was regarded as the stay of Athens – both
because it was rooted on the nether rock and linked to the powers
of the underworld, and therefore its physical basis was linked with a
religious safeguard.

Theseus son of Aegeus: Theseus was the son of Aegeus (or of
Poseidon the sea-god) and the national hero of Athens. He was a
friend of Heracles. When Aegeus left Troezen he left instructions
with Aethra, Theseus' mother, that the boy should, when he was
able, lift a rock under which Aegeus had hidden sandals and a
sword. At sixteen Theseus did this and went by land to Attica
having various dangerous encounters on the way. Arrived in Attica
he was sent against the Marathonian bull (through Medea's
intrigues). Next he formed part of the tribute of youths sent annually
to Crete to the Minotaur, which he killed with the help of Ariadne.

She fled with him and he deserted her at Naxos. He succeeded his father and united the communities of Attica, making Athens the capital. He fought the Amazons with Heracles and when the Amazons attacked Athens in turn they were finally defeated. Pirithous the Lapith became a friend of Theseus who helped him in the fight of Lapiths and Centaurs, and, later, aided him in an attempt to rescue Persephone from the lower world. He was rescued by Heracles, but Pirithous remained below. He was supposed in one legend to have been banished after a rebellion, and then murdered at Scyros. See note on **540**.

son of Laius: see *Oedipus the King, passim*. Oedipus killed his father   **528**
Laius and then married his own mother Jocasta, Laius's widow.

Thessalian sunbonnet: a felt hat with a brim worn by travellers.   **531**
Etna: Sicily had a reputation for both its horses and its mules.
a long search: she had come from Thebes where she continued to live.

like those Egyptians: Jebb thinks this is probably an echo by   **532**
Sophocles of Herodotus's account of the Egyptians' customs: he translates the Greek as 'For there the men sit weaving in the house but the wives go forth to win the daily bread' (p. 63). Masqueray comments: 'Polynice et Étéocle sont restés à Thèbes, tandis que leurs soeurs courent les routes, pour venir en aide à leur père. Les fils, les filles d'Œdipe vivent donc comme les Égyptiens, chez qui les femmes vont au marché et fond du trafic, tandis que les hommes restent à la maison à tisser. Sophocle avait lu Herodotus II, 35 (cf. vol. I, p. 74 seq.) le qui trahit l'imitation, c'est que la comparaison ne serait juste que si Polynice et Étéocle restaient inactifs à Thèbes, or, dit Ismène, une querelle terrible vient de s'élever entre eux.' *Sophocle*, II, 2nd ed., 1934, p. 168.

younger [son]: Eteocles.   **533**
Argos: in the Greek the adjective κοῖλον is applied to Argos, lying in a hollow, because the Argive plain is surrounded by hills

on its north, east and west sides, and on the south by the sea. The whole area rather than the city is indicated.

534   *the messengers of Delphi*: the men who went to Delphi to consult the oracle there. See note on Apollo below.

Apollo: the oracle at Delphi was Apollo's. See note on *Oedipus the King*, lines 43-4, p. 182.

540   *I myself have been in exile*: Aethra, mother of Theseus, was the daughter of Pittheus, King of Troezen; Theseus grew up not knowing his father was Aegeus, King of Athens. He was acknowledged as the heir of Aegeus after he arrived in Attica and killed the sons of his uncle Pallas who were intriguing against his father. See note on *Theseus*, **523**.

543   *Colonus' horses*: see note on **522**, *SD*.

544   *Semele's lad*: Dionysus, son of Zeus and of Semele, a daughter of Cadmus. Hera, who was jealous of her association with Zeus, disguised herself and advised Semele to test the divinity of her lover by asking him to come to her in his true shape. Semele tricked Zeus into granting her whatever she would ask, and she was killed by the fire of his thunderbolts. Zeus put the unborn child in his thigh. He was born at full time, went into Hades and brought Semele up and she became an Olympian goddess.

the gymnasts' garden: the Lyceum at Athens on the banks of the river Cephisus, a sacred grove.

olive-tree: cf. the sixth stanza of 'Nineteen Hundred and Nineteen' (*CP* 232):

> But is there any comfort to be found?
> Man is in love and loves what vanishes
> What more is there to say? That country round
> None dared admit, if such a thought were his,
> Incendiary or bigot could be found
> To burn that stump on the Acropolis,
> Or break in bits the famous ivories
> Or traffic in the grasshoppers and bees.

The grasshoppers and bees derived from Thucydides I, vi, and 'that stump', the 'ancient image made of olive wood' in the poem's first stanza, derived from this Sophoclean image and possibly from the original story in Herodotus VIII, 65, where the sacred olive is recounted to have grown a cubit (Pausanian, I, 27, 2 improved on the story by making the plant grow a shoot two cubits long in the same day) by the second day after the Persians had sacked and burnt Athens, including the old Erectheum which contained the spring of salt water and the sacred olive which were created by Erectheus and Athene in their rivalry to become deity of the city.

grey-eyed Athene: was the patron goddess of Athens; she produced the olive tree in a struggle with Poseidon for ownership of the land in Attica and won the contest. 'Grey-eyed' was one of the standard descriptions of the goddess.

Great Mother: Demeter, mourning for Persephone.

abounding Cephisus: river in Attica.

Poseidon: god of horses and the sea; see note on **523**.

Sun-god: the god Helios.   **550**

Pythian strand: the shore of the bay of Eleusis just beyond the   **556**
pass of Daphne about six miles from Colonus. Pythian according to Jebb (*Sophocles*, II, p. 167) alludes to the Ionic temple of Apollo in the highest narrowest part of the pass of Daphne. He discounts the argument of others for the temple of Ochoe, also sacred to Apollo. See following note.

immortal spirits: Demeter and Persephone.

the life of the blessed . . . to let none living know: the Greek means those who have been initiated by the Eumolpid hierophant at Eleusis and bound by him to secrecy. The Eleusinian mysteries offered some prospect of bliss after death.

Son of Rhea: Poseidon, who was Hippios, lord of the horses. Rhea, daughter of Uranus and Gaia, wife of Kronos and mother of the gods. See Jebb, *Sophocles*, II, 171: 'The cult was that of the Phrygian Mother Cybele; in Attica it was connected with the Eleusinian cult of Demeter.

God's daughter Pallas Athene: Athene was the daughter of Zeus. Zeus is apostrophised earlier in the Greek text.

557   *Apollo and Artemis*: here in their guise of hunting god and goddess, Artemis being a 'smiter of deer'.

561   *The second best's a gay goodnight . . . away*: Yeats wrote to Olivia Shakespear on 13 March 1927 that 'the last line is very bad Grecian but very good Elizabethan and so it must stay.' (*L* 723)

    Polyneices: the elder son of Oedipus.

562   *Mercy*: compassion, Αἰδώς. Αἰδώς had an altar at Athens.

563   *Adrastus*: the son of Talaus, King of Argos. He was the only person to escape from the attack on Thebes, and this was because of his horse Arion. He later led the sons of the seven, the Epigoni, against Thebes with more success, but his son was killed in this contest. He himself is reputed to have died of grief on the way home.

    Seven leaders . . . Amphiaraus: son of Oecles who foresaw the issue of the war; his wife Eriphyle, sister of Adrastus, persuaded him to go, and when all the leaders except Adrastus had fallen the Theban earth swallowed Amphiaraus and his chariot.

    Capaneus: the giant of this legend.

    Parthenopaeus of Arcadia, son of Atalanta: by Meilanion, who beat her in the famous foot race.

568   *God's winged thunder*: the thunder of Zeus.

570   *the dragon's teeth*: Cadmus, engaged in founding Thebes, needed water from a well guarded by a dragon, begotten by Ares, god of war. He killed it, sowed its teeth in the ground, armed men sprang up from the earth and killed each other. Five survived and became the ancestors of the Cadmeans. See note on **475**.

    Hermes: he was the guide of souls, and also the guide of the living on dangerous errands.

    the Goddess of the Dead: Persephone.

Hades: a son of Kronos, lord of the lower world. He married Persephone.

the Furies: the Erinyes.   571
Stygian hall: the Styx was the main river in Hades, the lower world.
hundred-headed dog: Cerberus, a monstrous dog who guarded the entrance to the lower world. He is variously described as having fifty or three heads.
the daughter of Earth and Tartarus: Jebb's version (p. 243) gives 'son'; Masqueray's (p. 216) 'Fille'. The daughter of Earth and Tartarus (her son) was Echidna, half-woman, half-serpent.
the brazen steps: see note on **523**.

the four sacred things, the basin of brass, the hollow pear-tree, the marble   572
tomb, the stone from Thoricus: the pear tree may have marked the place of Persephone's rape. Thoricus was a town and deme of Attica.

The Resurrection

Yeats began to write this play in 1925 or 1926. See Hone (*WBY* 417) for a reading of the play in 1925; see Lady Gregory (*J* 263) for the second stanza of the 'Song for the unfolding and folding of the curtains' being written on 24 May 1926. The first printed version appeared in *The Adelphi*, June 1927. It was not reprinted until it was included in *Stories of Michael Robartes and His Friends*, Dublin, 1931. Subsequently it was published in *Wheels and Butterflies*, London, 1934; New York, 1935; *The Collected Plays of W. B. Yeats*, London, 1934; New York, 1935; and in *The Collected Plays of W. B. Yeats*, London, 1952; New York, 1953 (repr. London 1953, 1960, 1963, and 1966). It is included in *Selected Plays* (Papermac edition, ed. A. Norman Jeffares, London, 1964 and *Eleven Plays of William Butler Yeats*, ed. A. Norman Jeffares, New York, 1964. The first printed version in *The Adelphi* is different from all the other versions; its text is supplied in the *Variorum Edition of the Plays of W. B. Yeats*, ed. Alspach, London, 1966, pp. 901–31. Yeats in a letter of 27 December 1930 to Olivia Shakespear remarked that he 'wrote a chaotic dialogue on this theme some years ago. But now I have dramatic tension throughout'. (*L* 780)

The play was first performed by the National Theatre Society Ltd, at the Abbey Theatre, Dublin on 30 July 1934. Yeats commented that he permitted it to be performed there after great hesitation as it was not intended for the public theatre, and added 'Owing perhaps to a strike which has prevented the publication of the religious as well as of the political newspapers and reviews, all is well' (*W&B* vii). The cast was: The Hebrew, A. J. Leventhal; The Greek, Denis Carey; The Syrian, J. Winter; The Christ, Liam Gaffney; Musicians, Michael J. Dolan, Robert Irwin.

Curtis Bradford (*YW* 238–9) finds the play's genesis

in two scenarios, different from each other and quite unlike either the 1927 or 1931 versions. Then Yeats wrote two manuscript versions of the play before its first printing; the second manuscript is very like the *Adelphi* text. He returned to the play in 1930 and wrote two more manuscript versions of it. In the fourth manuscript he nearly finished the play as we know it.

He has traced the different printed versions of the play to their respective MS versions (*YW* 261) which he calls the A and B versions; he summarises what happened between their composition (*YW* 266). He also draws attention to Yeats's having written in the Journal he began in 1908 a paraphrase of Heraclitus's words with which the play ends: 'The immortals are mortal, the mortals immortal, each living the other's death and dying the other's life.'

The play can be linked with his prose and poetry, to the 'Dove or Swan' section of *A Vision* (*AV* A) 180–215) and to many poems, notably 'The Second Coming' (*CP* 209). Yeats himself linked this poem with the play in a footnote to his Introduction to *The Resurrection* (*E* 393). In it we have the antithetical views of the Hebrew, who believes Christ is merely a man and must die, and the Greek, who believes that Christ is merely a god and cannot die. The Syrian, however, experiences an awareness of a miraculous category, a man/god who both does and does not die.

[Introductory prose passage] *Before I had finished this play*: see Curtis Bradford (*YW* 237–67) for details; Hone (*WBY* 430) describes Yeats as absorbed with the prose drafts of the lyrics in January 1929 and he was putting the last touches to the play in December 1930 (*L* 780). *The Peacock Theatre*: a small theatre attached to the Abbey Theatre, Dublin.

a staring virgin . . . holy Dionysus: Pallas Athene, the virgin goddess   **579** who snatched the heart from the body of Dionysus when he was torn to pieces by the Titans. She brought it on her hand to Zeus, who had begotten Dionysus on Persephone, whereupon he swallowed the heart, killed the Titans, and begat Dionysus again upon Semele. Both Persephone and Semele were mortal, Zeus an immortal; the first stanza of the poem draws parallels between Dionysus, offspring of gods and humans, and Christ, begotten by God upon the Virgin Mary, and examines the death and resurrection of both. See Ellmann (*IY* 260). The mythological material came from Yeats's reading Sir James Frazer's *The Golden Bough*, 1922, 388–9.

580   *that beating heart*: in the Introduction to the play Yeats gave Sir
William Crookes (1832–1919), an English chemist and physicist, as
his source for this image:

> 'What if there is always something that lies outside know-
> ledge, outside order? . . . What if the irrational return? What if
> the circle begin again?' Years ago I read Sir William Crookes'
> *Studies in Physical Research*. After excluding every possibility of
> fraud, he touched a materialised form and found the heart
> beating. I felt, though my intellect rejected what I read, the
> terror of the supernatural described by Job. Just before the
> war a much respected man of science entering a room in his
> own house found there two girl visitors – I have questioned
> all three – one lying asleep on the table, the other sitting on
> the end of the table screaming, the table floating in the air, and
> 'immediately vomited'. I took from the beating heart, from
> my momentary terror, from the shock of a man of science, the
> central situation of my play: the young man touching the
> heart of the phantom and screaming. It has seemed to me of
> late that the sense of spiritual reality comes whether to the
> individual or to crowds from some violent shock, and that
> idea has the support of tradition. (*W&B* 109–10; *VPl* 935)

the Muses sing/Of Magnus Annus: because they regard the ritual
death and rebirth of a god as a cyclic event in history. Ellmann
points out that both Gods, Dionysus and Christ 'had died and been
reborn in March when the sun was between the Ram and the Fish,
and when the moon was beside the constellation Virgo, who carries
the star Spica in her hand'. In these stanzas Yeats is thinking of
Virgil, *Eclogue*, IV, 6, '*Iam redit et Virgo* . . .' where Virgo, the
daughter of Jupiter and Themis, is the last to leave earth at the end
of the golden age; but will return bringing back the golden age.
This Virgilian prophecy was later read as a foretelling of the coming
of Mary (as Virgo) and Christ, the star of Bethlehem, (as Spica):

> 'The latest age of Cumean Song is at hand; the cycles in their
> vast array begin anew; Virgin Astrea comes, the reign of Saturn
> comes, and from the heights of Heaven a new generation of
> mankind descends . . . Apollo now is King and in your con-
> sulship, in yours, Pollio, the age of glory shall commence and
> the mighty months begin to run their course.' . . . Three hun-
> dred years, two degrees of the Great Year, would but corres-
> pond to two days of the Sun's annual journey, and his

transition from Pisces to Aries had for generations been associated with the ceremonial death and resurrection of Dionysus.
Near that transition the women wailed him, and night showed
the full moon separating from the constellation Virgo, with
the star in the wheatsheaf, or in the child, for in the old maps
she is represented carrying now one now the other. It may be
that instead of a vague line, the Sibyl knew some star that
fixed the exact moment of transition. I find but four explanations compatible with man's agency, and all four incredible,
for Christ being born at or near the moment of transition.
(*AV*(A) 152, 156–7)

Yeats discussed the Virgilian prophecy in *A Vision* (1937) in Book
IV, entitled 'The Great Year of the Ancients':

When a religious-minded Roman of the first century before
Christ thought of the first month of a new Great Year, did he
think of some ideal king such as Virgil foretold, or think of
Attis who died and rose again at the beginning of their old
lunar year? Which did he prefer of those incompatible ideas,
Triumph or Sacrifice, Sage or Victim? When did he expect the
one or the other?

To the time when Marius sat at home planning a sedition
that began the Roman civil wars, popular imagination attributed many prodigies; the wooden support of the eagles burst
into flames; three ravens brought their young into the open
field, picked their bones and carried the bones back into the
nest; a mouse gnawed the consecrated corn in the temple and
when caught brought forth five young and devoured them;
and, greatest marvel of all, out of the calm and clear sky came
the sound of a trumpet. The Etruscans declared that this trumpet meant 'the mutation of the age and a general revolution of
the world'. A generation later Virgil sang his song: 'the latest
age of the Cumaean song is at hand; the cycles in their vast
array begin anew; Virgin Astraea comes, the reign of Saturn
comes, and from the heights of Heaven a new generation of
mankind descends . . . Apollo now is king and in your Consul-
ship, in yours, Pollio, the age of glory shall commence and the
mighty months begin their course.' (*AV*(B) 243–4)

In the third part of this section he discussed what he meant by the
phrase:

'By common consent men measure the year', wrote Cicero, 'by the return of the sun, or in other words by the revolution of one star. But when the whole of the constellations shall return to the positions from which they once set forth, thus after a long interval re-making the first map of the heavens, that may indeed be called the Great Year wherein I scarce dare say how many are the generations of men.' But that Great or Greatest Year was sometimes divided into lesser periods by the return of the sun and moon to some original position, by the return of a planet or of all the planets to some original position, or by their making an astrological aspect with that position; and sometimes it was dissociated from the actual position of the stars and divided into twelve months, each month a brightening and a darkening fortnight, and at the same time perhaps a year with its four seasons. I do not remember the brightening and darkening fortnights in any classical author, but they are in the Upanishads and in the Laws of Manu for the Great Year and its Months pervaded the ancient world. Perhaps at the start a mere magnification of the natural year, it grew more complicated with the spread of Greek astronomy, but it is always the simpler, more symbolic form, with its conflict of light and dark, heat and cold, that concerns me most. (*AV*(B) 245–6)

The question of a new epoch is also discussed:

Syncellus said that a new epoch began when the constellation Aries returned to its original position, and that this was the doctrine of 'Greeks and Egyptians . . . as stated in the *Genetica* of Hermes and in the Cyrannic books'. Was Ptolemy the first to give a date to that return? The inventor of the ninth sphere, whether Ptolemy or another, was bound to make that calculation. What was the date? I have not read his *Almagest*, nor am I likely to, and no historian or commentator on his discoveries known to me has given it. It would depend on the day he selected for the equinox (at Rome March 25th), and upon what star seemed to mark the end of Aries and the beginning of Pisces. It was certainly near enough to the assassination of Caesar to make the Roman Empire seem miraculous, near enough to the Crucifixion to confer upon the early Church, had it not been committed to its war with Grecian fatalism, the greatest of its miracles:

> Then did all the Muses sing
> Of Magnus Annus at the spring.

(*AV*(B) 253–4)

Yeats's Introduction to the play also explains his concept, and in contemporary political terms:

In 1894 Gorky and Lunacharsky tried to correct the philosophy of Marxian socialism by the best German philosophy of their time, founding schools at Capri and Bologna for the purpose, but Lenin founded a rival school at Paris and brought Marxian socialism back to orthodoxy: 'we remain materialist, anything else would lead to religion.' Four of five years later Pius X saw a Commission of Catholic scholars considering the text of the Bible and its attribution to certain authors and dissolved the Commission: 'Moses and the Four Evangelists wrote the Books that are called by their names; any other conclusion would lead to scepticism.' In this way did two great men prepare two great movements, purified of modernism, for a crisis when, in the words of Archbishop Downey, they must dispute the mastery of the world.

So far I have the sympathy of the Garrets and Cellars, for they are, I am told, without exception Catholic, Communist, or both! Yet there is a third myth or philosophy that has made an equal stir in the world. Ptolemy thought the precession of the equinoxes moved at the rate of a degree every hundred years, and that somewhere about the time of Christ and Caesar the equinoctial sun had returned to its original place in the constellations, completing and recommencing the thirty-six thousand years, or three hundred and sixty incarnations of a hundred years apiece, of Plato's man of Ur. Hitherto almost every philosopher had some different measure for the Greatest Year, but this Platonic Year, as it was called, soon displaced all others; it was a Christian heresy in the twelfth century, and in the East, multiplied by twelve as if it were but a month of a still greater year, it became the Manvantra of 432,000 years, until animated by the Indian jungle it generated new noughts and multiplied itself into Kalpas.

It was perhaps obvious, when Plotinus substituted the archetypes of individual men in all their possible incarnations for a limited number of Platonic Ideas, that a Greatest Year for whale and gudgeon alike must exhaust the multiplication table. Whatever its length, it divided, and so did every unit whose multiple it was, into waxing and waning, day and night, or summer and winter. There was everywhere a conflict like that of my play between two principles or 'elemental forms of the mind', each 'living the other's life, dying the other's death.'

I have a Chinese painting of three old sages sitting together, one with a deer at his side, one with a scroll open at the symbol of yen and yin, those two forms that whirl perpetually, creating and re-creating all things. But because of our modern discovery that the equinox shifts its ground more rapidly than Ptolemy believed, one must, somebody says, invent a new symbolic scheme. No, a thousand times no; I insist that the equinox does shift a degree in a hundred years; anything else would lead to confusion.

All ancient nations believed in the re-birth of the soul and had probably empirical evidence like that Lafcadio Hearn found among the Japanese. In our time Schopenhauer believed it, and McTaggart thinks Hegel did, though lack of interest in the individual soul had kept him silent. It is the foundation of McTaggart's own philosophical system. Cardinal Mercier saw no evidence for it, but did not think it heretical; and its rejection compelled the sincere and noble Von Hügel to say that children dead too young to have earned Heaven suffered no wrong, never having heard of a better place than Limbo. Even though we think temporal existence illusionary it cannot be capricious; it is what Plotinus called the characteristic act of the soul and must reflect the soul's coherence. All our thought seems to lead by antithesis to some new affirmation of the supernatural. In a few years perhaps we may have much empirical evidence, the only evidence that moves the mass of men to-day that man has lived many times; there is some not yet perfectly examined – I think of that Professor's daughter in Palermo. This belief held by Plato and Plotinus, and supported by weighty argument, resembles the mathematical doctrines of Einstein before the experimental proof of the curvature of light.

We may come to think that nothing exists but a stream of souls, that all knowledge is biography, and with Plotinus that every soul is unique; that these souls, these eternal archetypes, combine into greater units as days and nights into months, months into years, and at last into the final unit that differs in nothing from that which they were at the beginning: everywhere that antinomy of the One and the Many that Plato thought in his *Parmenides* insoluble, though Blake thought it soluble 'at the bottom of the graves'. Such belief may arise from Communism by antithesis, declaring at last even to the common ear that all things have value according to the clarity of their expression of themselves, and not as functions of changing economic conditions or as a preparation for some Utopia. There is perhaps no final happy state except in so far as men may gradually grow better; escape may be for individuals alone who know how to exhaust their possible lives, to set, as it were, the hands of the clock racing. Perhaps we shall learn to accept even innumerable lives with happy humility – 'I have been always an insect in the roots of the grass' – and putting aside calculating scruples be ever ready to wager all upon the dice.

Even our best histories treat men as function. Why must I think the victorious cause the better? Why should Mommsen think the less of Cicero because Caesar beat him? I am satisfied, the Platonic Year in my head, to find but drama. I prefer that the defeated cause should be more vividly described than that which has the advertisement of victory. No battle has been finally won or lost; 'to Garret or Cellar a wheel I send.' (*W&B* 104–9; *VPl* 933–5)

the spring: the death and rebirth in March.

Another Troy . . . bauble yet: These lines develop Virgil's *Eclogue*, IV, 31–6:

Yet shall some few traces of olden sin lurk behind, to call men to essay the sea in ships, to gird towns with walls, and to cleave the earth with furrows. A second Tiphys shall then arise, and a second Argo to carry chosen heroes; a second warfare, too, shall there be, and again shall a great Achilles be sent to Troy.

Cf. a passage in a rewritten version of 'The Adoration of the Magi' where while one of these old men is reading out 'the Fifth *Eclogue* of Virgil' he falls asleep and 'a strange voice spoke through him, and bid them set out for Paris, where a dying woman would give them secret names and thereby so transform the world that another Leda would open her knees to the swan, another Achilles beleaguer Troy' (*M* 310).

There is another reference to this in *Samhain* (1904): 'for has not Virgil, a knowledgeable man and a wizard, foretold that other Argonauts shall row between cliff and cliff and other fair-haired Achaeans sack another Troy?' (*E* 150)

Yeats is also echoing the imagery of Shelley's *Hellas*, lines 1060–79, though not the optimistic tone of these lines:

The world's great age begins anew,
    The golden years return,
The earth doth like a snake renew
    Her winter weeds outworn:
Heaven smiles, and faiths and empires gleam,
Like wrecks of a dissolving dream.

A brighter Hellas rears its mountains
    From waves serener far;
A new Peneus rolls his fountains
    Against the morning star.
Where fairer Tempes bloom, there sleep
Young Cyclads on a sunnier deep.

A loftier Argo cleaves the main,
    Fraught with a later prize;
Another Orpheus sings again,
    And loves, and weeps, and dies.
A new Ulysses leaves once more
Calypso for his native shore.

Oh, write no more the tale of Troy,
    If earth Death's scroll must be!
Nor mix with Laian rage the joy
    Which dawns upon the free:
Although a subtler Sphinx renew
Riddles of death Thebes never knew.

Another Athens shall arise,
    And to remoter time
Bequeath, like sunset to the skies,
    The splendour of its prime;
And leave, if nought so bright may live,
All earth can take or Heaven can give.

Saturn and Love their long repose
    Shall burst, more bright and good
Than all who fell, than One who rose,
    Than many unsubdued:
Not gold, not blood, their altar dowers,
But votive tears and symbol flowers.

Oh, cease! must hate and death return?
    Cease! must men kill and die!

> Cease! drain not to its dregs the urn
>   Of bitter prophecy.
> The world is weary of the past,
> Oh, might it die or rest at last!

Cf. the image in 'The Gyres' (*CP* 337): 'Hector is dead and there's a light in Troy'.

Another Argo's painted prow: the prow was itself prophetic, cf. William Morris, *Life and Death of Jason IV*, where this is stressed:

> For just as a part of the ship Argo, keel or prow, was made of the Dodonalan oak, and Argo's crew heard with astonishment the ship herself prophesy to them on the sea. But Jason and the milder Argus knew whereby the prow foretold things strange and new.

The Roman Empire stood appalled: because though there were but six million Christians in the Roman Empire of sixty million people the world would become Christian and Christianity would destroy the Empire (cf. *AV*(A) 190). This was Gibbon's view, shared by Yeats. Yeats, while recognising it was 'of course impossible to do more than select a more or less arbitrary date for the beginning of Roman decay', saw this change coming in the period A.D. 1 to A.D. 1050 and described it in *A Vision*:

> God is now conceived of as something outside man and man's handiwork, and it follows that it must be idolatry to worship that which Phidias and Scopas made, and seeing that He is a Father in Heaven that Heaven will be found presently in the Thebaid, where the world is changed into featureless clay and can be run through the fingers; and these things are testified to from books that are outside human genius, being miraculous, and by a miraculous church, and this church, as the gyre sweeps wider, will make man also featureless as clay or sand. Night will fall upon man's wisdom now that man has been taught that he is nothing. He had discovered, or half-discovered, that the world is round and one of many like it, but now he must believe that the sky is but a tent spread above a level floor, and – that he may be stirred into a frenzy of anxiety and so to moral transformation – blot out the knowledge or half-knowledge that he has lived many times, and think that all eternity depends upon a moment's decision, and Heaven itself – transformation finished – must appear so vague and

motionless that it seems but a concession to human weakness. It is even essential to this faith to declare that God's messengers, those beings who show His will in dreams or announce it in visionary speech were never men. The Greeks thought them often great men of the past but now that concession to mankind is forbidden. All must be narrowed into the sun's image cast out of a burning-glass and man be ignorant of all but the image.

The mind that brought the change, if considered as man only, is a climax of whatever Greek and Roman thought was most a contradiction to its age; but considered as more than man He controlled what Neo-Pythagorean and Stoic could not – irrational force. He could announce the new age, all that had not been thought of or touched or seen, because He could substitute for reason, miracle. (*AV*(A) 185–6)

the reins of peace and war: because its system would give way to irrational force. Yeats put this idea in terms of sculpture in *A Vision*.

Roman sculpture – sculpture made under Roman influence whatever the sculptor's blood – did not for instance reach its full vigour, if we consider what it had of Roman as distinct from Greek, until the Christian Era. It even made a discovery which affected all sculpture to come. The Greeks painted the eyes of marble statues and made out of enamel or glass or precious stones those of their bronze statues, but the Roman was the first to drill a round hole to represent the pupil, and because, as I think, of a preoccupation with the glance characteristic of a civilisation in its final phase. The colours must have already faded from the marbles of the great period, and a shadow and a spot of light, especially where there is much sunlight, are more vivid than paint, enamel, coloured glass or precious stone. They could now express in stone a perfect composure, the administrative mind, alert attention where all had been rhythm, an exaltation of the body, uncommitted energy. [These sentences read differently in *AV*(B): 'They could now express in stone a perfect composure. The administrative mind, alert attention had driven out rhythm, exaltation of the body, uncommitted energy.'] May it not have been precisely a talent for this alert attention that had enabled Rome and not Greece to express those final *primary* phases? One sees on the pediments troops of marble Senators, officials serene and watchful as befits men who know that all the power of the world moves before their eyes, and needs, that it may not dash itself to pieces, their unhurried unanxious never-ceasing care. Those riders upon the Parthenon had all the world's power in their moving bodies, and in a movement that seemed, so were the hearts of man and beast set upon it, that of a dance; but presently all would change and measurement succeed to pleasure, the dancing-master outlive the dance. What need had those young lads for careful eyes? But in Rome of the first and second centuries where the dancing-master himself has died, the delineation of character as shown in face and head, as with us of recent years, is all in all, and sculptors seeking the custom of occupied officials stock in their workshops toga'd marble bodies upon which can be screwed with the least possible delay heads modelled from the sitters with the most scrupulous realism. When I think of Rome I see always those heads with their world-considering eyes, and those bodies as conventional as the metaphors in a leading article, and compare in my imagination vague Grecian eyes gazing at nothing, Byzantine eyes of drilled ivory staring upon a vision, and those eyelids of China and of India, those veiled eyes weary of world and vision alike.

Meanwhile the irrational force that would create confusion and uproar as with the cry 'The Babe, the Babe, is born' – the women speaking unknown tongues, the barbers and weavers expounding Divine revelation with all the vulgarity of their servitude, the tables that move or resound with raps – still but creates a negligible sect. (*AV*(A) 187–9).

that fierce virgin and her star: Ellmann (*IY* 261) remarks that this daringly asserts a parallelism and even identity between the three pairs, Astraea and Spica, Athene and Dionysus, and Mary and Christ. Cf. Lady Gregory (*J* 263) for an early version with 'Virgo [the constellation] and the mystic star.'

the fabulous darkness: this phrase comes from a description of Christianity by a fourth century Neo-Platonic philosopher, Proclus, whom Yeats read in a translation made by Thomas Taylor and published in 1816. Cf. Wilson (*Y&T* 59), and (*AV*(B) 277–18 and *AV*(A) 185 ff, particularly this passage:

All about it is an *antithetical* aristocratic civilisation in its completed form, every detail of life hierarchical, every great man's door crowded at dawn by petitioners, great wealth everywhere in few men's hands, all dependent upon a few, up to the Emperor himself who is a God dependent upon a greater God, and everywhere in court, in the family, an inequality made law, and floating over all the Romanised Gods of Greece in their physical superiority . . . the world became Christian and 'that fabulous formless darkness' as it seemed to a philosopher of the fourth century, blotted out 'every beautiful thing', not through the conversion of crowds or general change of opinion or through any pressure from below, for civilisation was *antithetical* still, but by an act of power. (*AV*(A) 189–90)

581 . . . *the dead had broken out of their cemetries*: cf. Matthew xxvii, 52–3: 'And the graves were opened; and many bodies of the saints which slept arose, and came out of the graves after his resurrection, and went into the holy city and appeared unto many.'

the Eleven: the disciples, without Judas.

James . . . Nathaniel: disciples.

thirteen: Jesus and the twelve disciples.

Jesus divided bread and wine: the last supper followed Jewish traditions for the Sabbath, when bread is broken and wine drunk. See Matthew xxvi, 26–8:

> And as they were eating, Jesus took bread, and blessed it, and brake it, and gave it to the disciples, and said, Take eat; this is my body. And he took the cup, and gave thanks, and gave it to them, saying, Drink ye all of it; for this is my blood of the new testament, which is shed for many for the remission of sins.

The account is also in Mark xiv, 22–4:

> And as they did eat, Jesus took bread, and blessed, and brake it, and gave to them, and said, Take, eat: this is my body. And he took the cup, and when he had given thanks, he gave it to them; and they all drank of it. And he said unto them, This is my blood of the new testament which is shed for many.

And in Luke xxii, 19–20:

> And he took bread, and gave thanks, and brake it, and gave unto them, saying, This is my body which is given for you: this do in remembrance of me. Likewise also the cup after supper, saying, This cup is the new testament in my blood which is shed for you.

Is it true . . . he denied it?: cf. Matthew xxvi, 69–75; Mark xiv,   **582**
66–72; Luke xxii, 56–62; John xviii, 25–7.

Nobody . . . had so pitied human misery: cf. *A Vision*:   **583**

The sacrifice of the 22nd Phase is voluntary and so we say to
Him that He was love itself, and yet that part of Him which
made Christendom was not love but pity, and not pity for
intellectual despair, though the man in Him, being *antithetical*
like His age, knew it in the Garden, but *primary* pity, that for
the common lot, man's death seeing that He raised Lazarus,
sickness seeing that He healed many, Sin seeing that He died.
(*AV*(A) 186–7)

the Messiah: see Daniel ix, 25 and John i, 25–40.

three days ago: Yeats seems to have in mind the reference to   **584**
Christ's rising again on the third day after the crucifixion. See
Matthew xxvii, 63 and Luke xxiv, 7. The action of the play is
therefore taking place on the day of the resurrection. See the speech
of the Greek, **586**, which ends 'Three days after the full moon, a
full moon in March, they sing the death of the God and pray for
his resurrection.'

the god and the Titans that murdered him: Dionysus. See **544**.   **586**

Astrea's holy child: Astraea, daughter of Zeus, who aided humans
on earth during the Golden Age. She was a goddess of justice and
sometimes she was regarded as a daughter of Astraeus the Titan,
by Eos. In her heavenly transformation she was Virgo.

the goddess came to Achilles: Athene, cf. 'The Phases of the Moon'   **587**
(*CP* 183). The phrase comes from Homer, *Iliad*, xxii, 330; or i, 197.
The line in 'The Phases of the Moon' described the twelfth phase,
the phase of the hero, one of violent, heroic action (see *AV*(A)
61–3; *AV*(B) 126–9).

Lucretius: Titus Lucretius Carus (*c* 99–55 B.C.), the author of *De Rerum Natura*, a philosophical poem written in hexameters in six books. This adopts the atomic theories of Epicurus, his aim being to show that the nature of the world can be explained without resorting to divine intervention. He wanted to free men from their fear of the Gods.

588   *He . . . copies their gestures . . . their acts. What seems their indifference is but their eternal possession of themselves*: a passage in *A Vision* describing the hero shows some of this thought. The man of the twelfth phase overcomes himself:

> . . . and so no longer needs . . . the submission of others, or . . . conviction of others to prove his victory. Solitude has been born at last, though solitude invaded, and hard to defend . . . The man is pursued by a series of accidents, which, unless he meet them *antithetically*, drive him into all sorts of temporary ambitions, opposed to his nature, unite him perhaps to some small protesting sect . . . and these ambitions he defends by some kind of superficial action, the pamphlet, the violent speech, the sword of the swashbuckler. He spends his life in oscillation between the violent assertion of some common-place pose, and a dogmatism which means nothing apart from the circumstance that created it.
>
> If, however, he meets these accidents by the awakening of his *antithetical* being, there is a noble extravagance, an over-flowing fountain of personal life. He turns towards the True *Mask* and having by philosophical intellect (*Creative Mind*) de-livered it from all that is topical and temporary, announces a philosophy which is the logical expression of a mind alone with the object of its desire. The True *Mask* . . . is the reverse of all that is emotional, being emotionally cold; not mathema-tical, for intellectual abstraction ceased at Phase 11, but marble pure. (*AV*(B) 127–8)

the Galilean women . . . Christ had arisen: cf. Matthew XXVIII, 1:

In the end of the Sabbath, as it began to dawn toward the first day of the week, came Mary Magdalene and the other Mary to see the sepulchre. And, behold, there was a great earthquake: for the Angel of the Lord descended from heaven, and came and rolled back the stone from the door, and sat upon it. His countenance was like lightning, and his raiment white as snow: and for fear of him the keepers did shake, and became as dead men. And the angel answered and said unto the women, Fear not ye: for I know that ye seek Jesus, which was crucified. He is not here: for he is risen, as he said. Come, see the place where the Lord lay. And go quickly, and tell his disciples that he is risen from the dead; and, behold, he goeth before you into Galilee; there Ye shall see him; as I have told you. And they departed quickly from the sepulchre with fear and great joy; and did run to bring his disciples word.

The version in Mark xvi, 1–8 is slightly different:

And when the sabbath was past, Mary Magdelene, and Mary the mother of James, and Salome, had brought sweet spices, that they might come and annoint him. And very early in the morning the first day of the week, they came unto the sepulchre at the rising of the sun. And they said among themselves, who shall roll away the stone from the door of the sepulchre? And when they looked, they saw that the stone was rolled away; for it was very great. And entering the sepulchre, they saw a young man sitting on the right side, clothed in a long white garment; and they were affrighted. And he saith unto them, Be not affrighted: Ye seek Jesus of Nazareth, which was crucified: he is risen; he is not here: behold the place where they laid him. But go your way, tell his disciples and Peter that he goeth before you into Galilee: there shall ye see him, as he said unto you.

And they went out quickly, and fled from the sepulchre; for they trembled and were amazed: neither said they any thing to any man; for they were afraid.

The version in Luke xxiv, 1–9 differs somewhat from Matthew and Mark:

Now upon the first day of the week, very early in the morning, they came unto the sepulchre, bringing the spices which they had prepared, and certain others with them. And they found the stone rolled away from the sepulchre. And they entered in, and found not the body of the Lord Jesus. And it came to pass, as they were much perplexed thereabout, behold, two men stood by them in shining garments: And as they were afraid, and bowed down their faces to the earth, they said unto them,

Why seek ye the living among the dead? He is not here, but is risen: remember how he spake unto you when he was yet in Galilee. Saying, The Son of man must be delivered into the hands of sinful men, and be crucified, and the third day rise again. And they remembered his words. And returned from the sepulchre, and told these things unto the eleven, and to all the rest.

In John xx, 1–10, the details are again different:

The first day of the week cometh Mary Magdalene early, when it was yet dark, unto the sepulchre, and seeth the stone taken away from the sepulchre. Then she runneth, and cometh to Simon Peter, and to the other disciple, whom Jesus loved, and saith unto them, They have taken away the Lord out of the sepulchre, and we know not where they have laid him. Peter therefore went forth, and that other disciple, and came to the sepulchre. So they ran both together: and the other disciple did outrun Peter, and came first to the sepulchre. And he stooping down, and looking in, saw the linen clothes lying; yet went he not in. Then cometh Simon Peter following him, and went into the sepulchre, and seeth the linen clothes lie, And the napkin, that was about his head, not lying with the linen clothes, but wrapped together in a place by itself. Then went in also that other disciple, which came first to the sepulchre, and he saw, and believed. For as yet they knew not the scripture, that he must rise again from the dead. Then the disciples went away again unto their own home.

589   *stood a man all shining*: the word 'shining' occurs in Luke xxiv, 4, applied to two men 'in shining garments'.

590   *great stone . . . over . . . the tomb*: cf. Matthew xxvii, 66: 'So they went and made the sepulchre sure, sealing the stone, and setting a watch.' See also Mark xv, 46: 'And he brought fine linen, and took him down . . . and laid him in a sepulchre which was hewn out of a rock, and rolled a stone into the door of the sepulchre.' John xix, 41, reads: 'Now in the place he was crucified there was a garden; and in the garden a new sepulchre, wherein was man never laid. There they laid Jesus because of the Jews' preparation day; for the sepulchre was nigh at hand.' The version in Luke XXIII, 53 runs: 'And he took it down . . . and laid it in a sepulchre that was hewn in stone, wherein never man before was laid.'

The Romans heard . . . people planned to steal the body and to put abroad a story that Christ had risen . . . The Romans put sentries at the tomb: This follows Matthew XXVII, 62–5:

> Now the next day, that followed the day of the preparation, the chief priests and Pharisees came together unto Pilate, Saying, Sir, we remember that that deceiver said, while he was yet alive, After three days I will rise again. Command therefore that the sepulchre be made sure until the third day, lest his disciples come by night, and steal him away, and say unto the people, He is risen from the dead: so the last error shall be worse than the first. Pilate said unto them, Ye have a watch: go your way, make it as sure as ye can.

Another Argo . . . another Troy: see note on *Another Troy*, **580**.

What if there is something: see Introduction to the play in *Wheels* **591** *and Butterflies*, pp. 109–10, *VPl* 935, quoted in note on 'that beating heart', **580**, p. 196.

What if . . . that something appears? . . . What if the circle begin again?: The Introduction in *Wheels and Butterflies* traces Yeats's preoccupation with cyclical events back to his youth and links the idea of an incarnation that would herald a new age with 'The Second Coming' (*CP* 210).

> For years I have been preoccupied with a certain myth that was itself a reply to a myth. I do not mean a fiction, but one of those statements our nature is compelled to make and employ as a truth though there cannot be sufficient evidence. When I was a boy everybody talked about progress, and rebellion against my elders took the form of aversion to that myth. I took satisfaction in certain public disasters, fet a sort of ecstasy at the contemplation of ruin, and then I came upon the story of Oisin in Tir-nan-oge and reshaped it into my *Wanderings of Oisin*. He rides across the sea with a spirit, he passes phantoms, a boy following a girl, a hound chasing a hare, emblematical of eternal pursuit, he comes to an island of choral dancing, leaves that after many years, passes the phantoms once again, comes to an island of endless battle for an object never achieved,

leaves that after many years, passes the phantoms once again, comes to an island of sleep, leaves that and comes to Ireland, to S. Patrick and old age. I did not pick these images because of any theory, but because I found them impressive, yet all the while abstractions haunted me. I remember rejecting, because it spoilt the simplicity, an elaborate metaphor of a breaking wave intended to prove that all life rose and fell as in my poem. How hard it was to refrain from pointing out that Oisin after old age, its illumination half accepted, half rejected, would pass in death over another sea to another island. Presently Oisin and his islands faded and the sort of images that come into *Rosa Alchemica* and *The Adoration of the Magi* took their place. Our civilization was about to reverse itself, or some new civilization about to be born from all that our age had rejected, from all that my stories symbolised as a harlot, and take after its mother; because we had worshipped a single god it would worship many or receive from Joachim de Flora's Holy Spirit a multitudinous influx. A passage in *La Peau de chagrin* may have started me, but because I knew no ally but Balzac, I kept silent about all I could not get into fantastic romance. So did the abstract ideas persecute me that *On Baile's Strand*, founded upon a dream, was only finished when, after a struggle of two years, I had made the Fool and Blind Man, Cuchulain and Conchubar whose shadows they are, all image, and now I can no longer remember what they meant except that they meant in some sense those combatants who turn the wheel of life. Had I begun *On Baile's Strand* or not when I began to imagine, as always at my left side just out of the range of the sight, a brazen winged beast that I associated with laughing, ecstatic destruction? Then I wrote, spurred by an external necessity, *Where There is Nothing*, a crude play with some dramatic force, since changed with Lady Gregory's help into *The Unicorn from the Stars*. A neighbourhood inflamed with drink, a country house burnt down, a spiritual anarchy preached! Then after some years came the thought that a man always tried to become his opposite, to become what he would abhor if he did not desire it, and I wasted some three summers and some part of each winter before I had banished the ghost and turned what I had meant for tragedy into farce: *The Player Queen*. Then unexpectedly and under circumstances described in *A Packet to Ezra Pound* came a symbolical system displaying the conflict in all its forms:

Where got I that truth?
Out of a medium's mouth,
Out of nothing it came,
Out of the forest loam,
Out of dark night where lay
The crowns of Nineveh.
(*W&B* 101–4; *VPl* 932–3)

their god arises every year: F. A. C. Wilson argues that this play **592**
owes much to Nietzsche's influence. He thinks that Yeats, wanting
to find a place for Christianity in his system of thought,

substituted it for Dionysus worship at his negative or 'objective' pole: it taught as much of any of Nietzsche's preferred
faiths the extinction of the individual will and personality,
culminating in the absorption of the 'I' in Godhead in its extro-
verted aspect, while in purity as in universality it was clearly
the most significant faith of its kind. Remembering that
Socrates also thought of the One or Good as something external to man, Yeats finds objective tendencies in his philosophy
also. He notes as objective characteristics 'denial of Self' and
belief in a single, indivisible God, symbolises the negative pole
as 'night', and repudiates Nietzsche's suggestion that Christianity and Platonic thought are of no value:

Why does Nietzsche think that the night has no stars,
nothing but owls and bats and the insane moon?

In later life Yeats wrote *The Resurrection* out of his confident
belief that Dionysus worship, in its pure form as a mystery
religion, was a more primitive faith of the same order as
Christianity, and this of course is a natural development of the
arguments I have set out above. As for the subjective synthesis, Yeats's annotations do no more than cite Homer as its
poet, and to list as characteristic virtues belief in 'many Gods',
affirmation of the 'Self' and of 'life': attributes which enable
us to associate Indian Shintoist and pagan Irish religion with
the Homeric Greek. All this is expressed in the notes Yeats
wrote on Nietzsche, in the following form:

Night: Socrates, Christ – one god – denial of Self – the
soul turned outwards towards [the external aspect
of] spirit, seeking knowledge.
Day: Homer – many gods – affirmation of Self-life.
We have in these words a complete system of world-religions,
in which any creed can be found a place.

I have hardly the space to say more here of the relation between Yeats's and Nietzsche's thought, but it will be useful to conclude this survey with a general comparison. Nietzsche rationalised Yeats's opinions and converted what had been loose emotion into intellectual substance: he gave him the core of his theories both of human personality and of religion, for *The Birth of Tragedy* is concerned with man's mind at least as much as God. He gave him even the terms 'subjective' and 'objective' for the divisions of the human psyche, and (since Dionysus-worship is an Asian and Homeric religion an Aryan emanation) the substance for the Yeatsian belief that subjective and objective religion originated respectively in the *west* and *east*. Both *Calvary* and *The Resurrection*, works concerned with God and the psyche, are owed to Nietzsche's influence, while we may trace a considerable debt in Yeats's later experiments with the Dionysus myth, *The King of the Great Clock Tower* and *A Full Moon in March*. At the same time we must remember how thoroughly Yeats transformed his authority. Nietzsche, it seems to me, was a man of violent and thus unphilosophical temperament; Yeats was far more tolerant and, on metaphysical questions, far better informed. In the field of subjective religious experience, Nietzsche had of course everything to learn from him, and in the negative or objective field, though both men had to build upon merely theoretical understanding, Nietzsche deliberately alienates the whole body of Christian mysticism, which Yeats retrieves. The result, if I am not mistaken, is that Yeats converted a minor and erratic theory into one of first importance, and conferred on Nietzsche's arguments a distinction they do not in themselves perhaps deserve. (*YI* 182–3)

He continues to comment on Yeats's use of traditional philosophical precedents, notably the cycle of rebirth in the Upanishads:

The cycle of the 'brightening fortnight' Yeats equated with Nietzsche's subjective temperament, so that it follows that the soul has fourteen 'Apollonian' lives; while the inferior, 'darkening' cycle was one of self-abnegation, and these would be the Dionysiac rebirths. Beyond the Upanishads, Yeats found precedent in the psychological theories of Heraclitus and Philolaus, both of whom had divided humanity into two opposite spiritual types: they had named these the 'lunar' and 'solar' personalities, and there were the strongest reasons for identifying the lunar and Apollonian temperaments, and for seeing in the

'solar' personality a soul dominated by an (external) God.
(cf. *Essays* 1931–6 pp. 112–6 and Burnet, *Early Greek Philosophy*
(1892), pp. 156, 173, 176. But whatever Yeats says in his
Essays, my references in Burnet suggest that he founded on
Heraclitus at a time when he still doubted the ultimate efficacity
of subjective religion. 'Lunar' souls are immature.) Yeats had
thus both Indian and Greek authority for taking Nietzsche's
as the traditional theory, or at least as a theory which the
traditionalist might reasonably believe.

When Yeats had aligned himself to the traditional doctrine
of reincarnation, he still had a further problem of integration:
he had to establish a connection with his cyclic theory of history
also. Nietzsche had presented his two principles as alternating
through recorded history, citing Babylon and the German
Middle Ages as objective periods and heroic Greece as a subjective culture, and it was necessary to find proper sanction for
such beliefs. Plato's system of 'superior' and 'inferior' cycles
provided a convenient means by which this could be done: in
an inferior (objective) cycle the Dionysiac temperament would
predominate, and in a superior the Apollonian. A further
passage in Plato, with the commentaries in Burnet's *Early
Greek Philosophy*, seemed to Yeats to authorise even his poly-
theism. In a celebrated text in his *Sophist*, Plato gives Empe-
docles and Heraclitus as his sources in affirming that 'in one
cycle of civilisation' God will be seen as unity and 'in the next'
as 'Many' (Plato: *Sophist*, 242,D,E.); a statement which Yeats
takes to mean that the Apollonian will worship the archetypal,
'visible' Gods, and the Dionysiac the concept of the Victim-
Saviour. Here is his own commentary on the passage:

> 'I think that two conceptions, that of reality [*sc.* 'Godhead]
> as a congeries of beings, that of reality as a single being,
> alternate in our emotion and in history and must always
> remain something that human reason, because subject
> always to one or the other, cannot reconcile ... I think
> that there are historical cycles when one or the other pre-
> dominates and that a cycle approaches when all shall be as
> particular and concentrate as human intensity allows.
> (1930 *Diary*, p. 18)

And Yeats goes on to present himself as the Virgil of that
approaching cycle, its vatic singer, conditioned by its proximity to envisage divinity always as multiplicity:

> Again and again I have tried to sing that approach, 'The
> Hosting Of The Sidhe', 'O sweet everlasting voices', and

those lines about 'The lonely majestical multitude', and have almost understood my intention. Again and again with remorse, a sense of defeat, I have failed when I would write of [a single] God, written coldly and conventionally. (ibid)

In this way Yeats found authority for an early and quite personal theory, with which I have shown him occupied in the alchemical tales. (*YI* 184-5)

593   *The heart of a phantom is beating*: see note on **580**.
Thomas has put his hand into the wound: cf. John xx, 26-9:

And after eight days again his disciples were within and Thomas with them; then came Jesus, the doors being shut, and stood in the midst, and said Peace be unto you. Then saith he to Thomas, Reach hither thy finger, and behold my hands; and reach hither thy hand, and thrust it into my side: and be not faithless but believing. And Thomas answered and said unto him, My Lord and my God. Jesus saith unto him, Thomas, because thou hast seen me, thou hast believed: blessed are they that have not seen and yet have believed.

594   *Your words are clear at last . . . God and man die each other's life, live each other's death*: see p. 195 for Curtis Bradford's citing a paraphrase of the Heraclitus quotation which appeared in Yeats's Journal for 1908 (*YW* 266). As Henn points out (*LT* 194) the antithesis corresponds with the movement of Yeats's gyres. Heraclitus (*c.* 500 B.C.), an Ephesian philosopher who held that fire was the primary element and that everything was in a state of flux ($\pi\alpha\nu\tau\alpha$ $\dot{\rho}\epsilon\hat{\imath}$) and that the universe was a conflict of opposites controlled by eternal Justice. The cosmos or world order was not made by God or man, but 'always was, is and will be everlasting fire being kindled and quenched in due measures.'

Galilean turbulence . . . Babylonian starlight: this was foretold by astronomers in Babylon who, according to Yeats, reduce man's status by their science. Man is being taught that he is insignificant in comparison to the universe, even featureless:

God is now conceived of as something outside man and man's handiwork, and it follows that it must be idolatry to worship

that which Phidias and Scopas made, and seeing that He is a
Father in Heaven, that Heaven will be found presently in the
Thebaid, where the world is changed into a featureless dust
and can be run through the fingers; and these things are testi-
fied to from books that are outside human genius, being miraculous, and by a miraculous Church, and this Church, as the
gyre sweeps wider, will make man also featureless as clay or
dust. Night will fall upon man's wisdom now that man has
been taught that he is nothing. . . .

The mind that brought the change, if considered as man
only, is a climax of whatever Greek and Roman thought was
most a contradiction to its age; but considered as more than
man He controlled what Neo-Pythagorean and Stoic could not
– irrational force. He could announce the new age, all that had
not been thought of, or touched, or seen, because He could
substitute for reason, miracle. (*A V*(B) 273 ff)

*Odour of blood when Christ was slain/Made all Platonic tolerance vain/
And vain all Doric discipline*: the effect of Christianity is to substitute the miraculous for the rational. Cf. the account in *A Vision*:

After Plato and Aristotle, the mind is as exhausted as were
the armies of Alexander at his death, but the Stoics can discover morals and turn philosophy into a rule of life. Among
them doubtless – the first beneficiaries of Plato's hatred of imitation – we may discover the first benefactors of our modern
individuality, sincerity of the trivial face, the mask torn away.
Then, a Greece that Rome has conquered, and a Rome conquered
by Greece, must, in the last three phases of the wheel, adore,
desire being dead, physical or spiritual force.

This adoration which begins in the second century before
Christ creates a world-wide religious movement as the world
was then known, which, being swallowed up in what came
after, has left no adequate record. One knows not into how
great extravagance Asia, accustomed to abase itself, may have
carried what soon sent Greeks and Romans to stand naked in
a Mithraic pit, moving their bodies as under a shower-bath
that those bodies might receive the blood of the bull even to
the last drop. The adored image took everywhere the only form
possible as the *atnithetical* age died into its last violence – a
human or animal form. Even before Plato that collective image
of man dear to Stoic and Epicurean alike, the moral double of
bronze or marble athlete, had been invoked by Anaxagoras

when he declared that thought and not the warring opposites created the world. At that sentence the heroic life, passionate fragmentary man, all that had been imagined by great poets and sculptors began to pass away, and instead of seeking noble antagonists, imagination moved towards divine man and the ridiculous devil. Now must sages lure men away from the arms of women because in those arms man becomes a fragment; and all is ready for revelation.

When revelation comes athlete and sages are merged; the earliest sculptured image of Christ is copied from that of the Apotheosis of Alexander the Great; the tradition is founded which declares even to our own day that Christ alone was exactly six feet high, perfect physical man. Yet as perfect physical man He must die, for only so can *primary* power reach *antithetical* mankind shut within the circle of its senses, touching outward things alone in that which seems most personal and physical. When I think of the moment before revelation I think of Salome – she, too, delicately tinted or maybe mahogany dark – dancing before Herod and receiving the Prophet's head in her indifferent hands, and wonder if what seems to us decadence was not in reality the exaltation of the muscular flesh and of civilisation perfectly achieved. Seeking images, I see her anoint her bare limbs according to a medical prescription of that time, with lion's fat, for lack of the sun's ray, that she may gain the favour of a king, and remember that the same impulse will create the Galilean revelation and deify Roman Emperors whose sculptured heads will be surrounded by the solar disk. Upon the throne and upon the cross alike the myth becomes a biography. (*A V*(B) 272–3)

This 'odour of blood' is related to the irrational streams of blood which 'are staining earth' in 'The Gyres' (*CP* 337) and there is an echo of this in the 'blood-dimmed tide' of 'The Second Coming' (*CP* 211).

Everything that man esteems/Endures a moment or a day/
Love's pleasure drives his love away: cf. a passage in Yeats's letter of 17 April 1929 to T. Sturge Moore, quoted in Hone (*WBY* 405):

Ezra Pound has just been in. He says 'Spengler is a Wells who has founded himself on German scholarship instead of English journalism'. He is sunk in Frobenius, Spengler's German source, and finds him a most interesting person. Frobenius suggested the idea that cultures (including arts and

sciences) arise out of races, express those races as if they were
fruit and leaves in a preordained order and perish with them. . . .
He proved from his logic – some German told Ezra – that a
certain civilisation must have once existed at a certain spot in
Africa and then went and dug it up. He proved his case all
through by African research. I cannot read German and so must
get him second hand. He has confirmed a conception I have
had for years, a conception that has freed me from British
Liberalism and all its dreams. The one heroic sanction is that of
the last battle of the Norse gods, of a gay struggle without
hope. Long ago I used to puzzle poor Maud Gonne by always
avowing ultimate defeat as a test – our literary movement would
be worthless but for its defeat. Science is the criticism of myths,
there would be no Darwin had there been no Book of Genesis,
no electrons but for the Greek atomic myth, and when the
criticism is finished there is not even a drift of ashes on the pyre.
Sexual desire dies because every touch consumes the Myth, and
yet a Myth that cannot be so consumed becomes a spectre.

the painter's brush consumes his dreams: the ideas of lines 14–21
appear in a different guise in *Autobiographies* also:

Our love-letters wear out our love; no school of painting out-
lasts its founders, every stroke of the brush exhausts the impulse,
Pre-Raphaelitism had some twenty years; Impressionism
thirty perhaps. Why should we believe that religion can never
bring round its antithesis? Is it true that our air is disturbed,
as Mallarmé said, by 'the trembling of the veil of the Temple',
or that 'our whole age is seeking to bring forth a sacred book'?
Some of us thought that book near towards the end of last
century, but the tide sank again. (*A* 315)

*The Words upon the
Window-Pane*

Yeats wrote this play during 1930. It was written at Coole, as the
dedication to Lady Gregory, in whose house it was written, makes
clear.

Yeats wrote to Olivia Shakespear on 23 October 1930, in a gay
letter, largely about his high blood-pressure, that he had 'just
finished a play on Jonathan Swift' (*L* 777). Earlier in 1930 he had
written to Lady Gregory from Rapallo, on 7 April, that when he
was not reading detective stories he was reading 'Swift, the *Diary to
Stella*, and his correspondence with Pope and Bolingbroke; these
men fascinate me, in Bolingbroke the last pose and in Swift the
last passion of the Renaissance, in Pope, whom I dislike, an imitation, both of pose and passion' (*L* 773). On 1 June he wrote to
Olivia Shakespear that he read Swift 'constantly' (*L* 776). The
play's starting point was Yeats's finding an inscription cut on a
bedroom window in Oliver St John Gogarty's Dublin house,
Fairfield. This read:

> Mary Kilpatrick – very young
> Ugly face and pleasant tongue.

Yeats wrote to Gogarty on [?] 22 June 1937 from the Athenaeum
to say that he thought he had found out who she was. If the date of
the inscription was 1778

> my discovery is certain. She was the sister of the Earl of Ossory
> and married the second Lord Holland and died of consump-
> tion beloved by everybody in 1778. See her portrait by Gains-
> borough in *The Homes of the Hollands* by the Earl of Ilchester.
> (*L* 891)

The play was first performed on 17 November 1930, at the Abbey
Theatre, Dublin. The cast was: Miss McKenna, Shelah Richards;
Dr Trench, P. J. Carolan; John Corbet, Arthur Shields; Cornelius

Patterson, Michael J. Dolan; Abraham Johnson, F. J. McCormick; Mrs Mallet, Eileen Crowe; Mrs Henderson, May Craig. The play was produced by Lennox Robinson.

Yeats wrote to Olivia Shakespear on 2 December 1930 that he thought the play 'a much greater success than I had ever hoped and beautifully acted' (*L* 779). The play was first published as *The Words upon the Window Pane*, Cuala Press ed., Dublin, 1934; then in *Wheels and Butterflies*, London, 1934; New York, 1935; *The Collected Plays of W. B. Yeats*, London, 1934; New York, 1935; *Nine One-Act Plays*, London, 1937 and *The Collected Plays of W. B. Yeats*, London, 1952; New York, 1953 (repr. London, 1953, 1960, 1963, 1966). It is included in *Selected Plays*, Papermac edition, ed. A. Norman Jeffares, London, 1964, and *Eleven Plays of William Butler Yeats*, ed. A. Norman Jeffares, New York, 1964. 'The Words upon the Window-Pane: A Commentary' first appeared in the *Dublin Magazine*, October–December 1931 and January–March 1932. Yeats was writing the Introduction in November 1930 (see *L* 779); this was dated November 1930 and November 1931 respectively in the two parts in the two issues of the *Dublin Magazine*.

[*Dedication to*] *Lady Gregory*:   **596**

Lady Augusta Gregory (1852–1932), Irish playwright and translator, widow of Sir William Gregory. She was a close friend of Yeats from 1896, and collaborated with him in establishing an Irish theatre.

the Corbets of Ballymoney: Yeats had Corbet relatives. (His father   **597** stayed with them in Sandymount Castle, Dublin, when he was an undergraduate. See A. Norman Jeffares, *The Circus Animals*, 1970, p. 119. His grandfather the Rev. William Butler Yeats retired and died at Sandymount Castle in 1862. They are alluded to as 'Sandymount Corbets' in 'Are You Content?' (*CP* 370) but this name and that of Ballymoney are probably employed to indicate a young man of some social and intellectual standing. There are many towns, villages or townlands in Ireland called Ballymoney, for instance, in Antrim, Cork, Wexford etc.)

598   *Myers'* Human Personality: a book written by F. W. H. Myers (1843–1901) and published in two volumes in 1903.

a wild book by Conan Doyle: this could be either *A New Revelation*, 1918, or a *History of Spiritualism*, 2 vols., 1926, by Sir Arthur Conan Doyle, author of the Sherlock Holmes stories.

Lord Dunraven, then Lord Adare: probably introduced in order to 'place' Dr Trench's standing. The full title of this Irish peerage created for the Quin family was Earl of Dunraven and Viscount Adare. Yeats probably is referring to Edward Wyndham-Quin, the third Earl, who was a scholar, interested in archaeology and literature. Yeats may have been amusing himself in calling one character 'Dr. Trench'. He referred to Professor Wilbraham Trench, who succeeded to Professor Edward Dowden's chair of English at Trinity College, Dublin in November 1913, as 'a man of known sobriety of manner and of mind' in his Introduction to Arland Ussher's translation of the Irish poem *The Midnight Court*. There had been some question of Yeats's being appointed to the chair in 1910. See Philip Edwards, 'Yeats and the Trinity Chair', *Hermathena*, CI, autumn 1965, 5–12.

David Home: this is probably an error; Yeats presumably intended Daniel D. Home (1833–86), a Scottish spiritualist and medium.

599   *Emanuel Swedenborg*: (1688–1772), Swedish scientist and mystic philosopher who devoted his life after 1745 to interpreting the scriptures, his being a theosophical system well known to Yeats. (For his influence on Yeats see A. Norman Jeffares, 'Gyres in Yeats's Poetry', *The Circus Animals*, 1970, pp. 103–14, and Wilson, *Y & T*, 78–9, 108–11, 145–6, 203 and 265.)

Harold's Cross: a South Dublin suburb where the Yeats family lived, 1885–7.

wonderful room for a lodging house: many seedy or slum streets or squares in Dublin had seen better days by the twentieth century; originally many of them were the town houses of well-to-do families in the eighteenth century.

Grattan: Henry Grattan (1746–1820), Irish barrister and M.P. He carried an address demanding legislative independence in 1782. The Irish parliament which lasted until the Act of Union in 1800 was known as Grattan's parliament, and the Anglo-Irish reached their high point in the 1780s, a period when much of Dublin's finer building took place.

Curran: John Philpot Curran (1750–1817), Irish barrister and M.P. He defended the prisoners in the trials which took place after the 1798 rebellion and opposed the Union.

Jonathan Swift: (1667–1745) Dean of St Patrick's Cathedral, Dublin.

Stella: Swift's name for Esther Johnson (1687–1728). He met her in Sir William Temple's household at Moor Park when he was secretary there. She moved to Ireland, they remained close friends till her death, and Swift was buried by her side in St Patrick's Cathedral. He described her on the night of her death as 'the truest, most virtuous and valuable friend that I, or perhaps any other person, was ever blessed with.'

Journal to Stella: a series of letters written between 1710 and 1713, addressed to Stella and Rebecca Dingley her companion.

Vanessa: Swift's name for Esther (or Hester) Vanhomrigh (1690–   **600**
1723) whom he met in London in 1708. She fell in love with him, and Swift's *Cadenus and Vanessa* is an account of their unhappy relationship.

lines . . . upon the window-pane: these lines (7–10, **601**) come from the poem quoted in the following note.

part of a poem . . . for Swift's fifty-fourth birthday: this is 'Stella to Dr. Swift on his birth-day November 30, 1721':

> St. Patrick's Dean, your Country's Pride,
> My early and my only Guide,
> Let me among the Rest attend,
> Your pupil and your humble Friend,
> To celebrate in female Strains
> The Day that paid your Mother's Pains;
> Descend to take that Tribute due
> In Gratitude alone to you.
>
> When Men began to call me fair,
> You interposed your timely Care:
> You early taught me to despise
> The Ogling of a Coxcomb's Eyes;
> Show'd where my Judgement was misplaced;
> Refined my Fancy and my Taste.
> Behold that Beauty just decay'd,
> Invoking Art to Nature's Aid:

Forsook by her admiring Train,
She spreads her tatter'd Nets in vain;
Short was her Part upon the Stage;
Went smoothly on for half a Page;
Her Bloom was gone, she wanted Art
As the Scene changed, to change her Part;
She, whom no Lover could resist
Before the second Act was hissed.
Such is the Fate of female Race
With no endowments but a Face;
Before the thirtieth Year of Life,
A Maid forlorn or hated Wife.

Stella to you, her Tutor, owes
That she has ne'er resembled those;
Nor was a Burthen to Mankind
With half her course of Years behind.
You taught how I might Youth prolong
By knowing what was right and wrong;
How from my Heart to bring Supplies
Of Lustre to my fading eyes;
How soon a beauteous Mind repairs
The loss of changed or falling Hairs;
How Wit and Virtue from within
Send out a smoothness o'er the Skin;
Your Lectures could my Fancy fix,
And I can please at thirty-six.
The Sight of Chloe at fifteen
Coquetting, gives me not the Spleen;
The Idol now of every Fool
Till Time shall make their Passions cool;
Then tumbling down Time's steepy Hill,
While Stella holds her Station still.

O! turn your Precepts into Laws,
Redeem the Women's ruined Cause,
Retrieve lost Empire to our Sex,
That Men may bow their rebel Necks.
Long be the Day that gave you Birth
Sacred to Friendship, Wit and Mirth;
Late dying may you cast a Shred
Of your rich Mantle o'er my Head;
To bear with dignity my Sorrow,
One Day alone, then die Tomorrow.

three poems of hers: in addition to the poem quoted above she wrote   **601**
'Jealousy':

> O shield me from his rage, celestial pow'rs,
> This tyrant, that imbitters all my hours:
> Ah, love, you've poorly play'd the hero's part,
> You conquer'd, but you can't defend my heart.
> When first I bent beneath your gentle reign
> I thought this monster banish'd from your train;
> But you would raise him, to support your throne
> And now he claims your empire for his own.
> Or tell me tyrants, have you both agreed
> That where one reigns, the other shall succeed?

For the third poem see *Swift: Poems*, ed. Harold Williams, 1958,
pp. 736–9.

Donne: John Donne (1572–1631), Dean of St Paul's from 1621
to his death. He began life as a Roman Catholic. He was secretary
to Sir Thomas Egerton, but alienated him by secretly marrying
Anne More, his wife's niece. He sailed in Essex's two expeditions,
to Cadiz and to the Islands. In 1615 he took orders in the Anglican
Church and became a magnificent preacher. He wrote satires,
epistles, elegies and miscellaneous poems and was the best known
of the metaphysical poets. Most of his work was not published till
after his death.

Crashaw: Richard Crashaw (?1612–49), whose father was a noted
anti-papal preacher, himself entered the Roman Catholic Church.
He went to Paris, and through Queen Henrietta Maria and Cardinal
Pallotto, the Governor of Rome, obtained a benefice in Loretto.
His main work was *Steps to the Temple*, religious and devotional
poems, showing the influence of Marino and the Spanish mystics.

'*You taught . . . fading eyes*': from Stella's poem, quoted above in
note on **600**, p. 223. Stella had used spectacles from about her
twenty-second year. Cf. Yeats's 'A Song' (*CP* 156):

> I thought no more was needed
> Youth to prolong
> Than dumb-bell and foil
> To keep the body young.

She followed him to Dublin: she took a house at Celbridge in Co. Dublin in 1714. See note on **609,** p. 239, *I followed you to Ireland* . . .

Everything great in Ireland and in our character . . . *comes from that day*: this statement is glossed in Yeats's Introduction:

'In Swift's day men of intellect reached the height of their power, the greatest position they ever attained in society and and the State. . . . His ideal order was the Roman Senate, his ideal men Brutus and Cato; such an order and such men had seemed possible once more.' The Cambridge undergraduate into whose mouth I have put these words may have read similar words in Oliver, 'the last brilliant addition to English historians,' for young men such as he read the newest authorities; probably Oliver and he thought of the influence at Court and in public life of Swift and of Leibniz, of the spread of science and of scholarship over Europe, its examination of documents, its destruction of fables, a science and a scholarship modern for the first time, of certain great minds that were medieval in their scope but modern in their freedom. I must, however, add certain thoughts of my own that affected me as I wrote. I thought about a passage in the Grammont *Memoirs* where some great man is commended for his noble manner, as we commend a woman for her beauty or her charm; a famous passage in the *Appeal from the New to the Old Whigs* commending the old Whig aristocracy for their intellect and power and because their doors stood open to like-minded men; the palace of Blenheim, its pride of domination that expected a thousand years, something Asiatic in its carved intricacy of stone.

'Everything great in Ireland and in our character, in what remains of our architecture, comes from that day . . . we have kept its seal longer than England.' The overstatement of an enthusiastic Cambridge student, and yet with its measure of truth. The battle of the Boyne overwhelmed a civilisation full of religion and myth, and brought in its place intelligible laws planned out upon a great blackboard, a capacity for horizontal lines, for rigid shapes, for buildings, for attitudes of mind that could be multiplied like an expanding bookcase: the modern world, and something that appeared and perished in its dawn, an instinct for Roman rhetoric, Roman elegance. It established a Protestant aristocracy, some of whom neither called themselves English nor looked with contempt or dread upon conquered Ireland. Indeed the battle was scarcely over when Molyneux, speaking in their name, affirmed the sovereignty of the Irish Parliament. No one had the right to make our laws but the King, Lords and Commons of Ireland; the battle had been fought to change not an English but an Irish Crown; and our Parliament was almost as ancient as that of England. It was this doctrine that Swift uttered in the fourth *Drapier Letter* with such astringent eloquence that it passed from the talk of study and parlour to that of road and market, and created the political nationality of Ireland. Swift found his nationality through the *Drapier Letters*, his convictions came from action and passion, but Berkeley, a much younger man, could find it through contemplation. He and his fellow-students but knew the war through the talk of the older men. As a boy of eighteen or nineteen he called the Irish people 'natives' as though he were in some foreign land, but two or three years later, perhaps while still an undergraduate, defined the English materialism of his day in three profound sentences, and wrote after each that 'we Irishmen' think otherwise – 'I publish ... to know whether other men have the same ideas as we Irishmen' – and before he was twenty-five had fought the Salamis of the Irish intellect. The Irish landed aristocracy, who knew more of the siege of Derry and the battle of the Boyne delineated on vast tapestries for their House of Lords by Dublin Huguenots than of philosophy, found themselves masters of a country demoralised by generations of war and famine and shared in its demoralisation. In 1730 Swift said from the pulpit that their houses were in ruins and no new building anywhere, that the houses of their rack-ridden tenants were no better than English pigsties, that the bulk of the people trod barefoot and in rags. He exaggerated, for already the Speaker, Connolly, had built that great house at Celbridge where slate, stone and furniture were Irish, even the silver from Irish mines; the new Parliament House had perhaps been planned; and there was a general stir of life. The old age of Berkeley passed amid art and music, and men had begun to boast that in these no country had made such progress; and some dozen years after Berkeley's death Arthur Young found everywhere in stately Georgian houses scientific agriculturalists, benefactors of their countryside, though for the half-educated, drunken, fire-eating impoverished lesser men he had nothing but detestation. Goldsmith might have found likeable qualities, a capacity for mimicry perhaps, among these lesser men, and Sir Jonah Barrington made them his theme, but detestable or not, they were out of fashion. Miss Edgeworth described her *Castle Rackrent* upon the title-page of its first edition as 'the habits of the Irish squirearchy before 1782.' A few years more and the country people would have forgotten that the Irish aristocracy was founded like all aristocracies upon conquest, or rather, would have remembered, and boasted in the words of a medieval Gaelic poet, 'We are a sword people and we go with the sword.' Unhappily the lesson first taught by Molyneux and Swift had been but half learnt when the test came – country gentlemen are poor politicians – and Ireland's 'dark insipid period' began. During the entire eighteenth century the greatest land-owning family of the neighbourhood I best knew in childhood sent not a single man into the English army and navy, but during the nineteenth century one or more in every generation; a new absenteeism, foreseen by Miss Edgeworth, began; those that lived upon their estates bought no more fine editions of the classics; separated from public life and ambition they sank, as I have heard Lecky complain, 'into grass farmers.' Yet their genius did not die out; they sent everywhere administrators and military leaders, and now that their ruin has come – what resolute nation permits a strong alien class within its borders? – I would, remembering obscure ancestors that preached in their churches or fought beside their younger sons over half the world, and despite a famous passage of O'Grady's, gladly sing their song. (*W&B* 8–14; *VPl* 958–60)

Yeats's pride in the eighteenth century Anglo-Irish reached its peak in his speech on divorce to the Irish Senate in which he proudly proclaimed:

> We against whom you have done this thing are no petty people. We are one of the great stocks of Europe. We are the people of Burke; we are the people of Grattan; we are the people of Swift, the people of Emmet, the people of Parnell. We have created the most of the modern literature of this country. We have created the best of its political intelligence. (*SSY* 99)

The best account of Yeats's attitude to Swift and the eighteenth century is that which Torchiana gives in *Y&GI* 120–67, 'Imitate him if you Dare'. He emphasises the ethical rigourism and hatred of Whiggery in the play, and suggests that the key to it lies in Stella's words supposedly cut upon the window-pane:

'You taught how I might youth prolong
By knowing what is right and wrong,
How from my heart to bring supplies
Of lustre to my fading eyes!

He comments that:

Swift might teach modern Ireland, as he had taught Stella
and had not taught eighteenth-century Ireland, how to prolong its youth by knowing right from wrong and listening to
the promptings of the heart. Swift as a moral agent in modern
Ireland was a figure dear to Yeats in these years, as the following unpublished passage shows:

> ... if I communicate with the living mind of Shakespeare
> when I read of Coriolanus among the servants of Aufidius,
> do I not communicate with the living mind of Swift still
> in that almost equal moment when discovering that his
> life or liberty depended upon an unsatisfactory servant, he
> dismissed him that he might not through fear endure any
> man's negligence or insolence, & restored him & honoured
> him when all danger had passed. As the difference between
> these two acts is that Shakespeare had for object the crea-
> tion of a mental image, while Swift had for object an effect
> upon our life within defined limits; it would be more easy
> therefore to believe if we had only ties to cause it, his
> eternal moment, to become – through the universal mind
> – a conscious moral agent in our own lives.

Beyond showing Swift as a moral agent, the passage goes a long
way toward suggesting why Yeats chose to dramatize Swift.
Swift's idea for forming a nation – 'a self-imposed discipline, a
deliberate limit' – expressed the same truth to Yeats. He
seldom forgot the import of Swift's warning in the *Contests
and Dissensions*:

> The fate of empire is grown a common-place: that all
> forms of government having been instituted by men, must
> be mortal like their authors, and have their periods of dura-
> tion limited as well as those of private persons ... there
> are few, who turn their thoughts to examine, how those
> diseases in a state are bred, that hasten its end; which
> would however be a very useful enquiry. For, though we
> cannot prolong the period of a commonwealth beyond the
> decree of heaven, or the date of its nature, any more than
> human life beyond the strength of the seminal virtue; yet

we may manage a sickly constitution and preserve a strong one; we may watch and prevent accidents . . . and by these, and other such methods, render a state long lived, though not immortal.

What better words for a precarious new state – the Irish Free State – come to birth at the end of a great cycle of Western civilization? (*Y&GI* 135-7)

Bolingbroke, Harley, Ormonde: Henry St John Bolingbroke, first Viscount (1678-1751), friend of Swift, author, orator, and politician. He was in charge of the negotiations leading to the Peace of Utrecht in 1710. He was dismissed on the accession of George I and then fled to France whence he returned in 1723. Robert Harley, first Earl of Oxford (1661-1724), another friend of Swift, who was a moderate Tory. He persuaded his party to pass the Act of Settlement. He remained in a Whig ministry until 1708. In 1710 he and St John led the Tory Ministry which brought about the Treaty of Utrecht (1713). In 1714 he was dismissed, largely through the Jacobite intrigues of his colleague. James Butler, Duke of Ormonde (1610-88), was born of an ancient and distinguished Anglo-Irish family. He distinguished himself in Strafford's administration and was appointed Chief Commander of the army in the rebellions of 1640. James Butler, the second Duke of Ormonde (1665-1746) served in the army against Monmouth; he fought at the battle of the Boyne (1690); he was Lord Lieutenant of Ireland three times between 1703 and 1713. In 1705 he was impeached for high treason. He retired to Avignon. Swift admired him. Yeats (and his family) greatly valued their connection with the Butlers. In 1773 Benjamin Yeats married Mary Butler, and the Butler name was frequently used as a christian name by the Yeatses thereafter.

602   *the Roman Senate*: Yeats's view of the Roman achievement from Republic to the rule of the Emperors is put, in the passage from *A Vision* cited on p. 204, in terms of sculpture.

Brutus: Marcus Junius Brutus (85-42 B.C.). He joined Pompey but was pardoned by Caesar after the Battle of Pharsalia. He joined the conspiracy against Caesar. After Caesar's assassination Brutus and Cassius were defeated at Philippi and Brutus committed suicide.

Cato: There were two Catos who may have been intended. The first (234–149 B.C.) was a senator famous for his opposition to the luxury becoming fashionable in his day. He was known for his conviction that the existence of Carthage threatened the safety of Rome and ended all his Senate speeches with 'Delenda est Carthago' (Carthage must be destroyed). The second, and more likely (from his appearance, like Brutus, in Shakespeare's *Julius Caesar*), was Marcius Porcius Cato Uticensis (95–46 B.C.) a Roman stoic who supported Pompey and after his defeat, joined the Pompeians in Africa. After Caesar's victory at Thapsus, he committed suicide at Pharsalia.

the ruin to come, Democracy, Rousseau, the French Revolution: cf. the Introduction to the play:

> Did not Rousseau within five years of the death of Swift publish his *Discourse upon Arts and Sciences* and discover instinctive harmony not in heroic effort, not in Cato and Brutus, not among impossible animals – I think of that noble horse Blake drew for Hayley – but among savages, and thereby beget the sans-culottes of Marat? After the arrogance of power the humility of a servant. (*W&B* 30; *VPl* 967)

Jean Jacques Rousseau (1712–78), author and philosopher, was born at Geneva. His *Du Contrat Social* (1762) prepared the way for the French Revolution.

Gulliver, that is why he wore out his brain: *Gulliver's Travels* (1726). Swift probably intended this satire to form part of the *Memoirs of Scriblerus*, and worked on it from 1720. Yeats's comment shows how he saw Swift at work persuading his contemporaries of his views on the need for balance in the State:

> that is why he hated the common run of men, – 'I hate lawyers, I hate doctors,' he said, 'though I love Dr. So-and-so and Judge So-and-so,' – that is why he wrote *Gulliver*, that is why he wore out his brain, that is why he felt *saeva indignatio*, that is why he sleeps under the greatest epitaph in history.' The *Discourse of the Contests and Dissensions between the Nobles and the Commons in Athens and Rome*, published in 1703 to warn the Tory Opposition of the day against the impeachment of Ministers, is Swift's one philosophical work. All States depend for their health upon a right balance between the One, the Few, and the Many. The One is the executive, which may in fact be more than one – the Roman republic had two Consuls –

but must for the sake of rapid decision be as few as possible; the Few are those who through the possession of hereditary wealth, or great personal gifts, have come to identify their lives with the life of the State, whereas the lives and ambitions of the Many are private. The Many do their day's work well, and so far from copying even the wisest of their neighbours affect 'a singularity' in action and in thought; but set them to the work of the State and every man Jack is 'listed in a party', becomes the fanatical follower of men of whose characters he knows next to nothing, and from that day on puts nothing into his mouth that some other man has not already chewed and digested. And furthermore, from the moment of enlistment thinks himself above other men and struggles for power until all is in confusion. I divine an Irish hatred of abstraction likewise expressed by that fable of Gulliver among the inventors and men of science, by Berkeley in his *Commonplace Book*, by Goldsmith in the satire of *The Good-Natured Man*, in the picturesque, minute observation of *The Deserted Village*, and by Burke in his attack upon mathematical democracy. Swift enforced his moral by proving that Rome and Greece were destroyed by the war of the Many upon the Few; in Rome, where the Few had kept their class organisation, it was a war of classes, in Greece, where they had not, war upon character and genius. Miltiades, Aristides, Themistocles, Pericles, Alcibiades, Phocion, 'impeached for high crimes and misdemeanours . . . were honoured and lamented by their country as the preservers of it, and have had the veneration of all ages since paid justly to their memories.' In Rome parties so developed that men born and bred among the Few were compelled to join one party or the other and to flatter and bribe. All civilisations must end in some such way, for the Many obsessed by emotion create a multitude of religious sects but give themselves at last to some one master of bribes and flatteries and sink into the ignoble tranquility of servitude. He defines a tyranny as the predominance of the One, the Few, or the Many, but thinks that of the Many the immediate threat. All States at their outset possess a ruling power seated in the whole body as that of the soul in the human body, a perfect balance of the three estates, the king some sort of chief magistrate, and then comes 'a tyranny: first either of the Few or the Many; but at last infallibly of a single person.' He thinks the English balance most perfect in the time of Queen Elizabeth, but that in the next age a tyranny of the Many produced that of Cromwell, and that, though recovery followed, 'all forms of government must be mortal like their authors,' and he quotes from Polybius, 'those abuses and corruptions, which in time destroy a government, are sown along with the very seeds of it' and destroy it 'as rust eats away iron, and worms devour wood.' Whether the final tyranny is created by the Many – in his eyes all Caesars were tyrants – or imposed by foreign power, the result is the same. At the fall of liberty came 'a dark insipid period through all Greece' – had he Ireland in his mind also? – and the people became, in the words of Polybius, 'great reverencers of crowned heads.' (*W&B* 14–17; *VPl* 960–2)

saeva indignatio . . . *the greatest epitaph in history*: Swift's Latin epitaph in St Patrick's Cathedral reads as follows:

> *Hic* depositum est Corpus
> IONATHAN SWIFT S.T.D.
> Hujus Ecclesiæ Cathedralis
> Decani,
> *Ubi* saeva Indignatio
> Ulterius
> Cor lacerare nequit.
> Abi Viator
> Et imitare, si poteris,
> Strenuum pro virili
> Libertatis Vindicatorem
> Obiit 19° Die Mensis Octobris
> A.D. 1745 Anno Aetatis 78.

See J. V. Luce, 'A note on the composition of Swift's epitaph', *Hermathena*, CIV, spring 1967, 78–81. Yeats drafted his version of this at Coole in 1929, and completed it in September 1930. It is entitled 'Swift's Epitaph' (*CP* 277) and runs:

> Swift has sailed into his rest;
> Savage indignation there
> Cannot lacerate his breast.
> Imitate him if you dare,
> World-besotted traveller; he
> Served human liberty.

He has gone where fierce indignation can lacerate his heart no more: this is presumably meant to be Corbet's rendering of the Latin. Yeats's poem compresses and intensifies the Latin more.

Moody and Sankey: Dwight Lyman Moody (1837–99) and Ira David Sankey (1840–1908) were American Evangelists. Sankey was responsible for the compilation of the well-known *Sacred Songs and Solos* associated with their names.

603   *we treat them as our guests and protect them from discourtesy and violence, and every exorcism is a curse or a threatened curse*: Dr Trench rebukes the Rev. Johnson for a lack of courtesy to the spirits, and the difference between the two men perhaps echoes a Yeatsian view of the differences between north and south. Mr Johnson (**602**, lines 16–17) stresses the expense he has incurred in coming from Belfast; he is not getting value for his expenditure. The polarity of Belfast and Dublin is being quietly affirmed.

604   *Some spirits are earth-bound – they think they are still living and go over and over some action of their past lives*: the third book of *A Vision*, entitled 'The Soul in Judgment' deals with the question of the soul after death. See *AV*(A) 219–40. See quotations from this book on pp. 282–6.

Sometimes a spirit re-lives not the pain of death but some passionate or tragic moment of life. Swedenborg describes this and gives the reason for it: Yeats wrote in *A Vision*:

> The more complete the *Dreaming Back* the more complete the *Return* and the more happy or fortunate the next incarnation. (*AV*(B) 227)

and he added this footnote:

> Compare the account of the *Dreaming Back* in Swedenborg's *Heaven and Hell*. My account differs from his mainly because he denied or ignored rebirth. Sombody has suggested that he kept silent deliberately, that it was amongst those subjects that he thought forbidden. It is more likely that his instructors were silent. They spoke to the Christian Churches, explaining the 'linen clothes folded up', and even what they said or

sought to say was half-transformed into an opium dream by the faith of those Churches in the literal inspiration of the Bible. (*AV*(B) note 3, 227–8)

For Swedenborg see note on **599**.
There is an incident . . . in the Odyssey: A Vision clarifies this:

In the *Dreaming Back*, the *Spirit* is compelled to live over and over again the events that had most moved it; there can be nothing new, but the old events stand forth in a light which is dim or bright according to the intensity of the passion that accompanied them. They occur in the order of their intensity or luminosity, the more intense first, and the painful are commonly the more intense, and repeat themselves again and again. In the *Return*, upon the other hand, the *Spirit* must live through past events in the order of their occurrence, because it is compelled by the Celestial body to trace every passionate event to its cause until all are related and understood, turned into knowledge, made a part of itself. All that keeps the *Spirit* from its freedom may be compared to a knot that has to be untied or to an oscillation or a violence that must end in a return to equilibrium. I think of the Homeric contrast between Heracles passing through the night, bow in hand, and Heracles, the freed spirit, a happy god among the gods. I think of it in William Morris' translation:

> And Heracles the mighty I saw when these went by;
> His image indeed: for himself mid the gods that never die
> Sits glad at the feast, and Hebe fair-ankled there doth hold,
> The daughter of Zeus the mighty and Hera shod with gold.

After its imprisonment by some event in the *Dreaming Back*, the *Spirit* relives that event in the *Return* and turns it into knowledge, and then falls into the *Dreaming Back* once more. (*AV*(B) 226) See also notes on *The Dreaming of the Bones*, pp. 153–5 and 160.

requiescat in pace: R.I.P. May he/she rest in peace.

I feel like Job . . . you know the quotation: Job IV, 13–15   **605**
In thoughts form the visions of the night when deep sleep falleth upon men, fear came upon me, and trembling which made all my bones to shake. Then a spirit passed before my face; the hair of my flesh stood up.

606 *SD Hymn 564*: this is by John Keble (1792–1866), the English
churchman, who became a Fellow of Oriel College, Oxford in 1811.
He published *The Christian Year* in 1827, and developed a theory of
poetry when Professor of Poetry at Oxford (1831–41). In his circle
originated the Tractarian movement. Keble's sermon on National
Apostasy of 1833 began this, and the ninetieth in the series of
Tracts for the Times was published in 1941. Keble married in 1835
and spent the rest of his life in a living in Hampshire. The text of
the hymn, another verse of which is sung subsequently at lines 19–
22, follows. It is taken from the *Irish Church Hymnal*, 1960, in which
it is Hymn 28. This version dispenses with capitals for Thou, Thy,
Thine, etc. and has revised punctuation:

> Sun of my soul, thou Saviour dear,
> It is not night if thou be near;
> O may no earth-born cloud arise
> To hide thee from thy servant's eyes.
>
> When the soft dews of kindly sleep
> My wearied eyelids gently steep,
> Be my last thought, how sweet to rest
> For ever on my Saviour's breast.
>
> Abide with me from morn till eve,
> For without thee I cannot live;
> Abide with me when night is nigh,
> For without thee I dare not die.
>
> If some poor wandering child of thine
> Have spurned today the voice divine,
> Now, Lord, the gracious work begin;
> Let him no more lie down in sin.
>
> Watch by the sick: enrich the poor
> With blessings from thy boundless store;
> Be every mourner's sleep tonight,
> Like infants' slumbers, pure and light.
>
> Come near and bless us when we wake,
> Ere through the world our way we take;
> Till in the ocean of thy love
> We lose ourselves in heaven above.

The Lord Treasurer: Robert Harley, first Earl of Oxford (1661–   **608**
1724). See note on **601**, *Bolingbroke, Harley* . . .

Plutarch: (*c*. A.D. 46–120) Greek biographer who wrote lives of
twenty-three Greeks and twenty-three Romans.

Hester Vanhomrigh: see note on **599**, *Vanessa*.   **609**

Cato or Brutus: see notes on **602**.

her: Stella. See note on **599**, *Stella*.

I had sworn never to marry: Swift was attracted to several women
in his life. His flirtations with Betty Jones in Leicestershire in 1691,
probably led him to the remarks on marriage made a few months
later when he was at Moor Park:

> the very ordinary observations I made with going half a mile
> beyond the University, have taught me experience enough not
> to think of marriage till I settle my fortune in the world, which
> I am sure will not be in some years; and even then I am so
> hard to please that I suppose I shall put it off to the other
> world.

Again, in his infatuation for Varina (Jane Waring) in about 1696
he lived up to the description he gave of himself:

'. . . a thousand household thoughts, which always drive matrimony
out of my mind whenever it chances to come there, will, I am sure,
fright me from that' (*The Correspondence of Jonathan Swift*, ed. F.
Elrington Ball, 6 vols, 1910–14, I, 6, 18–19).

In his list headed 'When I come to be old 1689 –' he began the list
with 'Not to marry a young woman'. Yeats, however, makes
Swift's rejection of Vanessa part of his dislike of the coming age:

> . . . the intellect of Swift's age, persuaded that the mechani-
> cians mocked by Gulliver would prevail, that its moment of
> freedom could not last, so dreaded the historic process that it
> became in the half-mad mind of Swift a dread of parentage:
> 'Am I to add another to the healthy rascaldom and knavery of
> the world?' (*W&B* 30; *VPl* 967)

His primary suggestion, however, is that Swift was afraid of
madness:

> 'I have something in my blood that no child must inherit.'
> There have been several theories to account for Swift's

celibacy. Sir Walter Scott suggested a 'physical defect', but that seems incredible. A man so outspoken would have told Vanessa the truth and stopped a tragic persecution, a man so charitable have given Stella the protection of his name. The refusal to see Stella when there was no third person present suggests a man that dreaded temptation; nor is it compatible with those stories still current among our country people of Swift sending his servant out to fetch a woman, and dismissing that servant when he woke to find a black woman at his side. Lecky suggested dread of madness – the theory of my play – of madness already present in constant eccentricity; though, with a vagueness born from distaste of the theme, he saw nothing incompatible between Scott's theory and his own. Had Swift dreaded transmitting madness he might well have been driven to consorting with the nameless barren women of the streets. Somebody else suggests syphilis contracted doubtless between 1799 when he was engaged to Varina and some date soon after Stella's arrival in Ireland. Mr. Shane Leslie thinks that Swift's relation to Vanessa was not platonic, and that whenever his letters speak of a cup of coffee they mean the sexual act; whether the letters seem to bear him out I do not know, for those letters bore me; but whether they seem to or not he must, if he is to get a hearing, account for Swift's relation to Stella. It seems certain that Swift loved her though he called it by some other name, and she him, and that it was platonic love.

> Thou, Stella, wert no longer young,
> When first for thee my harp was strung,
> Without one word of Cupid's darts,
> Of killing eyes or bleeding hearts;
> With friendship and esteem possest,
> I ne'er admitted Love a guest.
> In all the habitudes of life,
> The friend, the mistress, and the wife,
> Variety we still pursue,
> In pleasure seek for something new;
> Or else comparing with the rest,
> Take comfort that our own is best;
> The best we value by the worst,
> As tradesmen show their trash at first;
> But his pursuits are at an end,
> Whom Stella chooses for a friend.

If the relation between Swift and Vanessa was not platonic there must have been some bar that affected Stella as well as Swift. Dr. Delaney is said to have believed that Swift married Stella in 1716 and found in some exchange of confidences that they were brother and sister, but Sir William Temple was not in Ireland during the year that preceded Swift's birth, and so far as we know Swift's mother was not in England.

There is no satisfactory solution. Swift, though he lived in great publicity, and wrote and received many letters, hid two things which constituted perhaps all that he had of private life: his loves and his religious beliefs. (*W&B* 26–9; *VPl* 965–6)

You came to my mother's house and began to teach me: Swift thought he first met Vanessa in 1708. Mrs Vanhomrigh brought her family to London from Dublin in December 1707 and they met Swift (en route to London from Leicester) at Dunstable.

I followed you to Ireland five years ago: this sets the conversation in 1719; Swift returned to Ireland in May 1714 to be installed as Dean of St Patrick's. He had warned Vanessa that if she was in Ireland 'while I am there I shall see you very seldom.' She arrived in the autumn of 1714 and took up residence at Kildrogest (now Celbridge) in a house she had inherited from her father. This was about eleven miles from Dublin, on the Liffey.

constant attacks of dizziness: see T. G. Wilson, 'Swift's Personality and Death Masks', *A Review of English Literature*, July 1962, 40–1:

It is now well-established that Swift suffered from his youth onwards from bilateral Ménière's disease, a most distressing complaint in which the patient suffers from periodic and some-times completely incapacitating attacks of giddiness and vomiting, accompanied by head-noises and increasing deaf-ness. Ménière's disease is caused by a disorder of the internal ear or labyrinth and there is every excuse for the earlier writers who failed to recognise it, for Ménière's disease was not described as an affection of the ear until 1861. Giddiness, deaf-ness and vomiting are apparently unrelated symptoms, and in the state of knowledge of the time there was no obvious reason to connect them with a single disease of the internal ear. Nevertheless, although Wilde [Sir William Wilde, a Dublin oculist, Oscar Wilde's father, who wrote *The Closing Years of Dean Swift's Life*, 1849] and the physicians of the middle of the nineteenth century thought Swift's symptoms were of separate origin, the doctors of the previous century realised that they were related symptoms. Since Wilde's time Swift's letters to Charles Ford have come to light. In his letter of 20th November 1733 he says: 'And although in the London Dispensatory approved by the Physicians there are Remedyes named both for Giddyness and deafness, none of them that I can find, were prescribed to me ... The Doctors here think that both these Aylments in me are united in their Causes, but they were not always so; for one has often left me when the other stayed.'

It is likely Swift first suffered from Ménière's disease in his early twenties, but there are many references to its effects throughout his life. A letter of 31 October 1710 to Stella complains of 'a fit of giddiness; the room turned round for about a minute, and then it went off, leaving me sickish but not very.' In 1724 he complained of being 'pestered with a return of the noise and deafness in my ears' and in a letter to Charles Ford of 9 October 1733 he wrote of his being 'some months in a bad dispirited way with Deafness, and Giddyness, and Fluxes.' He had been confined to the house for a month by the two former ailments. In 1737 he was ill in bed, giddy and deaf, but he dictated a reply to an address of gratitude and support with 'all the dignity of habitual pre-eminence and all the resignation of humble piety.'

surfeit of fruit: Swift traced his giddiness and 'coldness of stomach' to eating too many apples:

I got my giddiness by eating a hundred golden pippins at a time at Richmond ... four and a quarter years (later) having made a fine seat about twenty miles farther in Surrey (Moor Park, Sir William Temple's residence), where I used to read and sleep, there I got my deafness. (*Correspondence*, ed. Ball, III, 413–14)

Dr. Arbuthnot: John Arbuthnot (1667–1735), Queen Anne's doctor, a friend of Swift and Pope, and a member of the Scriblerus Club.

610   *a line of Dryden's*: 'great wits are sure to madness/Near allied' from Dryden's *Absalom and Achitophel*, I, 163.

healthy rascaldom and knavery: see quotation from *W&B* 30, in note on **609**, p. 237.

'*If some poor wandering child . . . no more lie down in sin.*': another   **611**
verse from Hymn 564 in the Irish Church Hymnal. See **606**.

my last birthday: 30 November 1721.   **612**
'*with no endowments but a face —*': this line immediately precedes
the next lines (23–4): 'Before the thirtieth year of life/A maid
forlorn or hated wife'. In 'Stella to Dr. Swift', quoted in note on
600, p. 223, T. G. Wilson comments that Swift constantly draws
attention to the changes wrought by time in her appearance:

> . . . but never fails to praise her qualities of mind and heart:

> > Stella this day is thirty-four
> > (We shan't dispute a year or more);
> > However, Stella, be not troubled.
> > Although thy size and years are doubled
> > Since first I saw thee at sixteen,
> > The brightest virgin on the green;
> > So little is thy form declined;
> > Made up so largely in thy mind.

In the verses for 1721 he wrote:

> Now, this is Stella's case in fact,
> An angel's face a little crack'd,
> Could poets or could painters fix
> How angels look at thirty-six:
> This drew us in at first to find
> In such a form an angel's mind;
> An every virtue now supplies
> The fainting rays of Stella's eyes.

Quite why he dwells so insistently on her physical deterioration is hard to understand; possibly it is to console her for the
obvious ravages of phthisis from which she suffered, like
Vanessa and so many of Swift's other women friends. She
herself refers to this change in her appearance in her poem,
St. Patrick's Dean, Your Country's Pride. In any case, raillery
of some sort is necessary in verses of this kind to prevent
them from becoming too extravagantly sentimental. Swift
also repeatedly reminds her that he too is growing old. Here
is what he says about Stella as a nurse:

> When on my sickly couch I lay
> Impatient both of night and day,
> Lamenting in unmanly strains,
> Call'd every power to ease my pains;
> Then Stella ran to my relief
> With cheerful face and inward grief,
> And, though by Heaven's severe decree
> She suffers hourly more than me,
> No cruel master could require
> From slaves employed for daily hire,
> What Stella, by her friendship warm'd
> With vigour and delight perform'd:
> My sinking spirits now supplies
> With cordials in her hands and eyes:
> Now with a soft and silent tread
> Unheard she moves about my bed
> I see her taste each nauseous draught,
> And so obligingly am caught;
> I bless the hand from whence they came
> Nor dare distort my face for shame.

If further proof of Swift's devotion is required, one only has to read his essay *On the Death of Mrs. Johnson*, written just after she died, a tribute charged with emotion in every line. ('Swift's Personality', *REL* 52–3).

Yeats also comments that Swift prayed to Stella when she was ill that 'all violent desire whether of life or death' be taken from her. (*W&B* 25)

Chrysostom: St John (*c*. A.D. 345–407), an eloquent (Chrysostom = golden-mouthed) Greek Father of the Church, who wrote commentaries on the Gospel of St Matthew and the Epistles to the Romans and Corinthians.

611   '*If some poor wandering child*': see note on **606,** p. 236.

613   '*You taught how I might youth prolong . . . Can spread a smoothness o'er the skin.*': a quotation from Stella's poem 'Stella to Dr. Swift', quoted in note on **600,** p. 223.

'*Late dying may you cast a shred . . . One day alone, then die to-morrow.*': another quotation from Stella's poem 'Stella to Dr. Swift', quoted in note on **600,** p. 223.

you will close my eyes: Stella died in 1728 in her late forties. She had nursed him when he was ill and he could hardly have expected her to die seventeen years before him. Stella was eight years old when Swift, then about twenty, first met her.

the explanations of Swift's celibacy offered by his biographers: see   **615** quotation from *W&B* 26–9, quoted in note on **609**, p. 237.

Was Swift mad?: probably not. See T. G. Wilson, 'Swift's Personality':

> The popular idea that Swift was mad seems to originate from biographies written by Dr. Johnson and Sir Walter Scott. Both these *Lives* contain phrases such as 'madness . . . compounded of rage and fatuity' and 'Frantic fits of passion' – but neither bring forward any real evidence to show that Swift's mind was diseased. The idea may have arisen in the first instance from Swift's habit of referring to his attacks of giddiness, deafness and sickness as 'fitts', 'fitts of deafness', 'a small giddy fitt and swimming in head'. This constant talk of 'fitts' also led to the theory being put forward that he suffered from epilepsy, but Swift was not an epileptic. It is quite obvious from reading his journals that he used the word 'fit' when we would say 'attack'.
>
> Swift was therefore a life-long sufferer from Ménière's disease, and he was not insane. But he was undoubtedly a psychopath. His constant references to the bodily excreta amount to a pathological obsession. Dr. Johnson wrote:
>
> > The greatest difficulty that occurs, in analysing his character, is to discover by what depravity of intellect he took delight in revolving ideas, from which almost every other mind shrinks with disgust. The ideas of pleasure, even when criminal, may solicit the imagination, but what has disease, deformity, and filth, upon which the mind can be allured to dwell?
>
> The answer, of course, is that Swift like John Donne, Charles Dickens and Johnson himself was an obsessional, and this was the form his obsession took. (*REL* 42)

his face covered with boils. Some disease had made one of his eyes swell up: **616** this comment on the swollen eye may have been suggested by Wilde.

Sir Walter Scott commented on the death-mask of Swift in Trinity College, Dublin. (This is now known as the first Trinity Death-mask, see T. G. Wilson's article cited above, p. 243).

> It is an impression taken from the mask applied to the face after death. The expression of countenance is most unequivocally maniacal and one side of the mouth (the left) horribly contorted downwards as if convulsed by pain.

Wilson comments:

> This is, of course, complete nonsense. The mask shows absolutely no trace of a maniacal expression, and one must conclude that Sir Walter Scott, in describing it, was rather unworthily allowing his powers of artistic expression to get the better of him. Wilde did not agree with Scott about this, for he says: 'Sir Walter has greatly exaggerated the amount of contortion which the face exhibits; on the contrary, the expression is remarkably placid, but (he goes on to say) there is an evident drag in the left side of the mouth, exhibiting a paralysis of the facial muscles of the right side . . .'
> Here one must disagree with Wilde also, for the lack of symmetry between the two sides of the mouth is clearly caused by the fact that the lower jaw had slipped to the left-hand side when the mould was taken. Wilde also thought that, 'the left eye was much less full and prominent than the right: in fact' he says, 'it is comparatively sunken and collapsed within the orbit'. He related this to the attack of orbital cellulitis from which Swift was said to have suffered some years previously. Wilde was usually a meticulously accurate observer, but once more we must contradict him, for the simple reason that this alleged sinking and collapse of the eye does not exist, as anyone can see from looking at the cast. (*REL* 62–3)

the man appointed to take care of him beat him : this may derive from Swift's own ironic 'Verses on the Death of Dr. Swift, written by Himself : November 1731'.

> He gave the little wealth he had
> To build a house for fools and mad.

Wilson comments aptly:

> As he grew older his mind turned again and again to a matter which had interested him in his younger days. Wandering through the Liberties of St. Patrick's he must have seen many of the mentally afflicted roaming the streets, accepted by the

common man as part of the social order of the day. To Swift their plight was a challenge. He worked and saved for fifteen years to establish a hospital for their care. That hospital still flourishes, still largely governed by the enlightened constitution which he devised. It is a sad postscript that so many people should still believe that he founded his hospital because he was afraid that he himself might become insane, and that he died as one of its inmates.

This, of course, is far from the truth. He died in his Deanery, of that saddest of diseases, senile decay. About the year 1741 or 1742 when he was about seventy-five years of age he began to lose his memory and to act irrationally, and it was evident to those about him that his brain had failed, and that he had lapsed into a state of

> Second childishness and mere oblivion
>
> Sans teeth, sans eyes, sans taste, sans everything.

He was, in fact, suffering from the disease which Dr. Oliver Gogarty somewhat cynically described as 'delayed burial'. He remained in this pathetic condition for three years before he died. (*REL* 57–8)

Perish the day on which I was born: from Job III, 3: 'Let the day perish wherein I was born.'

A Full Moon in March

The play was first printed in *Poetry* (Chicago), March 1935, and subsequently in *A Full Moon in March*, London, 1935; *The Herne's Egg and Other Plays*, New York, 1938; *The Collected Plays of W. B. Yeats*, London, 1952; New York, 1953 (repr. London, 1953, 1960, 1963, 1966); *Selected Plays*, Papermac edition, ed. A. Norman Jeffares, London, 1964; *Eleven Plays of William Butler Yeats*, ed. A. Norman Jeffares, New York, 1964.

Although this play is placed before *The King of the Great Clock Tower* in *CPl*, it was in fact written after it and is a development of it. 'In *The King of the Great Clock Tower*', wrote Yeats, 'there are three characters, King, Queen and Stroller, and that is a character too many; reduced to essentials, to Queen and Stroller, the fable should have greater intensity. I started afresh and called the new version *A Full Moon in March*.' (Preface, *FMM*) In a letter to Edmund Dulac Yeats refers to its 'blood-symbolism' (*L* 830), and in another to Dorothy Wellesley (*L* 843) he expressed his dislike of it – 'a fragment of the past I had to get rid of.'

As is to be expected interpretations of it have generally followed the lines of those laid down for *The King of the Great Clock Tower*. Nathan (*TD* 195) writes: 'the Queen, now an active agent, is clearly defined as a virgin goddess, cruel and beautiful, needing human love to achieve her full identity, needing, in fact, all that is opposite to her virgin beauty. Thus the Stroller becomes a filthy arrogant swineherd, whose sacrifice "fertilizes" the Queen's barren virginity so that it can achieve fulfilment at the full moon in March.' Vendler (*YV* 153) sees it in terms of 'the meeting of Muse and poet . . . in a vacuum, uninfluenced by time and the rational world, since this is a Queen without a King . . . The Stroller . . . has become a Swineherd, the ultimate symbol of the "mire and blood" of human veins, and of all that "desecrates" the Muse. The necessity of that desecration . . . is the theme of the play.' Bloom (*Y* 341) sees it as 'a final fable of the moon-like Muse and the self-sacrificing poet' in which a sadistic female will is victorious. Henn's comments (*LT* 270) in the same vein on *The King of the Great Clock Tower* also apply to this play, and Newton, in *Essays in Criticism*, VIII, 1958, points out that the sex-antagonism in the play, if presented in terms of Strindbergian naturalism, would be 'unbearably repellent and frightening.' Whitaker (*S&S* 291) by relating it to concepts drawn from Kabbalistic and alchemical doctrine expands what is in essence a ritualised projection of a psychic and aesthetic process: 'the dialogue of the stroller with his opposite, or the poet with the matrix of history which produces him, lures him onwards, brings him suffering and delight, and offers him the chance of a lifelong creative death.' Wilson (*Y&T* ch. 2) sees it as 'a simple account of the Saviour-God myth', but also makes room for an interpretation of the Platonic theory of the fusion of opposites in which the Queen is '"unmixed spirituality" as distinct from that energy whose symbol in Yeats is the sun. But she in her cold passivity had been as imperfect as the Swineherd in his brutal oblivion of her divine nature; heaven is no heaven until it has been fertilized by its opposite, the energy which is the property of time . . .' The Queen's coldness and cruelty 'is the mark that Godhead itself is imperfect when divorced from the spirit which has gone out into matter: heaven is incomplete in its separation from man, the timeless in its separation from the world of time.' Rajan's succinct comment is that it is a sexual, aesthetic and metaphysical parable, in which sacrifice is an essential part of love. For Moore (*MLD* 268), 'everything [in the play] is mythical; nothing historical or "real".' The Queen, in so far as she is pure soul is a complete opposite of the Swineherd, in so far as he is pure body. But their purity is their common factor. 'Body and Soul must equally be bruised to pleasure each other. Perfection, especially that bodiless perfection of the fifteenth phase whose emblem is the moon, *does* lack something – "desecration and the lover's night". Love is both a giving and a possessing. To sacrifice all is to gain all' (270). The play therefore 'dramatizes two attractions – raising the low through the power of the ideal to immortality and pulling the high down into the mortal but reproductive world of nature' (272).

621   *Title:*

A Full Moon in March: the full moon in Yeats's system is associated with Phase 15, a phase of complete beauty, where unity of being is achieved, and March with the moment at which one cycle ends or dies and another begins or is created.

'*Sing anything*': the introduction has not only been reduced to a bare minimum, but is in a sense irrelevant: the Attendants can sing anything they like since whatever is anticipated is bound to happen.

622   *Pythagoras*: the Greek philosopher of the sixth century who thought the universe had a mathematical basis. He believed in the Orphic doctrine of metempsychosis, the purificatory or punishing process in which souls transmigrated from man to man, or man to animal or animal to man. Pythagoras and every loutish lad are antithetical opposites. Perfected love, the interpenetration of opposites, makes the lout wise and the philosopher foolish. Pythagoras as the opposite of loutishness is established by 'Among School Children' (*CP* 242):

> Plato thought nature but a spume that plays
> Upon a ghostly paradigm of things;
> Solider Aristotle played the taws
> Upon the bottom of a king of kings;
> World-famous golden-thighed Pythagoras
> Fingered upon a fiddle-stick or strings
> What a star sang and careless Muses heard:
> Old clothes upon old sticks to scare a bird.

Yeats wrote to Mrs Shakespear on 24 September 1926 that he was reading Croce, writing verse and hence had nothing to say:

Here is a fragment of my last curse upon old age. It means that even the greatest men are owls, scarecrows, by the time their fame has come. Aristotle, remember, was Alexander's tutor, hence the taws (form of birch).

> Plato imagined all existence plays
> Among the ghostly images of things;
> Solider Aristotle played the taws
> Upon the bottom of the King of Kings;
> World famous, golden-thighed Pythagoras
> Fingered upon a fiddle stick, or strings,
> What the stars sang and careless Muses heard –
> Old coats upon old sticks to scare a bird.

Pythagoras made some measurement of the intervals between notes on a stretched string. (*L* 719)

As for the detail 'golden-thighed', John Wain quotes a passage from Diogenes Laertius to the effect that Pythagoras did have a great personal standing and was not unaware of it:

> Indeed his bearing is said to have been most dignified, and his disciples held the opinion about him that he was Apollo come down from the far north. There is a story that once, when he disrobed, his thigh was seen to be of gold. (*Interpretations*, London, 1961, 200–1)

Comm 304 derives it from Thomas Taylor's translation of Iamblichus, *Life of Pythagoras*, 1965, p. 49:

> Pythagoras, however, receiving the dart, and neither being astonished at the novelty of the thing, nor asking the reason why it was given to him, but as if he was in reality a god himself, taking Abacis aside, he showed him his golden thigh, as an indication that he was not [wholly] deceived [in the opinion he had formed of him.]

Yeats could have met it again in Ben Jonson, whom he quotes frequently: *Volpone*, 1, i, 117, 'His musics, his trigon, his golden thigh'.

yawned and stretched: Vendler (*YV* 153) suggests that this is **622** because the Queen is awakening from her hibernation and is preparing for the kiss of union with the solar Swineherd. The phrase is also used by Yeats to suggest the lassitude that follows sexual intercourse. If this is the connotation here, it is prophetic or anticipatory of her final union with the Swineherd. The earliest versions of the play associate the phrase with sexual surrender. (See Curtis Bradford, *YW* 271–82.) Their relation is predetermined by the necessary relationship of opposites: that they should seek fulfilment in their interpenetration.

dust and mire: cf. the 'mire and blood' of 'Byzantium' (*CP* 280). **623**

625   *trembling of my limbs*: again anticipatory of **629**, *SD*, 'Her body shivers . . .'

SD   Queen leaves . . . stage: in this voluntary act the Queen descends to the world of time and thus prepares for her own desecration.

Complexities of insult: cf. 'all complexities of mire and blood', 'Byzantium' (*CP* 280, line 24).

626   *A severed head . . . child*: again anticipatory. The Queen does take the severed head in her hands, **627**, *SD*, does sink in bridal sleep, **629**, *SD*, in which she conceives a child, **628** line 4.

SD   drops her veil: the Queen, in revealing herself, invites her own desecration.

627   *An ancient Irish Queen*: the reference here and in the lyric that follows is to the legend of Aodh and Dectira which Yeats wrote about in his early story 'The Binding of the Hair', first published in *The Savoy*, 1896, and again in the 1897 edition of *TSR*. In this, Aodh, a strolling minstrel, comes to Queen Dectira's court and falls in love with her while she is binding up her hair. He kneels before her and is about to sing her his love when he is interrupted by a disturbance in the hall. The Queen's enemies have invaded her territories and in the ensuing battle he is killed. Queen Dectira goes out at dawn to search for him but finds only a head hanging from a bush by its dark hair. The head sings the lyric 'He Gives His Beloved Certain Rhymes' (*CP* 71). The references in the third stanza are to the Empress Theophano, married by Romanus 11 *c.* A.D. 956, and to Helen of Troy.

628   *Child . . . cruelty*: Vendler (*YV* 155–6) treats this as a love song in explanation of the cruelty of the previous lyric, and comments:

> The havoc wreaked by the Muse on her devotees is a proof of her love: whom she loves she chastens, since all knowledge and power arise . . . from obstruction and terror.

not from me . . . cruelty: in distinguishing her self and her cruelty the Queen does not yet see herself as a complete entity: that has to wait for the climactic dance.

Great my love before you came: either refers back to the sexual symbolism of 'yawned and stretched', or implies that the whole process of the interpenetration of Queen and Swineherd is pre-ordained in the inevitable movement of the cycles.

When I loved in shame: possibly refers back to the dropping of her veil, an act which prepares for her defilement but which is still accompanied by a sense of shame, symbolised by her standing with her back to the audience. In the final dance, her defilement, her union with the Swineherd's severed head, is frontal and shameless.

SD lays the head upon the throne: the Queen has changed places with the Swineherd. She has descended, he has ascended.

Jack . . . in the sky: now the Swineherd's heart is resurrected as a   **629**
star, on one level 'the artifact itself' (Whitaker, *S&S* 290) or, as
Vendler (*YV* 156) comments: 'the lesser ecstasy of love is sacrificed
for the greater ecstasy of art . . . To achieve song . . . experience
must be immolated. In being made into a poem, life is detached,
made into something external and public, and sacrificed on the
altar of form.'

SD She dances: 'Woman craves for, is obsessed by, the sexual act.
Her dance before the severed head ends as she takes it to her
breast . . . Woman is eternally seeking this ravishment, within her
very being; because of the "craving in her bones"'; Henn (*LT*
288), who also connects the image of the severed head with the
Second Coming, quoting *AV*(B) 273:

> When I think of the moment before revelation I think of
> Salome . . . dancing before Herod and receiving the Prophet's
> head in her indifferent hands, and wonder if what seems to us
> decadence was not in reality the exaltation of the muscular
> flesh and of civilization perfectly achieved.

An earlier MS. version (see Curtis Bradford, *YW* 288) is more
explicit:

> He laughs again. The dance expresses refusal. She takes up the
> head and lays it upon the ground. She dances before it. Her
> dance is a dance of invitation. She takes up the head and dances
> with the head to drum taps which grow quicker and quicker.
> Her dance expresses the sexual act. She kisses the head. Her

body shivers. She sinks slowly down, holding the head against her breast. Song of the closing of the curtain or the unfolding and folding of the cloth. The song at the end of 'Clock Tower' with the line 'Their desecration and the lover's night'.

emblematic niches: cf. 'Sailing to Byzantium', *CP* 217:

> O sages standing in God's holy fire
> As in the gold mosaic of a wall.

desecration and the lover's night: cf. the last stanza of 'Crazy Jane Talks with the Bishop', *CP* 294:

> A woman can be proud and stiff
> When on love intent:
> But Love has pitched his mansion in
> The place of excrement:
> For nothing can be sole or whole
> That has not been rent.

Each category must seek its opposite; purity must seek desecration; 'eternity is love with the productions of time'. Moore (*MLD* 271) comments: 'perfection without love is sterile; the human use of beauty demands its desecration.'

The King of the Great Clock Tower

The play was originally written in prose, 'that I might be forced to write lyrics for its imaginary people', published in *Life and Letters* in November 1934, and performed at the Abbey Theatre on 30 July of that year, together with *The Resurrection*. This is a verse version of it. In a letter to Olivia Shakespear, Yeats wrote:

> My two plays [the prose version of *KGCT* and *The Resurrection*] . . . both deal with that moment – the slain God, the risen God. I think I read you and Dorothy *The King of the Great Clock Tower*. It has proved most effective – it was magnificently acted and danced. It is more original than I thought it, for when I looked up *Salome* I found that Wilde's dancer never danced with the head in her hands – her dance came before the decapitation of the saint and is a mere uncovering of nakedness. My dance is a long expression of horror and fascination. She first bows before the head (it is on a seat) then in her dance lays it on the ground and dances before it, then holds it in her hands. Send the enclosed cutting [from the *Sunday Times*] to show to Ezra Pound that I may confound him. He may have been right to condemn it as poetry but he condemned it as drama. (*L* 826–7)

Yeats himself called this prose version 'theatrically coherent, spiritually incoherent'; Pound had dismissed it in one word – 'putrid'.

On the change to verse he wrote in the Preface to *A Full Moon in March*, 1935:

> A friend I had asked to read *The Resurrection* . . . sought me out at the fall of the curtain full of enthusiasm, but said 'When I tried to read it I was so bored that I could not get beyond the second page'. I came to the conclusion that prose dialogue is as unpopular among my studious friends as dialogue in verse

among actors and playgoers. I have therefore rewritten *The King of the Great Clock Tower* in verse, but if anyone is inclined to play it, I recommend the prose version published by the Cuala Press last October . . .

The prose version is reprinted in *VPl.*

In the course of his Commentary on 'The Great Clock Tower' in the 1934 edition of the play, published by the Cuala Press, Yeats explained that he had given up the fight to combine words and music and

began writing little dance plays, founded upon a Japanese model, that need no scenery, no properties, and can be performed in studio or drawingroom, thinking that some group of students might make a little money playing them and gradually elaborate a technique that would respect literature and music alike. Whenever I produced one of these plays I asked my singers for no new method, did not even talk to them upon the subject. When The Abbey School of Ballet was founded I tried these plays upon the stage where they seemed out of place. Why should musician or actor fold and unfold a cloth when the proscenium curtain was there, why carry on to the stage drum, gong, and flute when the orchestra was there. *Fighting the Waves* and the present play so far imitate the Japanese model that they climax in a dance, substitute suggestion for representation, but like the Japanese plays themselves they are stage plays.

The orchestra brings more elaborate music and I have gone over to the enemy. I say to the musician 'Lose my words in patterns of sound as the name of God is lost in Arabian arabesques. They are a secret between the singers, myself, yourself. The plain fable, the plain prose of the dialogue, Ninette de Valois' dance are there for the audience. They can find my words in the book if they are curious, but we will not thrust our secret upon them. I can be as subtle and metaphysical as I like without endangering the clarity necessary for dramatic effect. The Elizabethan singer, according to Edmund Spenser, and his music was simpler than yours, read out his song before he sang it. We will adopt no such arbitrary practice; our secret is our religion.'

The dance with the severed head, suggests the central idea of Wilde's *Salome*. Wilde took it from Heine who has somewhere described Salome in hell throwing into the air the head of John the Baptist. Heine may have found it in some Jewish religious legend for it is part of the old ritual of the year; the mother goddess and the slain god. In the first edition of *The Secret Rose* there is a story based on some old Gaelic legend. A certain man swears to sing the praise of a certain woman, his head is cut off and the head sings. A poem of mine called 'He Gives His Beloved Certain Rhymes' [*CP* 71, see *Comm* 67] was the song of the head. In attempting to put that story into a dance play I found that I had gone close to Salome's dance in Wilde's play. But in his play the dance is before the head is cut off.

The Commentary ends with what is now the First Attendant's song in *FMM*, **627**. The story that Yeats refers to is 'The Binding of the Hair', published in the 1897 edition of *TSR*, in which the 'certain man' is a strolling minstrel, Aodh, and the 'certain woman', Queen Dectira.

As a play *The King of the Great Clock Tower* retains the characteristic features of Yeatsian Noh drama – the choric attendants, masks, climactic dance, and binding metaphors – and it moves even closer towards abstraction in that its characters seem more like participants in a rite than living personages. Interpretations are not lacking. Nathan (*TD* 194) sees it in terms of the completion of being: the Queen, a supernatural figure, needs to complete her being by uniting with her opposite, the Stroller. The moment of this union is midnight, at the height of the subjective phase. The place in which the dead and living kiss is the spiritual reality of being.

Whitaker (*S&S* 284) widens this theme: 'The matrix of history, she [the Queen] descends from her absolute realm to enter a slaying and fructifying union with the temporal – with the hero, poet or other manifestation of the solar cycle, who must die to create. At full moon in March, when all cycles begin, the new creation is born from the death of the old.' Kermode and Vendler, with the support of Bloom, who also links the Queen with Yeats's image of Maud Gonne, both interpret it in aesthetic terms. Kermode (*RI* 81) sees the Stroller as artist, the *poète maudit*, and the Queen as image, out of time, deathless, and having nothing to do with intellect. Vendler's account (*YV* 145) of the Queen is as follows:

It is clear from the description of Phase 14 given in *A Vision* ... that the Queen in *The King of the Great Clock Tower* and *A Full Moon in March* belongs to that phase of aloof beauty. As I have shown earlier, a beautiful and remote woman is Yeats's pre-eminent symbol of the poetic image – and consequently is also the symbol of the Muse. One distinction must be made here between Phase 14 and Phase 15. In Phase 14 the Image is considered as the thing-in-itself, unobserved, self-sufficient, like Helen in the poem, 'Long-Legged Fly'. In Phase 15 the Image is considered as something absorbed into the poetic consciousness – the Image has struck the poet, impinged on him, and can therefore be called the Muse. In both *The King of the Great Clock Tower* and *A Full Moon in March* the Queen is first an aloof and solitary object of worship, the remote subject of the poet's song, the Image; but during the dance and the kiss, she unites with the poet, causes him to sing through her inspiration, and at this point may rightly be named the Muse.'

The basis of Wilson's interpretation is that the play is a 'reconstruction of the Platonic myth of the relation between spirit and matter' (*Y&T* 72), in which the 'Stroller symbolises spirit in its fallen condition, after the descent into matter, but spirit which is nevertheless in love with the idea of Heaven, [symbolised by the Queen].' (*Y&T* 70–1) He gives this myth an Irish setting, extends it by associating the Stroller as Victim-God with the Attis-Dionysus figure, and the King and Queen with Zeus and Cybele, the masculine and feminine principles in deity. Moore (*MLD* 275–6) argues, however, that Yeats 'deliberately pared away such associations in order to get at something more immediate and more primitive', which he associates with the archetypal Freudian 'family romance', in which 'the Stroller can be imagined as a long lost son who challenges the dominance of the father, overcomes the intuitive repugnance of the mother, and effects an unspeakable union, only to pay the price of emasculation and transformation into a spirit'. He admits, however, that such a reading distorts Yeats's theme and 'is too reductive to do justice to his sense of the power of the imagination to conceive immortality.' Henn combines the mythic, the human and the aesthetic approaches in his succinct view: 'The symbolism is plain. It is that of the Mother-Goddess and the Slain God, the ultimate victory of man over perverse, even, vicious woman, obsessed with her "virgin cruelty", the poet triumphant after death through his magical and enduring art.' (*LT* 286)

The cast in the first performance at the Abbey Theatre on 30 July 1934 was as follows: The King, F. J. McCormick; The Queen,

Ninette de Valois; The Stranger, Denis O'Dea; 1st Musician, Robert Irwin; 2nd Musician, Joseph O'Neill.

The play was first printed in *A Full Moon in March*, London, 1935, and subsequently in *The Herne's Egg and Other Plays*, New York, 1938; *The Collected Plays of W. B. Yeats*, London, 1952; New York, 1953 (repr. London, 1953, 1960, 1963, 1966).

Tir-nan-oge: the Land of the Young, the Celtic Paradise, timeless.   **633**
There every lover . . . wound: for perfect love as the timeless interpenetration of opposites see 'Chosen', *CP* 311:

> If questioned on
> My utmost pleasure with a man
> By some new-married bride, I take
> That stillness for a theme
> Where his heart my heart did seem
> And both adrift on the miraculous stream
> Where – wrote a learned astrologer –
> The Zodiac is changed into a sphere.

Yeats's explanation of the Thirteenth Cycle or Thirteenth Cone runs as follows:

It is that cycle which may deliver us from the twelve cycles of time and space. The cone which intersects ours is a cone in so far as we think of it as the antithesis to our thesis, but if the time has come for our deliverance it is the phaseless sphere, sometimes called the Thirteenth Sphere, for every lesser cycle contains within itself a sphere that is, as it were, the reflection or messenger of the final deliverance. Within it live all souls that have been set free and every *Daimon* and *Ghostly Self*; our expanding cone seems to cut through its gyre; spiritual influx is from its circumference, animate life from its centre. 'Eternity also', says Hermes in the Aeslepius dialogue, 'though motionless itself, appears to be in motion.' When Shelley's Demogorgon – eternity – comes from the centre of the earth it may so come because Shelley substituted the earth for such a sphere.*
(*AV* (B) 210–11).

He also commented on it as follows:

* Shelley, who had more philosophy than men thought when I was young, probably knew that Parmenides represented reality as a motionless sphere. Mrs Shelley speaks of the 'mystic meanings' of *Prometheus Unbound* as only intelligible to a 'mind as subtle as his own'.

The *Thirteenth Cone* is a sphere because sufficient to itself; but as seen by Man it is a cone. It becomes even conscious of itself as so seen, like some great dancer, the perfect flower of modern culture, dancing some primitive dance and conscious of his or her own life and of the dance. There is a mediaeval story of a man persecuted by his Guardian Angel because it was jealous of his sweetheart, and such stories seem closer to reality than our abstract theology. All imaginable relations may arise between a man and his God. I only speak of the *Thirteenth Cone* as a sphere and yet I might say that the gyre or cone of the *Principles* is in reality a sphere, though to Man bound to birth and death, it can never seem so, and that it is the antinomies that force us to find it a cone. Only one symbol exists, though the reflecting mirrors make many appear and all different. (*AV*(B) 240)

speech of birds: Vendler (*YV* 142), associates with the Shrouds of 'Cuchulain Comforted', *CP* 395, who sing with the throat of birds.

For there the hound . . . hell: an echo of a passage from *The Wanderings of Oisin*:

> We galloped; now a hornless deer
> Passed by us, chased by a phantom hound
> All pearly white, save one red ear;
> And now a lady rode like the wind
> With an apple of gold in her tossing hand,
> And a beautiful young man followed behind
> With quenchless gaze and fluttering hair. (*CP* 413)

The source for the image is probably Brian O'Looney's translation of Michael Comyn's *The Lay of Oisin in the Land of Youth* (the Gaelic poem of the last century mentioned in Yeats's Notes):

> We saw also, by our sides
> A hornless fawn leaping nimbly,
> And a red-eared white dog
> Urging it boldly in the Chase

(See Russell K. Alspach, 'Some Sources of Yeats's "The Wanderings of Oisin"', *PMLA*, September 1943.) Cf. also 'He Mourns for the change . . .' *CP* 68:

> Do you not hear me calling, white deer with no horns?
> I have been changed to a hound with one red ear . . .

In the original version the following note was printed after the title:

In the old Irish story of Usheen's journey to the Islands of the Young, Usheen sees amid the waters a hound with one red ear, following a deer with no horns; and other persons in other old Celtic stories see the like images of the desire of the man, and of the desire of the woman 'which is for the desire of the man', and of all desires that are as these. The man with the wand of hazel may well have been Angus, Master of Love; and the boar without bristles is the ancient Celtic image of the darkness which will at last destroy the world, as it destroys the sun at nightfall in the west.

A fuller note in *WR* read:

My deer and hound are properly related to the deer and hound that flicker in and out of the various tellings of the Arthurian legends, leading different knights upon adventures, and to the hounds and to the hornless deer at the beginning of, I think, all tellings of Oisin's journey to the country of the young. The hound is certainly related to the Hounds of Annwvyn or of Hades, who are white, and have red ears, and were heard, and are, perhaps, still heard by Welsh peasants, following some flying thing in the night winds; and is probably related to the hounds that Irish country people believe will awake and seize the souls of the dead if you lament them too loudly or too soon. An old woman told a friend and myself that she saw what she thought were white birds, flying over an enchanted place, but found, when she got near, that they had dogs' heads; and I do not doubt that my hound and these dog-headed birds are of the same family. I got my hound and deer out of a last-century Gaelic poem about Oisin's journey to the country of the young. After the hunting of the hornless deer, that leads him to the seashore, and while he is riding over the sea with Niamh, he sees amid the waters – I have not the Gaelic poem by me, and describe it from memory – a young man following a girl who has a golden apple, and afterwards a hound with one red ear following a deer with no horns. This hound and this deer seem plain images of the desire of the man 'which is for the woman', and 'the desire of the woman which is for the desire of the man', and of all desires that are as these. I have read them in this way in *The Wanderings of Oisin*, and have made my lover sigh because he has seen in their faces 'the immortal desire of immortals'.

The man in my poem who has a hazel wand may have been Aengus, Master of Love; and I have made the boar without bristles come out of the West, because the place of sunset was in Ireland, as in other countries, a place of symbolic darkness and death. – 1899. (*CW* 1)

634   *a bell*: an echo of the 'brazen bell' of *The Wanderings of Oisin*: This is the bell which is said to strike at midnight 'when the old year dies', **637**, line 9. It is referred to in the song of the First Attendant as Head, **639**, and it strikes as the Queen dances, **640**, *SD*. It is also, of course, the bell of time and history – see Yeats's Commentary on 'Parnell's Funeral', *CP* 319, reprinted in *Comm* 399, with its view of history divided by Four Bells:

> When lecturing in America I spoke of Four Bells, four deep tragic notes, equally divided in time, so symbolising the war that ended in the Flight of the Earls; the Battle of the Boyne; the coming of French influence among our peasants; the beginning of our own age; events that closed the sixteenth, seventeenth, eighteenth and nineteenth centuries. My historical knowledge, such as it is, begins with the Second Bell. (*KGCT*)

The notion of eternity threatened by time is clearer in an earlier version of the opening song given in a letter to Olivia Shakespear:

First musician (singing)
I wait until the tower gives forth the chime;
And dream of ghosts that have the speech of birds;
Because they have no thoughts they have no words;
No thought because no past or future; Time
Comes from the torture of our flesh, and these,
Cast out by death and tethered there by love,
Touch nerve to nerve throughout the sacred grove
And seem a single creature when they please.

Second musician (singing)
I call to mind the iron of the bell
And get from that my harsher imagery,
All love is shackled to mortality,
Love's image is a man-at-arms in steel;
Love's image is a woman made of stone;
It dreams of the unborn; all else is nought;
To-morrow and to-morrow fills its thought;
All tenderness reserves for that alone.

The letter continues: 'The inner ideas in these lines are taken up later. One might say the love of the beloved seeks eternity, that of the child seeks time.' (*L* 817)

SD   one-foot Craig screens: for a comment on these screens, see notes   **634**
on *The Player Queen*, pp. 141–2.
    The King: Rajan (*YCI* 159), doubting Wilson's interpretation given above, p. 256, sees him as 'the unimaginative, everyday intelligence, baffled by forces which it cannot comprehend but which it is nevertheless forced to recognise as valid'.

I am a poet . . . face: cf. the figure of Mary Hynes, in 'The Tower',   **635**
II, *CP* 219, on whom the blind poet Raftery conferred 'so great a glory'. The identification of the Queen and Image is clearer in the prose version: 'You have kept silence long enough, sat there an image of stone or wood.'
    The image . . . goose: the prose version has 'I had a wife, but she was so much uglier than the image in my head, that I left her.'

a sacred man?: an echo of the esteem in which the bards of ancient   **636**
Ireland were held, but also because, as his next speech indicates, the poet is in touch with a truth that is corroborated by the Gods.

the Boyne Water: 'where the old Gods live', prose version.   **637**
    sea-mew: cf. *The Player Queen*, **407**, Decima's song. In both cases the sea-mew appears to herald the event which the cyclical movement must bring to pass. See the Stroller's next speech.
    Aengus: the Celtic God of youth, beauty and poetry.
    stroke of midnight: implies the end of life, the end of a cycle. Cf. 'Byzantium', *CP* 280:

> At midnight on the Emperor's pavement flit
> Flames that no faggot feeds, nor steel has lit,
> Nor storm disturbs, flames begotten of flame,
> Where blood-begotten spirits come
> And all complexities of fury leave . . .

'Ribh considers Christian Love insufficient', *CP* 330, lines 19–20:

> At stroke of midnight soul cannot endure
> A bodily or mental furniture.

'The Four Ages of Man', *CP* 332, lines 7–8:

> Now his wars on God begin:
> At stroke of midnight God shall win.

638   *You will not speak?*: in the prose version the silence of the Stroller is identified with a desire for sacrifice: 'it is plain that he wishes to sacrifice his life, to lay it down at your feet.'

rambling rogue: cf. **633**, line 2.

That sudden shudder: of the sexual, which is also the creative, act. Cf. 'On Woman', *CP* 164:

> Harshness of their desire
> That made them stretch and yawn,
> Pleasure that comes with sleep,
> Shudder that made them one.

The next stanza juxtaposes creation and destruction.

639   *abstracts*: mere shadows of supernatural union.

the nuptial bed of man: cf. 'The marriage-bed is the symbol of the solved antinomy, and were more than symbol could a man there lose and keep his identity, but he falls asleep. That sleep is the same as the sleep of Death.' (*AV*(B) 52)

640   *Sacred Virgil*: a view based on the medieval interpretation of Virgil's Fourth *Eclogue*, which appeared to have the force of a divine prophecy. For the association between Virgil and the ushering in of a new cycle, see 'Two Songs from a Play', *CP* 239; *Comm* 284, and notes on *The Resurrection*, pp. 196–7.

But there's a stone . . . tongue: the same image is used at the end of the first section of 'A Dialogue of Self and Soul', *CP* 265, when the Soul declares its inability to describe the mystical union of Is and Ought, Knower and Known – thought and its object:

. . . intellect no longer knows
Is from the *Ought*, or *Knower* from the *Known* –
That is to say, ascends to Heaven;
Only the dead can be forgiven;
But when I think of that my tongue's a stone.

SD   The Queen dances . . . presses her lips: this dance and kiss mark
the climax of the play, the moment when opposites are reconciled –
the living and the dead, the poet and image, the temporal and the
timeless.

Castle Dargan: The lighted house stands for a vision of perma-
nence. Cf. 'The Curse of Cromwell', *CP* 350, and 'Crazy Jane on
God', *CP* 293:

> Before their eyes a house
> That from childhood stood
> Uninhabited, ruinous,
> Suddenly lit up . . .

This is probably the ruined castle referred to in the Introduction to
The Words upon the Window-pane quoted above, and it was probably
Castle Dargan, near Sligo. This castle is also alluded to in *Autobiographies*, p. 53. Cf. also *A* 77 and the description of the ruined
house 'that was burnt down' in Yeats's play *Purgatory*, a window of
which is lit up with a young girl in it (**685–7**). There is also a possibility that Yeats had Leap Castle in mind, which 'though burnt
down during our Civil War and still a ruin, is haunted by what is
called an evil spirit which appears as a sheep with short legs and
decaying human head' (*AV*(B) 224). Wilson interprets it as the
'mansions of heaven' as well.

mouthful of air: cf. 'He Thinks of Those who have Spoken Evil   **640**
of his Beloved', *CP* 75. The phrase was also used by Yeats to
describe faeries, 'nations of gay creatures, having no souls; nothing
in their bright bodies but a mouthful of sweet air' ('Tales from the
Twilight', *SO*, 1 March 1890). See also **126**; *PYP* 72.

The last two stanzas balance the vision of the poet granted to
him in the momentary ecstasy of that union which seems to have
opened a gap into eternity – and thus it is in a way an answer to
the question: *What marvel is/Where the dead and living kiss?* (lines 3–4) –

against the vision of the tree, which at worst asserts the inescapable victory of time – and thus it is like the King – and at best either admits a hope, by nature unheroic, of the continuation of life, or gives to eternity the grudging benefit of possibility. Visually, as Rajan points out, the play ends with a glimpse of the Queen. Moore (*MLD* 280) comments: 'This is an assertion that lovely things . . . cannot die while there is an imagination to *see* them. They are the Idea of Beauty made visible to that inner eye that can never be blurred by the corruption of time.'

641   *Alternative Song for the Severed Head*:

This poem was probably written in 1934; it first appeared in *Life and Letters*, November 1934.

Ben Bulben and Knocknarea: mountains overlooking Sligo. Cf. 'Under Ben Bulben', *CP* 397, 'The Hosting of the Sidhe', *CP* 67 and 'Red Hanrahan's Song about Ireland', *CP* 90.

Rosses' crawling tide: sea coast and village near Sligo.

Iron bell: see note on **634**, p. 260.

Cuchulain that fought night long with the foam: cf. 'Cuchulain's Fight with the Sea', *CP* 37.

Niam that rode on it: cf. 'The Wanderings of Oisin', *CP* 409, for the

> . . . pearl-pale, high-born lady, who rode
> On a horse with bridle of findrinny;

and the opening lines of Book III, *CP* 431:

> Fled foam underneath us, and round us, a wandering
>   and milky smoke,
> High as the saddle-girth, covering away from our
>   glances the tide.

In the Fenian tale, *Oisin in the Land of the Young*, Niam, who is extremely beautiful, spirits Oisin off to the land of the young for three hundred years.

lad and lass: Naoise and Deirdre when captured by Conchubar (and kept in a guest house in a wood in Yeats's play, *Deirdre*). Naoise's speech, **189**, lines 24 ff, sees Deirdre and himself re-enacting the situation of Lugaidh Redstripe (a warrior of the Red Branch cycle of tales). Deirdre was formerly Conchubar's ward whom he

kept in the hills in the care of an old nurse, Lavarcham, intending
to marry her. Naoise, one of his warriors, saw her, fell in love with
her and ran away with her to Scotland, accompanied by his brothers,
the other sons of Usna. When they return to Ireland, and Fergus,
their safe-conduct, has had to leave them, Naoise says to Deirdre:

> What do they say?
> That Lugaidh Redstripe and that wife of his
> Sat at this chess-board, waiting for their end.
> They knew that there was nothing that could save them,
> And so played chess as they had any night
> For years, and waited for the stroke of sword.
> I never heard a death so out of reach
> Of common hearts, a high and comely end . . . (**189–90**)

Aleel, his Countess: the poet and the heroine in Yeats's play,
The Countess Cathleen.

Hanrahan: cf. 'The Tower', II, *CP* 219, line 57:

> And I myself created Hanrahan.

Hanrahan is a character created by Yeats, who appeared in *Stories
of Red Hanrahan*, 1904, and *The Secret Rose*, 1907. Giles W. L. Telfer,
Yeats's Idea of the Gael, 1965, points out that Hanrahan has a striking
resemblance to Eoghan Ruadh O Suileabhan (1748–84).

The King that could make his people stare,   **642**
Because he had feathers instead of hair . . .

cf. 'The Wisdom of the King' in *TSR* (*M* 165–70). The child of
the High Queen of Ireland was visited by the crones of the grey
hawk (the Sidhe), one of whom let a drop of her blood fall on the
infant's lips. Two years later the King died, and the child grew
very wise, but the feathers of the grey hawk grew in his hair. The
child was deceived by the poets and men of law about these feathers;
they told him everyone else had feathers too, and ordered that
everyone should wear them, but that anyone who told the child the
truth should be put to death. The reason for this was a law that no
one who had a bodily blemish could sit on the throne. The King
eventually discovered the truth, ordered that Eochaid should rule
in his stead and vanished.

K*

The Herne's Egg

The play, which abandons the austere concentration of the Noh-type drama and requires quite elaborate theatrical resources, was first printed in 1938. The Abbey Theatre intended to produce it but changed their minds, to Yeats's relief, evidently because he feared that its irreverent and Rabelaisian qualities would provoke riots. He himself described it as 'the strangest wildest thing I have written' (*L* 845), as amusing as *The Player Queen* but 'more tragedy and philosophic depth' (*L* 843). When it was taking shape in his mind in December 1935, he told Dorothy Wellesley that Shri Purohit Swami was with him and that the play was 'his philosophy in a fable, or mine confirmed by him' (*L* 844). Although he warned Ethel Mannin not to ask him what it meant, the play has not lacked interpreters.

Wilson (*Y&T* ch. 3) finds its source not only in Ferguson's poem *Congal*, but also in Balzac's *Seraphita*, and at the same time a Shakespearean analogy in which Congal plays Brutus to Aedh's Caesar. Taking his cue from the presence of the Indian Swami, he interprets the Great Herne as divine Selfhood, with which Attracta, a type of negative purity, desires a purely spiritual union, but which is also made sufficiently grotesque to balance the tragic-comic hero Congal, who is the antithesis of Attracta, being pride in the Self, which sets itself up against Godhead. Congal's theft of the egg, both forbidden fruit and the egg of Brahma, boundless infinity, is an act of *hubris* in that like Adam he is trespassing upon the divine prerogative, for which he is punished. But even while accepting his punishment, he retains his pride. Rajan (*YCI* 163–4), minimising the element of Indian thought that Wilson stresses, regards Congal's fall as 'a progress in *hubris* begun possibly in ignorance, but persisted in with a full knowledge of what it entails', conducted with a strong sense of the absurd. Man is not only defeated, but defeated without dignity. Bloom (*Y* 422) develops Nathan's view (*TD* 281), that it is 'an extravagant attempt to embody on the level of farce and travesty Yeats's theory of reality' and sees it as a squalid parody of his own mythology, while granting it a lasting imaginative power. Moore, acknowledging that 'Yeats came perilously close to disintegrating the poetic truth of myth in the acid of his irony' (*MLD* 54), sees this self-parody within the larger framework of a distrust in the moral purity of the heroic virtues themselves. He sees in the play 'the same action regarded from a "tough" pragmatic standpoint and then from a "noble" transcendent one. Both views are reduced to logical absurdity by deflation' (*MLD* 284). Melchiori (*WMA* 194–5) regards it as 'a transposition into a highly stylized deliberately sham old Irish legendary setting of such oriental doctrines as that of the World Egg dropped by a bird (the herne's egg) and of metempsychosis, rolled into one with the typically Yeatsian myth of Leda's egg . . . Attracta . . . is at one and the same time Salome (the type of the dance), Leda, the "mother" of new civilizations, and the Queen coupling with the Unicorn [of *The Player Queen*]. The idea of the new cycle of civilization is presented cryptically under the aspect of the Herne's Egg, and again . . . in the transmigration of the spirit of a king into that of a donkey.' For Vendler (*YV* 158–9), the play is primarily concerned with the relation of the artist to the Muse. The Great Herne is the Muse, Attracta the artist, and the egg a symbol of the product of the union of Muse and Poet – the completed poem. Congal and Attracta represent different views of art, Congal denying its supernatural, spiritual, origin and Attracta believing in nothing else. Both are changed by their experiences. Congal comes to believe in the existence of the Great Herne, and Attracta that conception needs not only spiritual but carnal experience, mediated through the imperfection of man. In her aesthetic allegory, neither Congal's view that art is sublimation nor Attracta's that art is the only reality is true. For Peter Ure, Congal's theft of the egg is a fall into disorder and his persistence in carrying out revenge on the God through the rape of Attracta, who represents the reality of the mystical life, and his assertion of freedom and selfhood against the thunder and the curse, though heroic in itself, are also foolish, because they are the product of his own ignorance of the mystery by which he himself and his men have been made the surrogates of the Great Herne, the god.

The play was first staged at the Abbey Theatre, Dublin, on Sunday

29 October 1950 by The Lyric Theatre Company; it was produced by Josephine Albericci and the cast was: Congal, King of Connaught George Green; Aedh, King of Tara, Edward Golden; Corney, Attracta's servant, Alex. Andrews; Mike, Jack MacGowran; Peter, Hugh Martin; Pat, Oliver Bradley; John, Gerald Mangan; James, Michael Reynaud; Malachi, Art O'Phelan; Mathias, Bart Bastable; Attracta, a Priestess, Eithne Dunne; Kate, Doreen Fitzpatrick; Agnes, Mary Fisher; Mary, Joan Stynes; A Fool, Patrick Nolan; Soldiers, Frank Daly, Kevin Naughton, Jack Quinn, Kevin Redmond, Peadar Murphy. The setting and costumes were by Anne Yeats.

The play was first published in *The Herne's Egg*, London, 1938, and subsequently in *The Herne's Egg and Other Plays*, New York, 1938; *The Collected Plays of W. B. Yeats*, London, 1952; New York, 1953 (repr. London, 1953, 1960, 1963, 1966); *Selected Plays*, Papermac edition, ed. A. Norman Jeffares, London, 1964; *Eleven Plays of William Butler Yeats*, ed. A. Norman Jeffares, New York, 1964.

645   *SD   the battle*: Rajan, Ure and Wilson all regard the stylised battle as representing a state of prelapsarian equilibrium. Vendler, however, interprets it as the empty gestures of a tradition in its final stages in Yeats's system, which no longer has any vivid meaning. Moore (*MLD* 296–7) basically agrees with Vendler, commenting that although Congal is a hero born who responds naturally to the idea that playing the game according to the rules is the important thing, rather than any ulterior motive such as riches or power, nevertheless this purity of masculine play has become barren and needs the fertilising invigoration symbolised by the herne's egg if heroic artifice is to be restored to life.

647   *What if before . . . hearts*: suggests the theory of metempsychosis, and, taken with **666**, line 3, the idea that in its previous incarnation the donkey was a highwayman.
SD   Congal, Pat . . . shields: the 'heroes' of the last scene without the trappings of their heroism. Only Congal retains a vestige of it. Wilson (*Y&T* 130) gives two interpretations of Congal's men: (i) following the Upanishads, Congal is *rajas*, or passion, and the

six men 'represent the "six enemies" which in Indian tradition wait upon passion: vanity, jealousy, sloth, anger, greed and lust'; (ii) following Christian tradition, Congal is pride and his followers make up the number of the seven deadly sins. Against this is the view that the only passions they represent are lust and cowardice.

SD   Corney plays flute: the music of 'The Great Herne's Feather', **648** which haunts Congal throughout the play, announces the presence of God, the Great Herne.

Tara: a hill in Co. Meath, the seat of government of the High Kings of Ireland.

And we have set . . . relish: the lines suggest that Congal's motive is the arbitrary assertion of the individual will directed towards his material satisfaction in a purely physical object.

Women thrown . . . snow: the lines relate Attracta to the cold, cruel **649** Queen of *FMM* – see **666**, line 2. Melchiori (*WMA* 196–7) draws attention to the source of the image in Arthur Symons's translation of Mallarmé's 'Hérodiade'. In 'The Trembling of the Veil' Yeats wrote:

I can remember the day in Fountain Court when Symons first read me Herodiade's address to some Sybil who is her nurse and, it may be, the moon also:

> *The horror of my virginity*
> *Delights me, and I would envelop me*
> *In the terror of my tresses, that, by night,*
> *Inviolate reptile, I might feel the white*
> *And glimmering radiance of thy frozen fire,*
> *Thou that art chaste and diest of desire,*
> *White night of ice and of the cruel snow!*
> *Eternal sister, my lone sister, lo*
> *My dreams uplifted before thee! now, apart,*
> *So rare a crystal is my dreaming heart,*
> *And all about me lives but in mine own*
> *Image, the idolatrous mirror of my pride,*
> *Mirroring this Herodiade diamond-eyed.*

Yet I am certain that there was something in myself compelling me to attempt creation of an art as separate from everything heterogeneous and casual, from all character and circumstance, as some Herodiade of our theatre, dancing seemingly alone in her narrow moving luminous circle. (*A* 321)

Danae's lap: the daughter of Acrisius, King of Argos, who shut her in a bronze tower because an oracle foretold that he would be killed by his daughter's son. Zeus fell in love with her and visited her in a shower of gold; their son was Perseus, who eventually did kill his grandfather by accident. Ovid tells her story in *Metamorphoses*. But the suggestion here is that both Danae and Leda subconsciously invite their desecration by Zeus. See *FMM*.

650   *There is no happiness . . . funeral urn*: Moore's comment (*MLD* 287) is valuable: "The familiar confrontation of principles is here again – the timebound and the timeless. Neither can comprehend the other; divine innocence and fallen experience, each has its wisdom but lacks the knowledge of the other and so is unfulfilled.'

652   *die upon some battlefield*: this is Congal's idea; it is not in the curse. In other words he cannot comprehend the Herne except in terms of his own categories of experience.

653   *Strong sinew . . . joy*: Wilson (*Y&T* III) compares Yeats's translation of part of the Katha-Upanishad (*The Ten Principal Upanishads*, 1938, p. 38): 'Man should strip him of the body [i.e. renounce the sensual life] as the arrow-maker strips the reed, that he may know God as perpetual and pure.' Moore (*MLD* 289) rightly points to the paradoxical use of this image, 'physical (and specifically phallic) to suggest a disembodied experience.'

654   *Look, look she takes . . . hen*: in other words the Great Herne, working through the tranced Attracta, thwarts Congal's will.

655   *The moon was full*: i.e. at Phase 15.

SD   they fight: this drunken brawl is clearly to be contrasted with   **659**
the stylised, gentlemanly battle of Scene 1.

And there are . . . again: a hint of the new cycle to come.   **660**
   Maybe the Great Herne's curse . . . not?: Congal's first admission of
the power of the Great Herne. He is gaining insight.

legally: law, as lines 27–8, **663** indicate, stands for rationality, the   **661**
antithesis of the mystical experience symbolised by Attracta's
marriage with the Great Herne. Ure (*YTP* 151) comments:

> In this scene Congal's 'law' itself may be read as the conse-
> quence of his fall into disorder and hence as incompetent to
> restore the old equilibrium. Attracta's condition during it
> [one of God-possessed trance], furthermore, suggests that all
> he does is done at the god's behest, that he is already playing
> the fool, ironically unaware that law and reason and revenge
> against the god are simply the motives that the Great Herne
> uses to effect his own end, which is the consummation of the
> marriage.

Moore (*MLD* 292–3) comments: 'In perfect keeping with the
technique of incongruity Yeats has devised for the play, the logic
and mathematics Congal has just praised so judiciously are reduced
to absurdity in application: the order of rape is to be decided by
having the men throw their skullcaps to see who is nearest the
mark.'

But he is god . . . him: the lines condense part of Scene III.   **662**
   And yet through . . . suffer: there is a parallel here with Satan's
motives.

SD   Thunder: corroborates Attracta and though it drives Congal   **669**
to his knees, it does not make him retract his version of events.
'That tragi-comic hero Congal has a natural aptitude for the heroic
role as long as it involves no reverence for an authority higher than
himself; he comes late and reluctantly to an understanding (if it

can truly be called that) of the mission incumbent on him to establish contact with godhead. He is duly punished for his recalcitrance. He may get another chance, but it will not be in the next generation certainly.' (Moore, *MLD* 55)

Slieve Fuadh: actually the highest mountain in the Fews range in Co. Armagh. Mountain tops are traditionally the home of the Gods.

670   *I know . . . come*: i.e. Congal accepts his heroic and tragic destiny, to die, as he thinks, by the hand of the Fool, who is also the gods' agent.

673   *He won the first . . . second*: the first was the fall into disorder and the death of Aedh; the second the rape of Attracta.

676   *But killed me . . . yours*: Congal escapes death at the hands of the Fool, but see note on **661**, *legally*.

677   *I will protect you*: it is difficult to see why Attracta, who has acted previously as the Great Herne's agent, should wish to thwart him now, unless it be that she has come to realise the weakness of her position. Wilson (*Y&T* 108), suggests that at this stage she has been transformed into a Swedenborgian angelic spirit and in this condition tries to save Congal from the punishment of metempsychosis decreed for him upon his death. There is no dramatic preparation, however, for this idea. The whole incident may owe something to Ferguson's *Congal*, in which Lafinda, once his betrothed and now a bride of Christ, comforts Congal as he lies dying.

SD He dies: his death completes the process by which at the completion of an era, announced as in *The Player Queen* by the braying of a donkey, Congal dies into his opposite: hero, subjective, asserting his own will, becomes fool, objective, completely absorbed in the will of the Great Herne. Moore (*MLD* 297) comments: 'It is hard to say whether he is more fool than hero.

But there is no doubt that in his own eyes he wins the battle to retain his human dignity. The play suggests, however, that the self-reliance of a hero is illusory; even Law and Justice degenerate into mechanical principles inadequate to their purpose when they are not informed by some spirit of divinity.'

Purgatory

Purgatory was first produced on 10 August 1938 at the Abbey Theatre, Dublin. The cast was: Old Man, Michael J. Dolan; Boy, Liam Redmond. There exists a scenario of eight pages, two manuscripts, from typescripts corrected by Yeats, and a set of corrected proofs, now all in the National Library, Dublin. For a transcript of some of this material see Curtis Bradford (*YW* 297–300) who has written of the scenarios:

> When working on a play he began with what he called a 'Scenario'. These are always in prose and are usually very roughly written. Yeats had a visionary mind, and his scenarios record visions of a dramatic action, sometimes intense visions. Yeats sees in his mind's eye, as it were, a dramatic action unfolding before him in a theatre. Some of the scenarios are short ... Others, for example, the scenarios of 'The Words upon the Window-Pane' and 'Purgatory', are longer and fully develop the plays that grew out of them. (*YW* 171)

The settings were designed by the poet's daughter Anne Butler Yeats. Yeats himself attended the performance at the Abbey Theatre and said at the conclusion of the play that he had put nothing in it because it seemed picturesque but had put there 'his own convictions about this world and the next' (Hone, *WBY* 472). Yeats probably began this play, which is dated April 1938 in *On the Boiler*, in mid-March 1938, as a letter of his, dated 15 March 1938, written from the Hotel Idéal Sejour to Edith Shackleton Heald indicates:

> I have a one-act play in my head, a scene of tragic intensity but I doubt if I will begin it until I get to Steyning, or perhaps not till I get to Ireland. I am so afraid of that dream. My recent work has greater strangeness and I think greater intensity than anything I have done. I never remember the dream so deep. (*L* 907)

Wade remarks (*L* 907, note) that Yeats did begin to write the play at the Chantry House, Steyning, Sussex, Edith Shackleton Heald's house.

In an interview published in the *Irish Independent* 13 August 1938, Yeats answered queries put by Father Connolly, an American Jesuit, at a lecture on Yeats given by F. R. Higgins on 11 August 1938:

> Father Connolly said that my plot is perfectly clear but that he does not understand my meaning. My plot is my meaning. I think the dead suffer remorse and re-create their old lives just as I have described. There are mediaeval Japanese plays about it, and much in the folklore of all countries.
>
> In my play, a spirit suffers because of its share, when alive, in the destruction of an honoured house; that destruction is taking place all over Ireland today. Sometimes it is the result of poverty, but more often because a new individualistic genera-tion has lost interest in the ancient sanctities.
>
> I know of old houses, old pictures, old furniture that have been sold without apparent regret. In some few cases a house has been destroyed by a *mesaillance*. I have founded my play on this exceptional case, partly because of my interest in certain problems of eugenics, partly because it enables me to depict more vividly than would otherwise be possible the tragedy of the house.
>
> In Germany there is special legislation to enable old families to go on living where their fathers lived. The problem is not Irish, but European, though it is perhaps more acute here than elsewhere. (*Y&GI* 357–8)

On 15 August Yeats wrote to Dorothy Wellesley enclosing an account of the production of the play, repeating his comment about putting his convictions about this world and the next into it (*L* 913). To Edith Shackleton Heald he reported on the same day that *Purgatory* had been:

> . . . a sensational success so far as the audience went . . . But I have had this before. The trouble is outside. The press or the clerics get to work – the tribal dance and the drums. This time the trouble is theological. As always I have to remain silent and see my work travestied because I will not use up my fragile energies on impermanent writing . . . My daughter's designs for it [On *Baile's Strand*] and *Purgatory* – especially for

this – were greatly admired. *Purgatory* perfectly acted. House crowded. (*L* 913–14)

In September 1938 he wrote to Edith Shackleton Heald that the religious controversy over *Purgatory* had died down. 'Most people seem to be on our side and the daily newspapers had leaders in our support'. (*L* 915)

The play was set for a Cuala Press edition, the proof of which Yeats read, but, according to Curtis Bradford, after Yeats's death Mrs Yeats decided that *On the Boiler* had been so carelessly printed that the edition would have to be scrapped; a new edition was set and published in 1939. (*YW* 294) The play was included in *Last Poems and Two Plays*, Dublin, 1939; *On the Boiler*, Dublin, 1939; *Last Poems and Plays*, London, 1940; New York, 1940; and in the *Collected Plays of W. B. Yeats* (in which it is dated 1939), London, 1952; New York, 1953 (repr. London, 1953, 1960, 1963, 1966). It is included in *Selected Plays*, Papermac edition, ed. A. Norman Jeffares, 1964; and in *Eleven Plays of William Butler Yeats*, ed. A. Norman Jeffares, New York, 1964. Variants are listed in *VPl* 1041–50.

Comments on the verse of the play have been made by Ellmann, who remarks on some of the 'clipped rhythm and intentionally awkward syntax which Auden had made available for confiscation' (*ED* 5) and on the Auden-like abruptness in the minor characters' speeches. He calls it fancifully 'sprung verse' in *The Herne's Egg* and *Purgatory* (*ED* 118). The same Auden-like qualities appear in the poem 'Meru', (*CP* 333) which deals with the uprooting of civilisation—'Egypt and Greece, good-bye, and good-bye, Rome!' Fuller comment on Yeats's 'boldly' departing from the traditional in the verse of the play is provided by Nathan (*TD* 243–4). And David Clark (*YTDR* 12 ff), gives an interesting discussion of the verse. There are many hints for *Purgatory* in Yeats's writings. His early novel *John Sherman* (1891) contained a ruined house under a curse and a barren pear tree. In 'Theologians', *The Celtic Twilight* (*CT*; *CW*, v, 59–61; *EPS* 1925), an old Galway man was described. He could see nothing but wickedness and, after a description of Hell, went on to describe Purgatory:

'It seemed to be in a level place, and no walls around it, but it all one bright blaze, and the souls standing in it. And they suffer near as much as in Hell, only there are no devils with them there, and they have the hope of Heaven.

'And I heard a call to me from there "Help me to come out o' this!" And when I looked it was a man I used to know in the army, an Irishman, and from this country and I believe him to be a descendant of King O'Connor of Athenry.

'So I stretched out my hand first, but then I called out, "I'd be burned in the flames before I could get within three yards of you." So then, he said, "Well, help me with your prayers," and so I do.

'And Father Connellan says the same thing, to help the dead with your prayers, and he's a very clever man to make a sermon, and has a great deal of cures made with the Holy Water he brought back from Lourdes.' (*EP&S* 190–1)

The castle may be related to Castle Dargan, described in *Autobiographies* (53–4) and in *The King of the Great Clock Tower*:

First Attendant.	O, but I saw a solemn sight;
	Said the rambling, shambling travelling-man;
	Castle Dargan's ruin all lit,
	Lively ladies dancing in it.
Second Attendant.	What though they danced! Those days are gone,
	Said the wicked, crooked, hawthorn tree;
	Lovely lady or gallant man
	Are blown cold dust or a bit of bone.
First Attendant.	O, what is life but a mouthful of air?
	Said the rambling, shambling travelling-man;
	Yet all the lovely things that were
	Live, for I saw them dancing there.
	(*CPl* **640**)

The image of the house suddenly lit up was used in 'Crazy Jane on God' (*CP* 294):

> Before their eyes a house
> That from childhood stood
> Uninhabited, ruinous,
> Suddenly lit up
> From door to top:
> *All things remain in God.*

And, somewhat differently, in 'The Curse of Cromwell' (*CP* 350):

> I came on a great house in the middle of the night,
> Its open lighted doorway and its windows all alight,
> And all my friends were there and made me welcome too;
> But I woke in an old ruin that the winds howled through.

See also comments on *The King of the Great Clock Tower*, p. 263, which list other allusions to ruined houses.

An early story of 1894, 'Those who live in the storm' (*The Speaker*, 21 July 1894), concerns a woman Oona Hearne who is in love with Michael Creed, despite his bad qualities and because of his strength. In this she resembles the Old Man's mother in *Purgatory*.

Yeats attached great importance to choice and wrote in 'If I were Four-and-Twenty' that 'a single wrong choice may destroy a family, dissipating its tradition or biological force, and the great sculptors, painters, and poets, are there that instinct may find its lamp' (*E* 274). There are other passages relating to genetics, including the lines in 'Three Songs to the One Burden'

> The common breeds the common,
> A lout begets a lout (*CP* 371)

The idea is also dealt with in the Introduction to *Fighting the Waves*:

> . . . States are justified, not by multiplying or, as it would seem, comforting those that are inherently miserable, but because sustained by those for whom the hour seems 'awful', and by those born out of themselves, the best born of the best. (*E* 376)

There is also a sermon on degeneracy in *On the Boiler*, on this text from Burton's *Anatomy of Melancholy*:

> So many different ways are we plagued and punished for our fathers' defaults: in so much that, as Fernelius truly saith, 'it is the greatest part of our felicity to be well born, and it were happy for human kind, if only such parents as are sound of body and mind should be suffered to marry. (*E* 418)

In the course of his essay Yeats wrote 'Unless there is a change in the public mind every rank above the lowest must degenerate, and, as inferior men push up into its gaps, degenerate more and more quickly.' (*E* 423)

His awareness of general degeneracy also appears in 'Meditations in Time of Civil War': 'Ancestral Houses', lines 23–4 (*CP* 225);

'Nineteen Hundred and Nineteen', 1 (*CP* 232); 'The Gyres' (*CP* 337); 'A Bronze Head' (*CP* 382); 'Under Ben Bulben', lines 70–3 (*CP* 387).

A possible source for the play may be a ghost story Yeats told at one of Charles Ricketts's Friday evenings. Hone gives this version of it:

Centuries ago there lived in a castle in Ireland a man and wife. To their abounding sorrow they remained childless despite prayers and pilgrimage. At last, when they had long given up all hope, the woman, to her joy, found herself pregnant. Her husband, who till then had been tender and trusting became sullen and suspicious, often giving himself up to lonely bouts of drinking. Barely had the child been born, when the man, roaring drunk, rushed into the upper chamber where his wife lay. With cries of 'Bastard, bastard' he wrested the baby from her breast, and with the screaming infant in his arms, strode raging from the room. Down the winding wooden stairs he ran into the hall where, all reason fled, he beat and beat the tiny thing against anything he could. From her bed the mother rose and followed . . . to arrive too late. Her son was dead. Picking him up from where he had been flung, she turned and slowly climbed the spiral stairs that led to the threshold of her room. She moved as in a trance till, through the open door, the sight of the bed brought her to earth with a spasm of despair. Vehemently clasping the child, in a flash she bent beneath the bar which fenced the stairs, and dropped, like a singed moth, to the stone floor below. The man, his frenzy spent, was overwhelmed with grief. He sought consolation in taking another wife by whom he had other sons. Thus a family was founded and generation followed generation, each living much the same uneventful bucolic lives as those whom they succeeded. Although they cared for their castle and husbanded its lands, each in turn from time to time abandoned himself to the same solitary bouts. The house as a rule was a happy place but, during those spells, when its master was saturated with drink, an ashen woman would drift past him, ascending the curved stairs. Transfixed, he would wait the tragedy that he knew he was doomed only to see when he was drunk. Always with the same simple gesture she would reach the topmost step; always in the same way, pause, then bend, to drop a fluttering mass. Yet when he peered down he could see nothing. With the years the family vice grew like a cancer until it ate away their entire fortune and they were reduced to poverty. To crown their misery fire gutted the castle. The descendant to whom it then belonged was without the money or the desire to re-build. Indolent and inane, he left with few regrets to live in far-distant Dublin. Thenceforth the family and its fount seemed after countless years to have severed every bond. But destinies and traditions are hard to break and one day the grandson of this deserter was drawn to the very spot. His boon companion, killed by the kick of a horse, was to be buried within sight of the crumbling towers. Moved partly by affection for his friend, partly by curiosity to see the place whence his stock had sprung, the survivor of this long line had journeyed to attend the funeral. He met many friends and tippled with them all and, drunk, he found himself at dusk before the sombre shell of a stronghold. There being no door, he walked straight into the empty well up the wall of which had twined the oaken stairs. As he gazed he saw a fragile dishevelled form glide past him up and round the walls as though the steps were still there. Almost at the top she stopped, then with a burst of emotion dived, to disappear. The man knew no surprise. He felt that he had watched this melancholy scene innumerable times before – and for an instant he dimly understood that neither his children nor yet his children's children could ever purge themselves of a crime that they had inherited with their blood. (Hone, *WBY* 283–4)

The experience alluded to as 'timeless individuality' in the Introduction to *The Words upon the Window-Pane* enters into the play. It contains:

archetypes of all possible existences whether of man or brute, and as it traverses its circle of allotted lives, now one, now another prevails. We may fail to express an archetype or alter it by reason, but all done from nature is its unfolding into time. Some other existence may take the place of Socrates, yet Socrates can never cease to exist ... Plotinus said that we should not 'baulk at this limitlessness of the intellectual; it is an infinitude, having nothing to do with number or part' (*Ennead* v.7.1.); yet it seems that it can at will re-enter number and part and thereby make itself apparent to our minds. If we accept this idea many strange or beautiful things become credible ... the Irish country-woman did see the ruined castle lit up, the bridge across the river dropping; ... All about us

there seems to start up a precise inexplicable teeming life, and
the earth becomes once more, not in rhetorical metaphor, but
in reality, sacred. (*W&B* 37–8)

Yeats formulated some of his thoughts on the continuity of
perception in his 1930 Diary, where he remembered discussing
mystical experience with Cabbalists, and particularly 'pictures in
the astral light' which seemed to him of two kinds:

There are those described in the last verse of *The Sensitive
Plant*:

> For love, and beauty, and delight
> There is no death nor change; their might
> Exceeds our organs, which endure
> No light, being themselves obscure.

To the second kind belongs that of the shade of Heracles in
the *Odyssey* drawing its bow as though still in the passion of
battle, while the true spirit of Heracles is on Olympus with his
wife Hebe. To it belong also those apparitions of the murderer still dragging his victim, of the miser still counting his
money, of the suicide still hanging from his rafter.

We become aware of those of the first kind when some
symbol, shaped by the experience itself, has descended to us,
and when we ourselves have passed, through a shifting of the
threshold consciousness, into a similar state.

The second kind, because it has no universal virtue, because
it is altogether particular, is related only to the soul whose
creation it is, although we can sometimes perceive it through
association of place or of some object. It was the opinion of
those Cabbalist friends that the actions of life remained so
pictured but that the intensity of the light depended upon the
intensity of the passion that had gone to their creation. This is
to assume, perhaps correctly, that the greater the passion the
more clear the perception, for the light is perception. 'Light',
said Grosseteste, 'is corporeality itself or that of which corporeality is made', whereas Bonaventura calls taste and smell forms
of light. The 'pictures' appear to be self-luminous because the
past sunlight or candle-light, suddenly made apparent, is as it
were broken off from whatever light surrounds it at the
moment. Passion is conflict, consciousness is conflict.

Blake did not use the word 'picture' but spoke of the bright
sculptures of Los's Halls from which all love stories renew
themselves, and that remain on, one does not see the picture

as it appeared to the living actor but the action itself, and that we feel as if we could walk round it as if there was no fixed point of view. Whose perception then do we share? I put this point once to my Instructors. They replied that the 'picture' had nothing to do with memory – it was not a remembered perception – and left me to find the explanation. I have to face Berkeley's greatest difficulty; to account for the continuity of perception, but my problem is limited to the continuity of the perception that constitutes, in my own and other eyes, my body and its acts. That continuity is in the Passionate Body of the permanent self or daimon. Should I see the ghost of murderer and victim I should do so because my Spirit has from those other Passionate Bodies fabricated light, or perception. That fabrication is not enforced by the Passionate Body, is an act of attention on my Spirit's part; but for the act the murderer's own Spirit must be present, for as the Passionate Body is not in space and can only be found through its Spirit or daimon which is only present during its moments of retrocession or sleep, I should have said not that the living mind of Keats or Shakespeare but their daimon is present and the Passionate Bodies that constituted its moment, for images in the mind acquire their identity also from the Passionate Body. The daimon of Shakespeare or Keats has, however, entered into a sleepless universality. (*E* 330–2)

The section on 'The Soul in Judgement' in *A Vision* (1937), pp. 219–40 is also relevant and indicates the well-known elemental of Leap Castle as a likely element in Yeats's thought. Yeats argued that the *Spirit* is not changing images but light, and draws back into itself all it has felt or known:

I am convinced that this ancient generalisation, in so far as it saw analogy between a 'separated spirit', or phantom and a dream of the night, once was a universal belief, for I find it, or some practice founded upon it, everywhere. Certainly I find it in old Irish literature, in modern Irish folk-lore, in Japanese plays, in Swedenborg, in the phenomena of spiritualism, accompanied as often as not by the belief that the living can assist the imaginations of the dead. (*AV*(B) 221)

or again,

Because we no longer discover the still unpurified dead through our own and others' dreams, and those in freedom through contemplation, religion cannot answer the atheist, and philosophy talks about a first cause or a final purpose, when we would know what we were a little before conception, what we shall be a little after burial. (*A V*(B) 223)

Another passage continues the discussion:

The period between death and birth is divided into states analogous to the six solar months between Aries and Libra. The first state is called *The Vision of the Blood Kindred*, a vision of all those bound to us through *Husk* and *Passionate Body*. Apparitions seen at the moment of death are part of the vision, a synthesis, before *disappearance*, of all the impulses and images which constitute the *Husk*. It was followed by the *Meditation*, which corresponds to what is called the 'emotion of sanctity' on the Great Wheel; the *Spirit* and *Celestial Body* appear. The *Spirit* has its first vision and understanding of the *Celestial Body*, but that it may do so, it requires the help of the incarnate, for without them it is without language and without will. During the *Meditation Husk* and *Passionate Body disappear*, but may persist in some simulacurm of themselves as do the *Mask* and *Will* in *primary* phases. If the *Husk* so persist, the *Spirit* still continues to feel pleasure and pain, remains a fading distortion of living man, perhaps a dangerous succuba or incubus, living through the senses and nerves of others. If there has been great animal egotism, heightened by some moment of tragedy, the *Husk* may persist for centuries, recalled into a sort of life, and united to its *Spirit*, at some anniversary, or by some unusually susceptible person or persons connected with its past life.

In the third discarnate state [cf. *A V*(B) 231 (as below)], a state I shall presently describe, it may renounce the form of a man and take some shape from the social or religious tradition of its past life, symbolical of its condition. Leap Castle, though burnt down during our Civil War and still a ruin, is haunted by what is called an evil spirit which appears as a sheep with short legs and decaying human head. I suggest that some man with the *Husk* exaggerated and familiar with religious symbolism, torn at the moment of death between two passions, terror of the body's decay with which he identified himself, and an abject religious humility, projected himself in this image. If the *Passionate Body* does not *disappear*, the *Spirit* finds the *Celestial Body*, only after long and perhaps painful dreams of the past, and it is because of such dreams that the second state is sometimes called the *Dreaming Back*. If death has been violent or tragic the *Spirit* may cling to the *Passionate Body* for generations. A gambler killed in a brawl may demand his money, a man who has believed that death ends all may see himself as a decaying corpse, nor is there any reason why some living man might not see reflected in a mirror or otherwise some beloved ghost, thinking herself unobserved, powdering her face as in Mr. Davies' poem.

> The first night she was in her grave,
> As I looked in the glass
> I saw her sit upright in bed;
> Without a sound it was;
> I saw her hand feel in the cloth
> To fetch a box of powder forth.
>
> She sat and watched me all the while
> For fear I looked her way;
> I saw her powder cheek and chin,
> Her fast corrupting clay.
> Then down my lady lay and smiled,
> She thought her beauty saved, poor child.
>
> *(AV*(B) 223–5)

The influence of the Noh drama is suggested in the passage beginning 'In the *Dreaming Back*, the *Spirit* . . .', quoted on p. 235. This passage ends with the words:

The *Spirit* finds the concrete events in the *Passionate Body*, but the names and words of the drama it must obtain, the *Faculties* having gone when the *Husk* and *Passionate Body disappeared*, from some incarnate Mind, and this it is able to do because all spirits inhabit our unconsciousness or, as Swedenborg said, are the Dramatic Personae of our dreams. One thinks of those apparitions haunting the places where they have lived that fill the literature of all countries and are the theme of the Japanese Nō drama. (*AV*(B) 226–7)

Critics have commented on this influence (see Ure, *YTP* 73, note), and Wilson, arguing that what attracted Yeats most was 'the Noh of ghosts' (*Y&T* 138), states that 'in *Motomezuka* the play to which he most frequently refers, the whole action is concerned with a girl's sufferings in the several circles of the Buddhist hell, from which in this case no prayer can get her free' (*Y&T* 139). Henn (*LT* 276) quotes an autobiographical memory of Yeats:

Lionel Johnson said to me, his tongue loosened by slight intoxication, 'I wish those people who deny eternity of punishment would realise their own unspeakable vulgarity.' I remember laughing when he said it, but for years I turned it over in
my mind and it always made me uneasy.

The continuous nature of the *Dreaming Back* (cf. 'The Cold
Heaven', lines 9–10 (*CP* 140) and 'Shepherd and Goatherd', lines
79–82 (*CP* 159) was explained in another passage of *A Vision*:

All the involuntary acts and facts of life are the effect of the
whirring and interlocking of the gyres; but gyres may be
interrupted or twisted by greater gyres, divide into two lesser
gyres or multiply into four and so on. The uniformity of
nature depends upon the constant return of gyres to the same
point. Sometimes individuals are *primary* and *antithetical* to one
another and joined by a bond so powerful that they form a
common gyre or series of gyres. This gyre or these gyres no
greater gyre may be able to break till exhaustion comes. We all
to some extent meet again and again the same people and certainly in some cases form a kind of family of two or three or
more persons who come together life after life until all passionate relations are exhausted, the child of one life, the husband,
wife, brother or sister of the next. Sometimes, however, a
single relationship will repeat itself, turning its revolving wheel
again and again, especially, my instructors say, where there has
been strong sexual passion. All such passions, they say, contain
'cruelty and deceit' – I think of similar statements in D. H.
Lawrence's *Rainbow* and in his *Women in Love* – and this *antithetical* cruelty and deceit must be expiated in *primary* suffering
and submission, or the old tragedy will be repeated.
    They are expiated between birth and death because they are
actions, but their victim must expiate between death and birth
the ignorance that made them possible. The victim must, in the
Shiftings [cf. 'the third disincarnate state' (*AV*(B) 224, 231)],
live the act of cruelty, not as victim but as tyrant; whereas the
tyrant must by a necessity of his or her nature becomes the
victim. But if one is dead and the other living they find each
other in thought and symbol, the one that has been passive and
is now active may form within control the other, once tyrant
now victim. If the act is associated with the *Return* or the
Purification the one that controls from within, reliving as a form
of knowledge what once was tyranny, gives not pain but
ecstasy. The one whose expiation is an act needs for the act

some surrogate or symbol of the other and offers to some other man or woman submission or service, but because the unconscious mind knows that this act is fated no new gyre is started. The expiation, because offered to the living for the dead, is called 'expiation for the dead' but is in reality expiation for the *Daimon*, for passionate love is from the *Daimon* which seeks by union with some other *Daimon* to reconstruct above the antinomies its own true nature. The souls of victim and tyrant are bound together and, unless there is a redemption through the intercommunication of the living and the dead, that bond may continue life after life, and this is just, for there had been no need of expiation had they seen in one another that other and not something else. The expiation is completed and the oscillation brought to an end for each at the same moment. There are other bonds, master and servant, benefactor and beneficiary, any relation that is deeper than the intellect may become such a bond. We get happiness, my instructors say, from those we have served, ecstacy from those we have wronged. (*A V*(B) 237–9)

However Bloom remarks that, while in the mythology of *A Vision* the dead can be redeemed from their remorse through a fullness of the past recaptured, a purging justice of completeness in the *dreaming back*, the ghosts in *The Dreaming of the Bones* are not redeemed from their remorse 'for the young revolutionary soldier is as remorseless as the dreadful old man of *Purgatory* and will not forgive the dead who cannot learn to forgive themselves.' (*Y* 307)

In this connection there is Yeats's exuberant line in 'A Dialogue of Self and Soul' where after following to its source every event in action or thought he is content to 'Measure the lot; forgive myself the lot!' (*CP* 267)

Yeats put his theories on eugenic reform in the play; the Old Man has, he says, killed his son:

> because had he grown up
> He would have struck a woman's fancy,
> Begot, and passed pollution on. (**688**, lines 22–4)

The scenario tells us the crime which began the curse began sixty-three years before the action (see Curtis Bradford, *YW* 296). He also thought that destruction was taking place all over the Ireland of his day, and the burnings of great houses in the civil war were in his mind. And he had a feeling for increasing degeneracy. See

Torchiana, *Y&GI* 362, who draws attention to a statement made to Synge by an old man and remembered by Yeats: 'The young people are of no use . . . I am not as good a man as my father and my son is growing up worse than I am ('The Great Blasket', *Spectator*, 2 June 1933, p. 798).

To these themes he adds the idea of the earth-bound ghost, so located because its crime has been so dreadful the spirit cannot forget it and relives its actions over and over again. To a certain extent, he formulates the query of his earlier play *The Countess Cathleen* of whether a soul can sacrifice itself for a good end. And the Old Man remarks, after he has murdered his son, 'Mankind can do no more': he has murdered in vain but out of a desire to free his mother of her crime. There are obvious overtones of Hamlet's view of Gertrude as well as those of Oedipus in the theme. (Professor Melchiori remarks, though with suitable qualifications, that in *Purgatory* Yeats wrote his own *Oedipus at Colonus* (*WMA* 253).)

Torchiana argues that Yeats is symbolising in *Purgatory* life in this individualistic world. He points to *On the Boiler*, the lecture 'Modern Ireland' (*Massachusetts Review*, v, 267) and Yeats's commentary on 'A Parnellite at Parnell's Funeral', where Yeats commented on 'Four Bells, four deep tragic notes, equally divided in time, so symbolising the war that ended in the Flight of the Earls; the Battle of the Boyne; the coming of French influence among our peasants; the beginning of our own age; events that closed the sixteenth, seventeenth, eighteenth and nineteenth centuries.' (*KGCT* (1935), *VPl* 832); Yeats thought his own historical knowledge began with the Second Bell. Torchiana (who draws upon Donald R. Pearce, 'Yeats's Last Plays: An Interpretation', *ELH*, xviii, March 1951, 71–75 and John Heath-Stubbs, *On a Darkling Plain*, 1950, p. 205) regards modern Ireland as the essential material of the play. 'From the destruction of the house', he writes, 'we see the decline of the family and the individual into the final spiritual anguish of souls in purgatory, while the Old Man lives in virtual hell on earth' (*Y&GI* 359). He suggests that the mother represents Yeats's second period, from the Battle of the Boyne, 1690, to the French Revolution, 1789. She departed from her tradition, as an inheritress of the Protestant Irish culture, by marrying a groom, and this is a parallel to 'the democratic seductions of the French Revolution', her choice of a groom symbolising Ireland's espousing the democratic politics of

O'Connell (*Y&GI* 360). The Old Man is seen by Torchiana as representative of nineteenth century Ireland under O'Connell; he is close to being a complete member of the garrison, whose Catholic father 'drunk on piety and politics, turned the house down and destroyed the last vestige of that Protestant past in denying Parnell.' (*Y&GI* 361) Torchiana remarks that he suggests so much more: he is linked to both Yeats's second and fourth periods and seems to have all three warring in his blood.

This play has received much attention from critics. T. S. Eliot remarked that it was not 'a world of real Good and Evil, of holiness or sin, but a highly sophisticated lower mythology' (*After Strange Gods*, New York, 1934, p. 50). Peter Ure provides a very sensible discussion of the question of the intervention of the living in the life of the dead, and remarks that in *Purgatory* 'the convictions [of Yeats *qua* philosopher] are dissolved into the life of the protagonist; our attention is fixed upon the Old Man's story and his divided nature. The dead of *A Vision* and of the other plays live, although their condition is vividly enough rendered, a schematic life, each in the appropriate circle of their purgatory; but in the last play the Old Man's attempt to break into the circle, driven by furious pity and by jealous hatred of his own evil as embodied in his son, is his own story and no ghost shares it' (*YTP* 112).

Helen Hennessy Vendler sees the play as a restless reliving of actions undertaken with mixed feelings and obligations. She thinks that hatred and rage had begun to seem to Yeats, at this point of his life, indispensable and that detachment – even the detachment necessary for creation – began to seem impossible, seemed to her to end on a note of frustration and incomprehension. (*YV* 200–2) Leonard E. Nathan remarks that for the play's almost brutal candour about the objective world it is unsurpassed in Yeats's work. He considered its success could be attributed to Yeats's solution of his problem of how to make the supernatural a central element in his dramatic form (*TD* 212–13, 223).

681   *Half-door*: many Irish cottages and farmhouses have a door made in two parts, the top half often being left open for extra light and ventilation.

threshold . . . pig-sty: cf. 'Upon a House shaken by the Land Agitation' (*CP* 106), 'Although mean roof-trees were the sturdier for its fall', a reference to the likely use of Coole Park's timbers in smaller dwellings, as the stones and timbers of the monasteries in England were sometimes used after the Dissolution in the building of private houses.

The moonlight . . . the shadow of a cloud . . . the house . . . that tree Torchiana regards these lines as 'a composite image of eighteenth century excellence fallen on evil days. A ruined house, ruined family and ruined tree suggest individual, familial, and national failures' (*Y&GI* 363–4). The tree, 'stripped bare' in line 20, is akin to earlier symbolic trees in Yeats. See the 'broken tree' ('The Lamentation of the Old Pensioner', *CP* 52); 'an old thorn tree' ('The Old Age of Queen Maeve', *CP* 451); 'an old tree' ('Red Hanrahan's Song about Ireland', *CP* 90); 'the tree is broken' (*The Shadowy Waters, CP* 473); 'a twisted tree' (*The Two Kings, CP* 503); 'the withered rose tree' ('The Rose Tree', *CP* 206); 'the old wind-broken tree' ('A Meditation in Time of War', *CP* 214); 'a pear tree broken by the storm' ('Meditations in Time of Civil War', v, *CP* 229); 'a tree that has nothing within it' ('Three Songs to the Same Tune', *CP* 320 and 'Three Marching Songs', *CP* 377); the 'leafless tree', and 'Who but an idiot would praise/A withered tree?' (untitled poem, *RPP*, *VE* 780); 'the wicked crooked hawthorn tree' (untitled poem, *KGCT*, *VE* 788).

a better trade: cf. 'The People' (*CP* 169):

> I might have used the one substantial right
> My trade allows: chosen my company
> And chosen what scenery had pleased me best.

See also 'A Statesman's Holiday' (*CP* 389): 'So I have picked a better trade.'

fifty years ago: Torchiana remarks that the Old Man would presumably have seen the house just before Parnell was rejected by his party in 1889, an act that split the nation (*Y&GI* 359).

But there are some . . . familiar spots: cf. *AV*(B) 227 for comment **682** quoted above on apparitions haunting the places where they have lived.

the mercy of God: many critics fail to note this presaging of the final prayer in the play, **689**, lines 11–14.

the big old house . . . burned down: a suggestion, here, of the burnings of 'big houses' in the civil war in Ireland.

683   *Curragh*: an area in Co. Kildare where many establishments for the breeding and training of racehorses are situated.

Great people . . . Magistrates, colonels, members of Parliament,/Captains and Governors: this is reminiscent of Yeats's comments on Coole, Lady Gregory's house, in 'Coole Park and Ballylee, 1931' (*CP* 275): 'Where none has reigned that lacked a name or fame.' See also Lady Gregory, *Coole*, 1971, particularly the chapters on the library and breakfast room of the house, and Yeats's description in *Dramatis Personae*:

> Richard [Gregory] had brought in bullock-carts through Italy, the marble copy of the Venus de' Medici in the drawing-room, added to the library the Greek and Roman Classics bound by famous French and English binders, substituted for the old straight avenue two great sweeping avenues each a mile or a little more in length. Was it he or his father who had possessed the Arab horses painted by Stubbs? It was perhaps Lady Gregory's husband, a Trustee of the English National Gallery, who had bought the greater number of the pictures. Those that I keep most in memory are a Canaletto, a Guardi, a Zurbarán. Two or three that once hung there had, before I saw those great rooms, gone to the National Gallery, and the fine portraits by Augustus John and Charles Shannon were still to come. The mezzotints and engravings of the masters and friends of the old Gregorys that hung round the small downstairs breakfast-room, Pitt, Fox, Lord Wellesley, Palmerston, Gladstone, many that I have forgotten, had increased generation by generation, and amongst them Lady Gregory had hung a letter from Burke to the Gregory that was chairman of the East India Company saying that he committed to his care, now that he himself had grown old, the people of India. In the hall, or at one's right hand as one ascended the stairs, hung Persian helmets, Indian shields, Indian swords in elaborate sheaths, stuffed birds from various parts of the world, shot by whom nobody could remember, portraits of the members of Grillion's Club, illuminated addresses presented in Ceylon or Galway, signed photographs or engravings of Tennyson, Mark Twain, Browning, Thackeray, at a later date paintings of Galway scenery by Sir Richard Burton, bequeathed at his death, and etchings by Augustus John. I can remember somebody saying: 'Balzac would have given twenty pages to the stairs' (*A* 390–1).

He described Lady Gregory's brothers, the Persses as 'soldiers, farmers, riders to hounds, and in the time of the Irish Parliament, politicians' (*A* 392). In his 'Commentary on a Parnellite at Parnell's Funeral' he wrote of the Protestant Ascendancy:

When Huguenot artists designed the tapestries for the Irish House of Lords, depicting the Battle of the Boyne and the siege of Derry, they celebrated the defeat of their old enemy Louis xiv, and the establishment of a Protestant Ascendancy which was to impose upon Catholic Ireland, an oppression copied in all details from that imposed upon the French Protestants. Did my own great-great-grandmother, the Huguenot Marie Voisin feel a vindictive triumph, or did she remember that her friend Archbishop King had been a loyal servant of James II and had, unless greatly slandered, accepted his present master after much vacillation, and that despite episcopal vehemence, his clergy were suspected of a desire to restore a Catholic family to the English throne. The Irish House of Lords, however, when it ordered the Huguenot tapestries, probably accepted the weavers argument that the Battle of the Boyne was to Ireland what the defeat of the Armada had been to England. Armed with this new power, they were to modernise the social structure, with great cruelty but effectively, and to establish our political nationality by quarrelling with England over the wool trade, a protestant monoply. At the base of the social structure, but hardly within it, the peasantry dreamed on in their medieval sleep; the Gaelic poets sang of the banished Catholic aristocracy; 'My fathers served their fathers before Christ was crucified' sang one of the most famous. Ireland had found new masters, and was to discover for the first time in its history that it possessed a cold, logical intellect. That intellect announced its independence when Berkeley, then an undergraduate of Trinity College, wrote in his *Commonplace Book*, after a description of the philosophy of Hobbes, Newton and Locke, the fashionable English philosophy of his day, 'We Irish do not think so.' An emotion of pride and confidence at that time ran through what there was of an intellectual minority. The friends who gave Berkeley his first audience, were to found 'The Dublin' now 'The Royal Dublin Society,' perhaps to establish that scientific agriculture described and praised by Arthur Young. The historical dialectic trampled upon their minds in that brutal Ireland, product of two generations of civil war, described by Swift in a well-known sermon; they were the trodden grapes and became wine. When Berkeley landed in America, he found himself in a nation running the same course, though Ireland was too close to England to keep its independence through the Napoleonic Wars. America, however, as his letters show, had neither the wealth nor the education of contemporary Ireland; no such violence of contraries, as of black upon white, had stung it into life. (*VE* 832–3)

Aughrim and the Boyne: the Battle of the Boyne, July 1690, when William defeated James II; at Aughrim an Irish force led by the French General St Ruth was defeated by William's General Ginkle, on 12 July 1691.

every spring . . . may-blossom in the park: see Yeats's 'Commentary on A Parnellite at Parnell's Funeral', where he remarked:

> The influence of the French Revolution woke the peasantry from the medieval sleep, gave them ideas of social justice and equality, but prepared for a century disastrous to the national intellect. Instead of the Protestant Ascendency with its sense of responsibility, we had the Garrison, a political party of Protestant and Catholic landowners, merchants and officials. They loved the soil of Ireland; the returned Colonial Governor crossed the Channel to see the May flowers in his park; the merchant loved with an ardour, I have not met elsewhere, some seaboard town where he had made his money, or spent his youth, but they could give to a people they thought unfit for self-government, nothing but a condescending affection. They preferred frieze-coated humanists, dare-devils upon horseback, to ordinary men and women; created in Ireland and elsewhere an audience that welcomed the vivid imaginations of Lever, Lover, Somerville and Ross. (*KGCT, VE* 833–4)

Lady Gregory probably provided the idea when she wrote in her *Journals* on 3 June 1922: 'Everything is beautiful, one must stand to look at blossoming tree after tree; the thorns in the Park that William [her late husband, Sir William Gregory, a former Governor of Ceylon] used to come over from London to see at this time of the year best of all' (*Journals*, ed. Lennox Robinson, 1946, p. 32).

intricate passages: cf. 'In Memory of Major Robert Gregory' (*CP* 148):

> What other could so well have counselled us
> In all lovely intricacies of a house.

to kill a house/Where great men grew up . . . a capital offence: cf. 'Upon a House shaken by the Land Agitation' (*CP* 106):

> How should the world be luckier if this house,
> Where passion and precision have been one
> Time out of mind, became too ruinous
> To breed the lidless eye that loves the sun? . . .
> How should their luck [the peasant successors of
> the 'big' house's inhabitants] run high enough to reach
> The gifts that govern men, and after these
> To gradual Time's last gift, a written speech
> Wrought of high laughter, loveliness and ease?

and 'These are the Clouds' (*CP* 107):

> The weak lay hand on what the strong has done,
> Till that be tumbled that was lifted high
> And discord follow upon unison,
> And all things at one common level lie.

The old man is, like Oedipus, condemning himself in these lines.

keep me upon his level: the degeneration of the family is a theme **684** used by Irish novelists, Maria Edgeworth, and notably Somerville and Ross in *The Big House of Inver*, 1925. See F. S. L. Lyons, 'The Twilight of the Big House', *Ariel*, 1, 3 July 1970.

old books . . . French binding: for a description of the library at Coole see Lady Gregory, *Coole*, 1931, p. 2, 'with its walls of leather and vellum' in which Yeats delighted and which he celebrated in 'Coole Park and Ballylee, 1931' (*CP* 275):

> Beloved books that famous hands have bound,
> Old marble heads, old pictures everywhere.

sixteen years old . . . Puck Fair: an annual fair held from 9–11 August at Killorglin, Co. Kerry, where a goat is crowned. The boy was born about 10 August 1922, the year the Irish Free State was founded, if we take the action as occurring when the play was first performed, on 10 August 1938. F. A. C. Wilson comments, 'This can, if we wish, be taken as a device for dating back the final stage in the deterioration of Ireland to 1922, the year of the adoption of the constitution and of the outbreak of the civil war. (*Y&T* 155)

685   *SD   A window is lit*: the house lit up is a symbol of the supernatural. See earlier quotation of passages from poems, and *Autobiographies*. See note on **687** below.

686   *Tertullian*: Quintus Septimus Floreus Tertullian (*c.* A.D. 160–
c. 220) a Christian writer who was converted *c.* 195. He followed the
Montanist heresy, and boldly attacked the official attitude to Christianity. Wilson suggests that Yeats had read Tertullian's treatise on
the mixed nature of the soul, *De Anima*, his proof that pleasure
and remorse exist in the soul after death, and refers to the anony-
mous translation of *Tertullian*, 3 vols, Edinburgh 1869–95, I, pp.
40–1 (*Y&T* 152, 265).

687   *get it and spend it*: possibly an echo of Wordsworth's sonnet:

> The world is too much with us; late and soon
>   Getting and spending, we lay waste our powers
> (Miscellaneous Sonnets, XXXII, *Poetical Works*, ed.
> Hutchinson, 1924, p. 259).

you were young . . . now I am young: cf. 'But I am old and you are
young' ('Two Years Later', *CP* 137); 'Girl's Song' (*CP* 296):

> Saw I an old man young
> Or young man old?

There are echoes of Blake is this: see also a passage in 'The Bounty
of Sweden':

'I was good-looking once like that young man, but my un-
practised verse was full of infirmity, my Muse old as it were;
and now I am old and rheumatic, and nothing to look at, but
my Muse is young. I am even persuaded that she is like those
Angels in Swedenborg's vision, and moves perpetually towards the day-spring of her youth'. (*A* 541)

Yeats used the antithesis in writing of his own poetry: 'now I am
old my muse grows younger.'

sixteen years: the Old Man was sixteen when his drunken father
destroyed the house. This would have occurred 'close to the death
of Parnell in 1891' according to Torchiana (*Y&GI* 359). The boy
is sixteen at the time of the play, see note on **684**.

the window is lit up: cf. *Autobiographies*, p. 77, for a description of a psychic happening accompanied by a blaze of light and for another of the 'Sky bright with strange lights and flames' when Parnell was buried, which recalled similar phenomena said to have been witnessed when tidings of the death of Saint Columba overran the north-west of Europe, see *VE* 834.

'*Then the bride-sleep fell upon Adam*': a misquotation from D. G. Rossetti's 'Eden Bower', line 165: 'Yea, where the bride-sleep fell upon Adam (*Alas the hour!*)' Cf. *The Player Queen*, 406, line 13.

Hush-a-bye baby . . . bright: the irony in this quotation being the   **688** low birth of the father.

I am a wretched foul old man: Wilson compares this line to *King Lear*, IV, VIII, 60: 'I am a very foolish, fond old man' (*Y&T* 266n).

O God: the prayer for release may stem from the belief Yeats put in *A Vision* that a Spirit may stay in the *Purification* for centuries. The *Purification* may

> require the completion of some syntheses left unfinished in its past life. Because only the living create it may seek the assistance of those living men into whose 'unconsciousness' or incarnate *Daimon*, some affinity of aim, or the command of the *Thirteenth Cone*, permits it to enter. (*AV*(B) 233–4)

The question remains as to whether or not the anguished concluding prayer reveals a way out of the situation in which Yeats depicts a cyclic repetition. (God is as silent as Rocky Voice in 'The Man and the Echo', *CP* 393) The question is put, according to Bloom (*Y* 427), in this speech of the Old Man:

> But there's a problem: she must live
> Through everything in exact detail,
> Driven to it by remorse, and yet
> Can she renew the sexual act
> And find no pleasure in it, and if not,
> If pleasure and remorse must both be there,
> Which is the greater?

Bloom regards the play as confused because neither the Old Man nor, he argues, Yeats, can answer the question: a view opposite to that taken by Whitaker (*S&S* 272) that the Old Man errs because, unlike Yeats, he tries to annihilate history. The prayer may provide the only solution however much it may have of Yeats's own despair, as he put it in *On the Boiler*:

> Unless there is a change in the public mind, every rank above the lowest must degenerate, and as inferior men push up into its gaps, degenerate more and more quickly. The results are already visible in the degeneration of literature, newspapers, amusements, and, I am convinced, in benefactions like those of Lord Nuffield, a self-made man, which must gradually substitute applied science for ancient wisdom. (*OTB* 18)

In 'The Man and the Echo' (*CP* 394) we get some of his own despair, his knowledge that he will not know the answers to the riddle of the afterlife:

> What do we know but that we face
> One another in this place.

In the face of his own ultimate uncertainty he shed the bravado of, say, 'The Gyres' (*CP* 337) in which he tried to face the coming ruin of civilisation with detached joy, as in 'Lapis Lazuli' (*CP* 338) he described the heroic gaiety that rebuilt such ruins: 'and those that build them again are gay'.

In *Purgatory* he wants his audience to realise the dangers of this degradation of the human stock and soul, to understand and, perhaps to try to stop the process by 'a change in the public mind'.

Yeats made a prose draft of this play at the Chantry House, Steyning, Sussex in September 1938 (Hone, *WBY* 474–5). He was working on it in October, as he told Ethel Mannin in a letter of 20 October 1938:

> I am writing a play on the death of Cuchulain, an episode or two from the old epic. My 'private philosophy' is there but there must be no sign of it; all must be like an old faery tale. It guides me to certain conclusions and gives me precision but I do not write it. To me all things are made of the conflict of two states of consciousness, beings or persons which die each other's life, live each other's death. That is true of life and death themselves. Two cones (or whirls), the apex of each in the other's base.

(*L* 917–18)

He finished it in December, as a letter written on New Year's Day 1939 to Edith Shackleton Heald indicates:

> ... too much excitement at finishing my play and reading it out ...
> I think my play is strange and the most moving I have written for some years (*L* 922).

Two days before his death, on 26 January 1939, he made further corrections to the play (Jeffares, *Y:M&P* 297).

The play was first performed at the Abbey Theatre, Dublin, on Sunday 2 December 1945 by the Lyric Theatre Company. It was produced by Evelyn MacNeice and the cast was: An Old Man, Art O'Murnaghan; Cuchulain, Enda McGarry; Eithne Inguba, Ronnie Masterson; Aoife, Marjorie Williams; Emer, Christine Kane; The Morrigu, Goddess of War, Máiréad Connaughton; A Blind Man, Oliver Bradley; A Servant, John O'Riordan; A Street Singer, Edward Farrell. The Flautist was played by Hilda Layng, and the settings and costumes were by Anne Yeats.

It was first published in *Last Poems and Two Plays*, Dublin, 1939, then in *Last Poems and Plays*, London, 1940; New York, 1940 and later in *The Collected Plays of W. B. Yeats*, London, 1952; New York, 1953 (repr. London, 1953, 1960, 1963, 1966).

Persons in the Play:

Cuchulain: the Hound of Ulster, a warrior in the Red Branch cycle of Gaelic mythology. See notes on pp. 87, 101, 301–6.

Eithne Inguba: see notes on pp. 111, 302.

Aoife: the female ruler of a tribe, defeated by Cuchulain, by whom he had a son. See notes on pp. 93, 302. Lady Gregory's sources for the chapter 'The Son of Aoife' in her *Cuchulain of Muirthemne* were Keating's *History of Ireland*, Curtain's *Folk Tales* and 'Some Gaelic ballads'.

Emer: Cuchulain's wife, the daughter of Forgall.

The Morrigu: a crow-headed war goddess in Gaelic mythology. See note on line 34 ff, p. 301.

the last of a series: the play fulfils Yeats's hope, expressed in 'Certain Noble Plays of Japan', prompted by a visit to Dulac's studio to see the mask and head-dress to be worn by the player speaking the part of Cuchulain in one of the dance plays (presumably *The Only Jealousy of Emer*), that he would write another play and thus 'complete a dramatic celebration of the life of Cuchulain planned long ago' (*E&I* 221–2). The other Cuchulain plays were *On Baile's Strand*, *Fighting the Waves* and *The Only Jealousy of Emer*.

the antiquated romantic stuff: possibly a reference back to the romanticised treatment Yeats initially gave the Gaelic legends in, say, 'Cuchulain's Fight with the Sea' (*CP* 37). The source is probably mainly the last two chapters of Lady Gregory's *Cuchulain of Muirthemne*.

the son of Talma: Francois Joseph Talma (1763–1826), a famous French actor. Henn (*LT* 248) records his performance as Charles IX in Paris in 1789 as having a profound influence on public opinion. Hence, perhaps, the lines in 'A Nativity' (*CP* 387)

> What hurries out the knave and dolt?
> Talma and his thunderbolt.

The reason why he is chosen is probably because the old man is out of fashion. Cf. a passage in *On the Boiler*:

> We who are the opposites of our times should for the most part work at our art and for good manners' sake be silent. What matter if our art or science lack hearty acquiescence, seem narrow and traditional? Horne built the smallest church in London, went to Italy and became the foremost authority upon Botticelli. Ricketts made pictures that suggest Delacroix by their colour and remind us by their theatrical composition that Talma once invoked the thunderbolt ... (*E* 417–18)

In 'A Nativity', Landor and Delacroix are included, and both knew Talma (cf. Henn, *LT* 247).

audience of fifty or a hundred: the size of the Peacock Theatre, Dublin. See general introduction to the *Plays for Dancers* which discusses Yeats's need for a small, select audience (p. 84).

first performance of Milton's Comus: Comus was first acted on 29 September 1634 at Ludlow Castle, seat of The Earl of Bridgewater who had been appointed President of the Council of Wales and Lord Lieutenant of Wales and the countries on the Welsh border in 1631. His children acted in the masque, Alice, his youngest daughter aged fifteen, playing the Lady, and his surviving sons, John, aged eleven, and Thomas aged nine, the Elder and Younger brothers. Henry Lawes, who wrote the music and played the Attendant Spirit, was their music teacher.

the old epics: the Gaelic epics. Perhaps the best introduction to them is provided by Lady Gregory's *Cuchulain of Muirthemne* and *Gods and Fighting Men*. An excellent translation of the *Tain* has recently been made by Thomas Kinsella, 1970.

Mr. Yeats' plays: perhaps in addition to the Cuchulain plays (*On Baile's Strand, Fighting the Waves* and *The Only Jealousy of Emer*) the other plays relating to Gaelic legends: *The Countess Cathleen*; *The King's Threshold*; *The Shadowy Waters*; *Deirdre*; *At the Hawk's Well*; *The Green Helmet*; *The Herne's Egg*.

694   *sciolists*: Wilson (*Y&T* 175) suggests that Yeats is remembering a favourite epigram of Synge's: 'the sciolist is never sad' ('The Cutting of an Agate', *E&I* 325).

as old . . . easy to get excited: cf. Yeats's own over-excitement in writing the play. Letter to Edith Shackleton Heald quoted p. 297.

the music of the beggar-man, Homer's music: the link between the music of Homer and the beggar-man may perhaps be that between the blind Irish poet Anthony Raftery (1784–1834) and Homer, which is suggested in 'The Tower', II (*CP* 219–20) where Mary Hynes was 'commended by a song' of Raftery's:

> Strange, but the man who made the song was blind;
> Yet, now I have considered it, I find
> That nothing strange; the tragedy began
> With Homer that was a blind man,
> And Helen has all living hearts betrayed.

severed heads: the theme probably comes from Salome, and Yeats used it in *The King of the Great Clock Tower* and *A Full Moon in March*. Henn (*LT* 344) suggested that Mantegna's painting 'Judith with the Head of Holofernes' may have influenced Yeats; the picture is in the National Gallery, Dublin. Yeats's play *The Green Helmet* (earlier prose version entitled *The Golden Helmet*) drew upon an eighth century saga, *Bricriu's Feast* in which a beheading is avoided. See note on *The Green Helmet*, p. 98.

I could have got such a dancer once but she has gone: possibly a reference to Ninette de Valois, who had greatly impressed Yeats by her dancing and acting in *The King of the Great Clock Tower*. He wrote on 7 August 1934 to Olivia Shakespear about this; the passage from his letter is quoted on p. 253.

Dame Ninette de Valois, the stage name adopted by Edris Stannus (b. 1898), a ballerina born in Ireland. She was director of ballet at the Abbey Theatre, but had left the Abbey Theatre by the time Yeats was writing *The Death of Cuchulain*, and had been director at Sadler's Wells for several years.

the dancers painted by Degas: Hilaire Germaine Edgar Degas (1834–1917), a French artist. Henn suggests a picture by Degas, 'Ballet Girls', is the origin of this passage (*LT* 344); the painting is part of the Edward Martyn (1859–1922) bequest in the National Gallery, Dublin. Martyn was an Irish landowner who was involved in the early period of the Irish Theatre, being a co-founder of the Irish literary theatre. He lived at Tulira Castle, Galway, and is described by George Moore in *Hail and Farewell*.

Rameses the Great: Pharaoh of Egypt (1311–1245 B.C.).

Maeve: Queen of Connaught. She is reputedly buried in the   695
cairn of Knocknarea, a mountain in Sligo.

Emain Macha: Armagh, named after Emain, daughter of Hugh Roe, who claimed to rule in her father's right after his death. She defeated Dihorba his brother in battle, captured his five sons by a stratagem and married his brother Cimbaeth. The five princes were compelled to build her a palace. She is described in 'The Dawn' (*CP* 164) as measuring the town 'with the pin of a brooch'. Emain Macha was the capital of Uladh or Ulster, and was south-west of the present Armagh. It was destroyed in A.D. 332. (See G. Keating, *The History of Ireland*, II, 1908, pp. 153–7, for two legends about its founding.)

Muirthemne: in Co. Louth.

your death may come of it: this message is contradicted by Emer's letter, line 18.

Conall Caernach: one of the Ulster heroes, next in prowess to Cuchulain. In Lady Gregory's version of the legend he avenges Cuchulain by killing Lugaid.

SD The Morrigu: a crow-headed war goddess, one of the three   696
daughters of Calatin, killed with his twenty-seven sons by Cuchulain at the great Battle of the Ford. After his death his wife gave birth to these three deformed creatures, the Morrigu, Badb, and Macha, who each had one eye in the middle of her forehead. Maeve adopted them and brought them up, had them taught sorcery, and imbued them with her hatred for Cuchulain. The Morrigu was associated in legend with Cuchulain's death. In one story, which Eleanor Hull recounts in *The Cuchullin Saga*, 1898, 105, when he met a woman and quarrelled with her over a cow she was transformed into a crow. Cuchulain said he had not realised who she was; had he known, he said,

'We should not have parted thus'. 'Whatever you have done', said she, 'will bring you ill-luck.' 'You cannot harm me,' said he. 'Certainly I can,' said the woman, 'I am guarding your death-bed, and I shall be guarding it henceforth.'

In one legend (*The Great Fall of Mag Muirthemne or the Death of Cuchulain*, see Birgit Bjersby's use of Thurneysen, *Die Irische Helden, und Königsage bis zum* 17: *en Jahrh.*, I–II, Halle, 1921, in *ICL* 52), Cuchulain is sent by Emer his wife to the Valley of the Dumb so he will not hear of Maeve's progress, because there is a legend that his fighting her will cause his death. Emer sends the girl Niamh to sleep with him so that he will stay in the Valley of the Dumb. In *The Death of Cuchulain* Yeats substitutes Eithne Inguba for Niamh. In the legend it is Badb who takes on Niamh's shape and urges Cuchulain to attack the enemy who are ravaging Dundalk and Muirthemne. In Yeats's version the Morrigu uses her magical powers to get Eithne Inguba to falsify Emer's message (lines 3–9 and 18–23). See Eleanor Hull, *The Cuchullin Saga*, pp. 102, 105, 239–40, 242–3, 248, 254, 260, 263; and Birgit Bjersby, *ICL* 52–6. In the Gaelic legend Cuchulain will not be diverted from his purpose when the real Niamh returns and tries to persuade him to stay.

Maeve put me in a trance: presumably acting through the Morrigu.

a younger man, a friendlier man: later Cuchulain tells his servant that if he does not return she is to be given to Conall Caernach 'because the women/Have called him a good lover' (**698**, lines 19–20).

697   *to send me to my death*: Cuchulain accepts the likelihood of his death; indeed Wilson (*Y&T* 171–2) regards this as a death-wish, quoting the legend:

> Moreover, loath as ye be to dismiss me into danger and against my foes, even so cheerful am I that now go to have my side bored and my body mangled, neither knowest thou better than I myself know that in this onset I must fall. No more then hinder my path and course; for whether I stay I am devoted to death, or whether I go my life's span is run out.

I went mad at my son's death: this refers to the material of the poem 'The Death of Cuchulain', founded on the eighth century legend of the tragical death of Cuchulain and Queen Aoife's son. Birgit Bjersby tells the story in *ICL* 23–5:

... Cuchulain after having made an offer of marriage to Emer, the beautiful, chaste and talented daughter of Forgail, went to Scathach, a female demon, who was to impart to him her skill in the use of all kinds of weapons and in every kind of warfare. During his stay there, Scathach urged war against Aoife, the female sovereign of a neighbouring tribe. In spite of Scathach's efforts to keep Cuchulain from this fight, he went out against Aoife, said to be terrible in battle. By making use of a crafty device, he managed to overpower Aoife, and in order to save her life, Aoife must promise him to be obedient to Scathach and to bear him a son, whom she must name Conla. When this son was seven years of age, she must send him to Ireland under the obligation (or *geas*, the expression used in the Irish sagas) not to refuse anyone a single combat nor to tell his name to anybody. On his arrival in Ireland, a single combat is fought between him and his father. According to the oldest tradition, the father, before the combat, is half conscious that Conla is his own son, but he will fight for the honour of Ulster, 'ein Halb unverstandener alter Rest,' as Thurneysen calls it. After having killed his son, the father carries him before the eyes of the heroes of Ulster, and then his death is keened.

This old saga has been popular for many centuries; it lived in the memory of the people and developed into many different versions. The form of it adopted by the Irish Literary Movement is a very late one, dating from the 18th and 19th centuries.

The most conspicuous differences are the following: not until the very moment of the death blow, does the boy tell Cuchulain that he is Conla, his own son. Then to save the Ulster men from Cuchulain's rage, King Conchubar gives his druids an urgent command to draw their magical circles round Cuchulain, to make him believe for the space of three days that he fights the wild waves of an angry sea.

Yeats' Cuchulain poem is consistent with this later version of the saga in so far as the son dies in single combat by the hand of his father, who afterwards himself finds his death in the waves. But otherwise the story is quite different. Emer, not Aoife, is the mother of the boy, whose name is Finmole and who has been brought up as a shepherd boy in the wood.

Driven by her jealousy, aroused by Cuchulain's unfaithfulness to her, Emer commands her son to go and kill his father, who is described as a man 'with gray hair,' 'old and sad with many wars.' Finmole goes, a little unwilling at first to fulfil his fatal task, and thus to find his own death. Before he dies, he

reveals his secret to his father: he is mighty Cuchulain's son.
The poem ends describing the father's death:

> For four days warred he with the bitter tide:
> And the waves flowed above him, and he died.

The precise sources for Yeats's treatment of the legend are difficult
to discover, as Birgit Bjersby points out (*ICL* 26–7):

In these early days Yeats did not yet know Lady Gregory
whom he met for the first time in 1896, nor her versions of the
sagas, which had not yet been published. Standish James
O'Grady's *History of Ireland* certainly inspired Yeats to write
on Cuchulain, and O'Grady does mention that there exists a
saga describing Cuchulain's single combat with his son, but he
did not include it in his *History*. The name Finmole Yeats might
also have got from this book, in which the name is met with –
not, however, as the name of Cuchulain's son, but as a king's
name.

Yeats' poem cannot be ascribed to any ancient saga version,
but rather to modern folktale versions which have combined
two saga motifs, the death of Cuchulain's son and that of Cuchulain himself. According to the ancient version of this tale,
Cuchulain does not die in the waves. It is, however, a popular
trait in Irish folktales to let a hero die fighting with the sea, and
therefore it is not surprising to find it connected with Cuchulain, the foremost hero . . .

The old tale of the tragical death of Aoife was a very popular
one, and in a Donegal folktale we actually meet the same ending as in Yeats' poem: Cuchulain dies fighting with the waves,
or, at any rate, becomes exhausted unto death during this fight.
It is not here necessary to re-tell the whole tale which relates
various experiences of Cuchulain, but the end of it is so similar
to that of Yeats' poem that it may here be quoted: (The other
heroes when realising that Cuchulain had killed his own son
were frightened of his wrath, and one of them said:) 'Go now
. . . and bind him to go down to Bale Strand and give seven
days' fighting against the waves of the sea, rather than kill us
all. So Fin bound him to go down . . . Then he (Cuchulain)
strove with the waves seven days and nights till he fell from
hunger and weakness and the waves went over him.'

We may rightly assume that at this time Yeats read or in any
case glanced through most of the popular publications of Irish
folktales and that he read Curtin's folktale on Cuchulain, as well

as several others. He might even have heard several versions in conversation.

Later on – probably in 1924 or 1925 when Yeats was re-writing several poems for a new edition – he also re-wrote this poem and gave it a more symbolic name, *Cuchulain's Fight with the Sea*. The changes do not, however, concern the contents – apart from·one small detail: the name Finmole has disappeared, and no other name is put in to replace it.

Yeats's treatment of the legend in *On Baile's Strand* is easier to trace, since it is based on Lady Gregory's *Cuchulain of Muirthemne*, pp. 313–20. See notes on *On Baile's Strand*, pp. 101–4.

it was my wife/That brought me back: Emer in *The Only Jealousy of Emer* renounces Cuchulain's love to save him from Fand, but Eithne Inguba says (**294**, lines 18–19):

> And it is I that won him from the sea,
> That brought him back to life.

Better women than I: cf. Eithne Inguba's speech in *The Only Jealousy of Emer* (**285**, lines 21–2).

> Women like me, the violent hour passed over,
> Are flung into some corner like old nut-shells.

It seemed that we should kill each other, then/Your body wearied and I   **699**
took your sword: possibly a reference to the trickery with which Cuchulain defeated Aoife.

six mortal wounds: those who delivered his wounds were themselves killed by Conall Cearnach. Bjersby comments:

> When he [Cuchulain] was dead a man called Lugaid cut his head off, but Conall Cearnach exacted a terrible vengeance on behalf of Cuchulain; according to one version he returned to the Ulstermen with Lugaid's head. According to another he brought the heads of all the chief men taking part in this last fight against Cuchulain. On his return he showed Emer the heads telling her of his exploits. She died and was laid beside her husband, and an inscription in Ogham [a kind of alphabet, see note, p. 51] was put above their grave. (*ICL* 53)

The Morrigu at the end of the play makes these happenings clear:

> This head is great Cuchulain's, those other six
> Gave him six mortal wounds. (**703**, lines 4–5)

my belt/About this stone: this is part of the legend:

He went to the pillar stone that was on the plain; and he put his breast-girdle round it so that he might not die seated nor lying down, but that he might die standing up. Then came the men around him, but they durst not go up to him, for they thought he was still alive.

Then came to Cúchulainn the Grey of Macha to protect him, so long as his soul was in him . . .

Then came the birds and settled on his shoulder.

'There were not wont to be birds about that pillar', said Erc, son of Cairpré. Then Lugain arranged Cúchulainn's hair over his shoulder and cut off his head. (*Y&T* 170–1)

die upon my feet: this is an example of the heroic gesture in defeat, akin to the chess-playing of Deirdre and Naoise in *Deirdre*, **189–90**, once they realise their situation is hopeless.

At the Hawk's Well: cf. Yeats's play of this name, begun in 1915, first performed in 1916, first published in 1917. In this play Yeats tells the story of how Cuchulain is lured away by the woman of the well and begets a son on her.

upon Baile's Strand: a reference to Yeats's play *On Baile's Strand*, where Cuchulain kills his son. Cf. also 'Cuchulain's Fight with the Sea' (*CP* 37).

the grey of Macha: one of Cuchulain's chariot horses, a lake-horse or kelpie.

700   *Conchubar forvaae it*: in *On Baile's Strand* Conchubar forbids the friendship growing between Cuchulain and Aoife's champion, the young man Cuchulain does not recognise as his son (see **264–70**).

witchcraft: Conchubar alleges that withcraft has maddened Cuchulain, a cry taken up by the other Kings, which Cuchulain believes (**270**).

702   *The shape that I shall take when I am dead,/My soul's first shape, a soft feathery shape*: the poem 'Cuchulain Comforted' (*CP* 395) is complementary to the play. The prose version, a dream of 7 January 1939, dictated at 3 a.m. on 13 January 1939, Yeats read to Dorothy Wellesley. The text is given in *DWL* 212 ff:

A shade recently arrived went through a valley in the Country of the Dead; he had six mortal wounds, but had been a tall, strong, handsome man. Other shades looked at him from among the trees. Sometimes they went near to him and then went away quickly. At last he sat down, he seemed very tired. Gradually the shades gathered round him, and one of them who seemed to have some authority among the others, laid a parcel of linen at his feet. One of the others said: 'I am not so afraid of him now that he is sitting still. It was the way his arms rattled.' Then another shade said: 'You would be much more comfortable if you would make a shroud and wear it instead of the arms. We have brought you some linen. If you make it yourself, you will be much happier, but of course we will thread the needles. We do everything together, so every one of us will thread a needle, so when we have laid them at your feet you will take which ever you like best.' The man with the six wounds saw that nobody had ever threaded needles so swiftly and so smoothly. He took the threaded needles and began to sew, and one of the shades said: 'We will sing to you while you sew; but you will like to know who we are. We are the people who run away from the battles. Some of us have been put to death as cowards, but others have hidden, and some even died without people knowing they were cowards.' Then they began to sing, and they did not sing like men and women, but like linnets that had been stood on a perch and taught by a good singing master.

The poem is similar; it was originally entitled 'The Death of Cuchulain' but this was changed when Yeats realised he had already used this title twice:

> A man that had six mortal wounds, a man
> Violent and famous, strode among the dead;
> Eyes stared out of the branches and were gone.
>
> Then certain Shrouds that muttered head to head
> Came and were gone. He leant upon a tree
> As though to meditate on wounds and blood.
>
> A Shroud that seemed to have authority
> Among those bird-like things came, and let fall
> A bundle of linen. Shrouds by two and three
>
> Came creeping up because the man was still.
> And thereupon that linen-carrier said:
> 'Your life can grow much sweeter if you will

> 'Obey our ancient rule and make a shroud;
> Mainly because of what we only know
> The rattle of those arms make us afraid.
>
> 'We thread the needles' eyes, and all we do
> All must together do.' That done, the man
> Took up the nearest and began to sew.
>
> 'Now must we sing and sing the best we can,
> But first you must be told our character:
> Convicted cowards all, by kindred slain
>
> 'Or driven from home and left to die in fear.'
> They sang, but had nor human tunes nor words,
> Though all was done in common as before;
> They had changed their throats and had the
>   throats of birds.
>
> (*CP* 395–6)

703   *Maeve's latest lover*: her amorousness was notorious.

her sons: in the oldest version of the legend Cuchulain is killed by Lugaid macCon Roi and Erc macCoirbri, by three magic spears prepared by the three sons of Calatin. Later versions add MacHied macFirin maic Rosa, to make one man for each spear. The fathers of all six had been killed by Cuchulain, hence their combining to kill him.

Conall avenged him: see note on **699**, *six mortal wounds*.

704   *SD   a few faint bird notes*: cf. note on **702** above, referring to 'Cuchulain comforted' and its prose draft quoted there. The souls in 'Sailing to Byzantium', *CP* 217, are described as clapping their hands and singing. Bird song is the communication of the spirit, see notes on *KGCT*, **633**, *speech of birds*.

Usna's boys: Naoise and his brothers Ardan and Ainle who accompanied him to Scotland when he ran away with Deirdre, King Conchubar's intended bride.

Maeve had three in an hour: see note on **703**. The harlot symbol is discussed in Wilson, *Y&T* 176–85.

can get/No grip upon their thighs: Wilson (*Y&T* 116) refers to the 'intractability of the ethereal body to mortal touch' and comments that the harlot cannot make love with the Sidhe, and quotes Plutarch on the subject.

I meet those long pale faces,/Hear their great horses: cf. 'Under Ben Bulben', *CP* 397:

Swear by those horsemen, by those women
Complexion and form prove superhuman,
That pale, long-visaged company
That air in immortality
Completeness of their passions won;
Now they ride the wintry dawn
Where Ben Bulben sets the scene.

I both adore and loathe: cf. 'The Lady's First Song' (*CP* 343)

> I am in love
> And that is my shame.
> What hurts the soul
> My soul adores,
> No better than a beast
> Upon all fours.

Cf. also 'Crazy Jane Grown Old Looks at the Dancers' (*CP* 295) where the dancing youth winds the girl's coal-black hair 'As though to strangle her' and the dancing girl 'Drew a knife to strike him dead'. Yeats wrote about this poem in a letter to Mrs Shakespear of 2 March 1929:

> Last night I saw in a dream strange ragged excited people singing in a crowd. The most visible were a man and woman who were I think dancing. The man was swinging around his head a weight at the end of a rope or leather thong and I knew that he did not know whether he would strike her dead or not, and both had their eyes fixed on each other, and both sang their love for one another. I suppose it was Blake's old thought 'sexual love is founded on spiritual hate'. (*L* 758)

See also 'Anima Hominis' where the warfare of man and demon is imaged in love (*M* 336–7).

the Post Office: the General Post Office, Dublin, held by the insurgents in the Easter rising, 1916, and the scene of their surrender. Cf. 'Three Songs to the One Burden', III, *CP* 373:

> Come gather round me, players all:
> Come praise Nineteen-Sixteen,
> Those from the pit and gallery
> Or from the painted scene
> That fought in the Post Office
> Or round the City Hall,
> Praise every man that came again,
> Praise every man that fell.

Pearse and Connolly are celebrated, 'the player Connolly' in the second stanza, Pearse in the third. He

> had said
> That in every generation
> Must Ireland's blood be shed.

The theme also occurs in the fourth stanza of *The Statues, CP* 375:

> When Pearse summoned Cuchulain to his side,
> What stalked through the Post Office? What intellect,
> What calculation, number, measurement replied?

In this poem Yeats saw Pearse as summoning intellectual and aesthetic forces into being (through his becoming part of the process of mythology).

Pearse: Patrick Henry Pearse (1879–1916), Irish poet and leader, shot for taking part in the 1916 rising, when he was president of the provisional government. Yeats wrote to Edith Shackleton Heald on 28 June 1938 that

> Pearse and some of his followers had a cult of him [Cuchulain]. The government has put a statue of Cuchulain in the rebuilt Post Office to commemorate this. (*L* 911)

Connolly: James Connolly (1870–1916), Irish trade-union leader and organiser of the Irish Citizen Army, shot for his part in the 1916 rising, not to be confused with 'the player Connolly' mentioned above.

705   *Oliver Sheppard*: (d. 1941), Irish sculptor. His statue of Cuchulain is in the present General Post Office, Dublin.

Critical comment on the play can be found in Bloom (*Y* 429–33); Henn (*LT* 277–9); Nathan (*TD* 196–202); Donald R. Pearce, *ELH*, xviii, 1951; Ure (*YTP* 77–83); Vendler (*YV* 236–47); Wilson (*Y&T* 162–95).

Gaelic Names

Yeats commented that when he wrote most of the poems in *P* (1895; rev. 1899) he had hardly considered seriously the question of the pronunciation of the Irish words. He had copied at times somebody's perhaps fanciful spelling, and at times the ancient spelling as he found it in some literal translation, pronouncing the words as they were spelt. In 1899 he supposed he would not at any time have defended this system, but he did not then know what system to adopt. He added:

> The modern pronunciation, which is usually followed by those who spell the words phonetically, is certainly unlike the pronunciation of the time when classical Irish literature was written, and, as far as I know, no Irish scholar who writes in English or French has made that minute examination of the way the names come into the rhythms and measures of the old poems which can alone discover the old pronunciation. A French Celtic scholar gave me the pronunciation of a few names, and told me that Mr Whitley Stokes had written something about the subject in German, but I am ignorant of German. If I ever learn the old pronunciation, I will revise all these poems, but at present I can only affirm that I have not treated my Irish names as badly as the mediaeval writers of the stories of King Arthur treated their Welsh names.

In a glossary he gave the old spelling in parentheses wherever he had adopted somebody's phonetic spelling in the poems. Information from this is supplied in this edition. In *CP* he adopted Lady Gregory's spelling of Gaelic names with two exceptions.

> The 'd' of Edain ran too well in my verse for me to adopt her perhaps more correct Etain, and for some reason unknown to me I have always preferred 'Aengus' to her 'Angus'. In her *Gods and Fighting Men* and *Cuchulain of Muirthemne* she went as close to the Gaelic spelling as she could without making the names unpronounceable to the average reader.

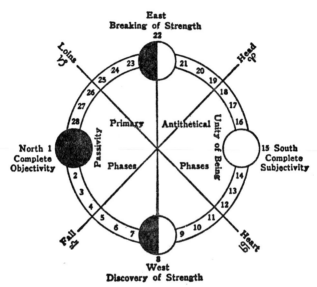

The Great Wheel of the Lunar Phases

Index to Titles

Page numbers in bold are those of the *Collected Plays*; those of the Commentary are in ordinary figures.